D1231941

THE

LEADER'S
BOOKSHELF

THE
LEADER'S
BOOKSHELF

ADM. JAMES STAVRIDIS, USN (RET.)

AND R. MANNING ANCELL

NAVAL INSTITUTE PRESS
Annapolis, Maryland

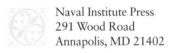

Naval Institute Press
291 Wood Road
Annapolis, MD 21402

Library of Congress Cataloging-in-Publication Data
Names: Stavridis, James, author. | Ancell, R. Manning, date, author.
Title: The leader's bookshelf / Adm. James Stavridis, USN (Ret.),
    R. Manning Ancell.
Description: Annapolis, Maryland : Naval Institute Press, [2017] |
    Includes bibliographical references.
Identifiers: LCCN 2016050134 (print) | LCCN 2017001341 (ebook) |
    ISBN 9781682471791 (hardback) | ISBN 9781682471807 (ePDF) |
    ISBN 9781682471807 (ePub) | ISBN 9781682471807 (mobi)
Subjects: LCSH: Command of troops—Bibliography. | Leadership—
    Bibliography. | United States—Armed Forces—Officers—Books and
    reading. | BISAC: EDUCATION / Leadership.
Classification: LCC Z6724.L4 S73 2017 UB210 (print) |
    LCC Z6724.L4 (ebook) | DDC 016.3553/3041—dc23
LC record available at https://lccn.loc.gov/2016050134

♾ Print editions meet the requirements of ANSI/NISO z39.48-1992
(Permanence of Paper).
Printed in the United States of America.

25 24 23 22 21 20   18 17 16 15 14

CONTENTS

PREFACE

This book grew out of a love of books. Throughout our professional lives we have purchased, read, discussed, and argued about books that illuminate the principles and ideals of leadership. While we both come from military backgrounds, it is clear that good leadership is central to success in any job, profession, or element of human activity. And while there are countless books that extoll the virtues and ideas of leadership, many of them languishing on shelves in airport bookstores, there are relatively few books that provide leadership lessons in a broader format. History, biography, autobiography and memoir, fiction, and geopolitics are all categories that teach us about leadership in indirect but powerful ways.

Given that Bob Ancell has spent decades interviewing very senior military leaders formally, and that Jim Stavridis engaged such leaders throughout his thirty-seven-year career, including nearly seven years as a four-star admiral, we felt strongly that we were in possession of the basic material to compile a "Leader's Bookshelf," could populate it with the very best books for emerging readers to peruse, and could clearly illuminate the lessons that can be drawn from them. We used formal interviews and informal conversations that both of us conducted over a period of years to build the list and focused on frequency of citation in creating the order—but in the end, this list is the result of our own views and experiences.

We gratefully acknowledge not only the help and guidance of the many four-star officers cited herein, but also the good work of the U.S. Naval Institute and especially our colleague and collaborator Capt. Bill Harlow, himself a keen student of leadership.

Leadership is certainly not learned solely from reading books, but a personal bookshelf—or even a library of thousands of volumes—can be critical to developing the ability to inspire others in the pursuit of worthy goals, which lies at the heart of what all leaders seek to accomplish in the challenging but rewarding tasks they take up.

Portions of this book were adapted from previous articles written by Admiral Stavridis. In particular he would like to thank the editors of *Signal* magazine for permission to adapt "Are Leaders Born or Made?" written for the April 1, 2015, edition, which forms part of chapter 1 of this book. He drew from an article he wrote for *The Atlantic* in crafting portions of chapter 2. Other material in the book was drawn from columns Admiral Stavridis wrote for *Foreign Policy*, the U.S. Naval Institute *Proceedings*, and his blog at the U.S. European Command.

The epigraphs at the beginning of each chapter are drawn from *The Reader's Quotation Book*, edited by Steven Gilbar (New York: Penguin Books, 1990).

THE

LEADER'S
BOOKSHELF

LEADERSHIP BY THE BOOK

Adm. James Stavridis

Reading is the sole means by which we slip, invol-
untarily, often helplessly into another's skin, another's
voice, another's soul.

—Joyce Carol Oates

Are the very best leaders born or made?
Over the course of my career and life, both in military operations and in the civilian world of academe, it has gradually become
clear to me that some gifts of leadership are indeed bestowed at birth:
high emotional intelligence, a pleasing appearance, a smooth and
soothing voice, a commanding physical presence—these are all helpful
attributes. Some aspects of leadership are in fact "present at the creation" of a woman or man.

But the *best* leaders, in my experience, do not spring forth fully
formed. They are forged through a combination of parenting, teaching, training, educating, and gaining vibrant real world experiences—
effectively *practicing* to be better leaders. The experiences that shape
them along the road of life matter deeply in the formation of effective
leaders. In other words, *both* heredity *and* environment matter in creating good leaders.

But I have come to believe that throughout all of those important developmental steps, perhaps the single best way a leader can learn and grow is through reading.

Think about iconic leaders in history: many of them have been senior military figures. Picture Caesar on the road in Gaul, his traveling library of scrolls with him, candles guttering in the cold French wind seeping through the sides of his tent. He is reading the classics of Greek and early Roman literature, studying, pondering, considering how best to lead his legions. Or Napoleon with his boxes of books that went everywhere with him, a link to French and Russian literature, a treasure trove of inspiration throughout his many triumphs and his shocking defeats. Throughout World War II, Admiral Nimitz and Admiral Spruance turned often to the literature of the sea, returning again and again to the classic sea stories even as they led the greatest fleet ever assembled across the Pacific. Gen. James Mattis, possessed of one of the largest libraries of any military figure in modern history, always traveled with his box of books into combat in Afghanistan. As I write this, the commander of all U.S. forces in the Pacific—Army, Navy, Air Force, and Marine Corps—is a Navy admiral, Harry Harris. He has collected hundreds of first editions of modern novels and is a voracious reader who is never without a book (or an e-reader) in his hands. And in my own house today reside more than four thousand books—much to the chagrin of my beloved wife, Laura, who has spent far too much of her life packing and unpacking them in postings all around the world. The personal business card I hand out today as I go about my duties as the dean of the Fletcher School of Law and Diplomacy at Tufts University has on its opposite side one of my favorite quotes from Thomas Jefferson: "I cannot live without books."

So many of our best leaders develop and enhance their ability to lead through endless contact with books.

Reading is central to leading for a variety of reasons:

First, it provides a chance for a young person (or indeed someone of any age, of course, but especially for the relatively unformed student of leadership) to experience an enormous variety of life experiences without leaving home or school. How else can a young aspiring leader learn how Ernest Shackleton managed to save his entire crew after his ship, *Endurance*, was crushed by ice and destroyed in Antarctica in 1915? Where else but through a novel like *Gates of Fire* by Steven Pressfield can a leader ponder the burden of command in the ancient world when all the odds seemed stacked against the commander, as they did for Leonidas at Thermopylae? The brilliant yet understated memoirs of Ulysses S. Grant, written as he lay dying of throat cancer at the end of his adventurous and tumultuous life, are a unique window into all that went into one leader's experience from small-unit command to the presidency of the United States.

Second, reading is the gateway to true self-evaluation. Every book is a kind of "complex simulator" that provides the means for a leader to read a story and ask, "What would I have done in that situation?" As I prepared myself for command of a Navy destroyer two decades ago, I read the classic sea novels of Patrick O'Brian and tried to think about what the best course of action would be for me as I prepared to face the fundamental challenges of both peace and war on a small combatant vessel. Many lessons of naval leadership are embedded in the twenty volumes of O'Brian's iconic seafaring series, beginning with *Master and Commander*, as the reader follows the long leadership journey of Royal Navy captain Jack Aubrey and his irascible sidekick, Dr. Stephen Maturin. I also read the sea novels of Joseph Conrad, each of them opening my mind to the challenges and opportunities of leading, as well as the stresses. Reading Conrad's iconic novella *The Secret Sharer*, for example, best prepared me for the realization that a ship captain occupies a lonely (if not a solitary) existence, no matter the size of his or her command.

Third, books allow us to think deeply about those individuals who are *our* heroes. As I think back on my lifetime of reading, many of the people I admire most deeply are known to me only through books— either by them or about them. Reading the aforementioned memoirs of Ulysses Grant or a biography of George Marshall—two of the greatest

U.S. Army generals—has helped me immeasurably as a leader. After reading a superb biography of "the Liberator," Simón Bolívar, I turned next to the powerful novel about his life and times, *The General in His Labyrinth*, by the Colombian Nobel laureate Gabriel García Márquez. Picking up Colin Powell's *An American Journey* permits a glimpse of all that he accomplished in an extraordinary career as the national security advisor, chairman of the Joint Chiefs of Staff, and secretary of state. Reading the autobiographical memoir *Duty* by former secretary of defense Robert Gates gave me an entirely new perspective on a leader I already thought I knew well, having worked directly for him over a considerable period as a combatant commander in both Latin America and NATO. A significant part of being a good leader comes from identifying the leadership traits of those we idolize personally and then seeking to replicate them—and all of that is catalyzed by reading.

Fourth, and perhaps most practically, we can use reading as a way to improve our own communication skills in writing. The more a young leader reads, the better she or he will be able to write. Often when I am struggling to find the right pattern of words for an essay or article, I will turn to one of Winston Churchill's magnificent books about World War II from his six-volume classic, *The Second World War*, or do as Churchill himself did and pull down the King James version of the Holy Bible, with its powerful cadences and vivid images. Simply reading a few paragraphs from such classics helps unlock the words in my own process of composition. Many styles of writing exist, of course—from the folksy twang of Mark Twain in *A Connecticut Yankee in King Arthur's Court* to the blunt, simple, but evocative prose of Gen. Dwight David Eisenhower in *Crusade in Europe*. Exploring various ways of writing through reading will inevitably make each of us a better writer in our own right. Good leaders must be good communicators, and the hard work of writing is best sharpened on the whetstone of reading.

Fifth, and finally, reading is a very *efficient* way to improve our leadership skills. Books are always at hand, can be stopped and started at a whim, are fine companions on boring journeys or when standing in a line, and can be used to fill in the small dead spaces in our working days. Even if only fifteen minutes are available, pulling out a book (especially easy in this age of small tablets or even the larger smartphones) is a very effective use of time. This is especially true today when we can load a couple of novels, a memoir, a handful of magazines, and even a graphic novel on a decent-sized tablet. What used to fill a briefcase and quickly became too heavy to lug around is now available on a slender six-ounce device! Ah technology . . .

Thus, reading is the pathway to leading—but how best to begin?

Once we understand how important reading is for leading, the next step, of course, is deciding *what* books to read. Here the ultimate dilemma for any reader is apparent—there are virtually an infinite number of books and an extremely finite number of hours to devote to actually reading. Voltaire observed in the eighteenth century that a man could begin his reading journey in the national library in Paris and die before he left the first alcove of shelves. So let's begin by discussing an organizational approach to systematically think about books that illuminate leadership as we move toward the immense thicket of the world's books.

Our thesis in this book is actually quite simple: by focusing on the reading patterns of the most senior officers in the U.S. military—certainly by any measure an organization that produces some of the best leaders in the world—we can create a set of books that makes sense for leaders in all walks of life. As this book unfolds, you will have a unique insight into the reading that the U.S. military undertakes as it produces leaders.

One interesting place to start is with reading lists. Unsurprisingly, given its need to develop good leaders, the U.S. military is a leader in the idea of culling the forest of books into coherent reading lists and providing recommendations. As a starter, each of the military service chiefs—Army, Navy, Marine Corps, Air Force, and Coast Guard—has produced reading lists that are reasonably useful. They are usually divided into basic, intermediate, and advanced books; and the reading often mirrors coursework at the various service and national war colleges.

But we believe that the best way to find the books that truly shape leaders is to simply ask senior leaders what they are reading and what books shaped them as leaders. Almost every senior military leader I have known is an avid reader, and most are happy to share their recommendations. For example, as a four-star combatant commander for nearly seven years in two very different commands (U.S. Southern Command, responsible for Latin America and the Caribbean, and U.S. European Command, responsible for the European theater and much of the Levant), I often blogged about my own reading and gladly took recommendations from every level in my organization that opened other fine books to me.

My coauthor, Bob Ancell, and I have been asking very senior leaders about their reading habits and favorite books for the past several years. Between us we have spoken with well over two hundred four-star officers, both on active duty and retired. All of those admirals and generals have given us lists of books that strongly influenced their leadership skills. We then collated the lists and determined which of the books were mentioned most frequently and ranked the highest among the participants in this admittedly nonscientific but fairly comprehensive survey. *The Leader's Bookshelf* is the result. It is centered on the list of the "Top 50" books that emerged from our conversations with the most senior and successful military leaders this nation has produced over recent decades. Along with this core of the very best books—including an analytical essay for each—are other ideas about the power of reading, how to assemble a library, reading in different genres, and other tricks of the trade in unlocking the power of "reading and leading."

We wish you "good reading," with the hope that what you find in this book will make you a fine reader (and leader) as well!

MAKING TIME FOR READING

Adm. James Stavridis

Books never annoy; they cost little, and they are always
at hand, and ready at your call.

—William Cobbett

First of all, we have to put "reading" in a context, because we are all *constantly* reading something. Today we live within a virtual torrent of written words pouring out of the proverbial fire hose twenty-four hours a day, seven days a week. The French have an evocative saying, "Ce n'est pas la mer de boire," which literally means, "This is not the sea to drink." They mean this in the sense that you don't have to do everything; maybe so, but unfortunately we all feel a certain obligation to "keep up" with our electronic mail, our virtual and real in-boxes, the constant news cycle, changes in pop culture, and thousands of other inputs—most of which require reading.

During my final year as the supreme allied commander at NATO in 2013, I wrote about what I tried to read in a given day in an article that appeared in *The Atlantic*, a leading literary magazine, and with the magazine's permission I repeat some of it here.

When I get up, the first thing I do is open up Gmail and check my personal email. Next I go through the headlines with Google News, which I find to be very accurate and broad-based. I have cues set at the moment for Afghanistan, the Balkans, Syria, Libya, Russia, piracy, cyber, missile defense, and a few other topics. After that, I'll read a compilation of daily news clips from various sources throughout Europe. I am also an active blogger: my latest effort is a post about Afghanistan; but I write about everything from the Balkans to piracy to summer reading lists and leadership successes and failures—including my own.

Over a cup of coffee, I'll then turn to my BlackBerry and my official email accounts to clear the myriad of messages that will have arrived overnight.

Over a second cup of coffee, I'll quickly skim the news and editorial pages of four papers online: *The Washington Post, The New York Times*, France's *Le Figaro* and Spain's *El Pais*—the latter two help me practice my working-level facility in those languages.

I am a huge consumer of social networks and I utilize Twitter, Facebook, and LinkedIn. I'm interested and am learning more about Tumblr and other visually dominant sites. I have about 30,000 friends on Facebook, contacts on LinkedIn, and followers (I hate that term), who form a wonderfully broad group of people with whom I can share ideas and get fresh perspectives. [Today that number has almost doubled, up to about 60,000 in total; not Lady Gaga but respectable for an admiral and dean.] This crowd is not shy about sharing opinions on what I write, which usually spurs me to dig even deeper into a topic.

As the day progresses, I get about a dozen or so hourly updates from various news services which hit my BlackBerry. I also keep CNN International going full time on background in my office. Although I have limited time to watch television,

I've been watching Hala Gorani, a Syrian-American who hosts a very good international show on CNN. On PBS I like Robert Nolan's *Great Decisions* series. Also, Ken Burns' documentaries are amazing in their ability to evocate with images and music.

At the end of the day, I'll read *The International Herald Tribune* [now *The International New York Times*], which is the English-language "paper of record" in Europe. I'll also look over *Stars & Stripes*, a European-focused military daily newspaper with a rich history that is kind of like the military's hometown paper when we are serving overseas.

I enjoy reading many columnists, but I regularly follow David Brooks, David Ignatius, Fareed Zakaria, Kathleen Parker, John Hamre, David Gergen, James Traub and Peggy Noonan. On the lighter side I like Chris Buckley (also one of the funniest novelists in America) and Dave Barry (ditto). For nonfiction books, I often turn to some of these columnists.

For periodicals, at the top of my list is *The Economist*, which I think word for word is the best written magazine for international relations in the world. I'm also a big fan of *The New Yorker*, especially for short fiction and poetry. I like *Foreign Affairs* published by the Council on Foreign Relations, of which I am a member.

The Atlantic is also very good, and I'm not just saying that—I've been a steady reader for over 30 years, and somewhere I have a few rejection slips from my early days both for short stories and nonfiction. I do try to write a little bit every day. Over the years I've managed to publish several books on topics ranging from ship handling to Latin American affairs and many articles. I have yet to publish any fiction, but I'm still hopeful.

Bloggers are too numerous to count, but a couple of sites I like are the *Foreign Policy* blogs, Small Wars Journal, and Slate. I occasionally dip into The Daily Beast and The Huffington Post.

I tend to gravitate toward reporters who cover all aspects of the story: from personal aspects to the big picture that answer the "so what" of a story. I appreciate those who do their home-work so the interview is an informed conversation from which we both learn. I have much less respect for those agenda-driven reporters who try for the short term "hit" without regard for context.

Additionally, there are times when the media get it wrong. The same is true in the military, of course. But, when a mistake is made I look for that organization or reporter to do the right thing by way of a correction or clarification to ensure the reader gets the real picture.

I enjoy the work done at *Wired*'s Danger Room. I've been mentioned there a few times both positively and negatively how-ever, I think they generally call 'em like they see 'em and have a good sense of humor with a healthy dash of irony: both good things.

I've never been in a "Twitter fight" though I've witnessed my fair share. I do enjoy vigorous and informed debate but the benefit is lost when the exchange becomes a series of petty ad hominem attacks. I don't see much value in it.

I am also a big reader of fiction, and enjoy accurate histori-cal fiction, which affords a chance to learn history painlessly. Generally, I try to make time to read at least one novel a week. Lately I've read *The Art of Fielding* by Chad Harbach, and *The Age of Miracles*, by Karen Thompson Walker, both coming-of-age novels by young American novelists. I also like the sea-going novels of Patrick O'Brian, like any Navy officer. Other authors I enjoy and read repeatedly include George MacDonald Fraser, Cormac McCarthy, John Updike, Ha Jin, Gary Shteyn-gart, Elmore Leonard, and Ian Fleming, among many others.

I also read poetry, especially from countries I am visiting in my current job (about 80 over the past several years). For example, before a recent trip to Madrid I went back and read some of the work of Frederico Garcia Lorca. I just read a book of poetry from a decade ago by Carl Dennis called *Practical Gods*, which impressed me. W. B. Yeats still amazes me with the freshness of his vision a century after much of his work was published.

Before bed, I'll try to read an article or two from the top military journals. As a Navy Officer, I am partial to the U.S. Naval Institute magazine, *Proceedings*, as well as the Army's top journal, *Military Review*.[1]

Whew. Looking back, I find it hard to believe I could get through so much; but like many of us, I am essentially reading constantly. While my reading "diet" has changed a bit over the past several years, the same fundamental idea holds true: as readers, we need a wide variety of input. In my reading as the dean of the Fletcher School at Tufts University, I continue to track a wide variety of global issues. Today I am focused on Syria, Iran, China, India, Russia/Ukraine, and North Korea in terms of nations. I am very concerned about the European Union and spend a fair amount of time staying current on what is happening as centrifugal forces continue to pull apart the European project. Insofar as transnational subjects, I track cyber, bio, violent extremism (especially Islamic radicalism such as the Islamic State and al-Qaeda), and the Arctic.

This kind of broad, subject- and inbox-oriented reading matters, of course—but it will not make you a better leader. Reading for leading generally requires reading *books*, and the time investment to get through longer works is a challenge. Indeed, I am often asked where I find the time to read.

First and foremost, you need to master the art of reading books in short bursts. In today's frenetic world, there are very few opportunities to stop, put up your feet, and read for several uninterrupted hours. Obviously that would be wonderful, but it is generally unrealistic for most of us. So my advice is to train yourself to read in short spurts, perhaps as little as ten to fifteen minutes. While not ideal, it is efficient. The key to making it useful is concentration and not keeping too many books going at once. I try to be reading one novel and one nonfiction book more or less simultaneously, going back and forth between them if I get bored.

Second, take notes. This can be done easily on electronic texts using the very convenient functions built into Kindles, Nooks, and most of the other tablets and devices today. If you are reading hard copy, jotting notes lightly in pencil on the margins is fine (unless you have a valuable first or signed edition and wish to preserve its value or you borrowed the book from the public library). Alternatively, you can fold a piece of paper, use it as a bookmark, and take your notes on that. I also use small sticky tabs to mark particularly cogent passages.

A third vital approach, and the heart of reading and leading, is to read with *purpose*. As you pick up a book with an eye to improving your own leadership style, begin by researching the author and his or her background. Understand all that you can about an author, particularly trying to think about why an author decided to write a particular book. Sometimes it is obvious—a memoir, for example, is normally an opportunity to illuminate a certain period in the author's life and provide a kind of historical coda to it. Why a particular novel is written can be obvious after reflection on the author's life and experiences— think Hemingway or James Jones on novels about combat—or entirely obscure. But as a reader seeking to glean ideas about leadership, it is helpful to think about why an author might have picked up the pen in the first place. Occasionally an author will explicitly describe why she or he chose to write a particular book in a foreword. There are often clues in the various reviews available online, as critics describe an author's background in an in-depth review. Even a Wikipedia-level glance at an author's biographical information is very helpful, and of course in today's transparent world there are generally interviews and coverage of readings and other events where an author will have spoken about her or his ideas and theories about the genesis of a book.

As you then begin to read the actual book, think consciously about what we discussed in chapter 1—how reading can help improve your leadership skills. As you move through the book, frequently and pointedly ask yourself, "What would I do in this situation?" Use the book as a "simulator" to hone your own ideas on leadership. Additionally, think about the leadership situations the author (in the case of pure fiction) places in front of the characters. In the worlds of nonfiction and historical fiction, consider the world situation and how events drive the central characters in leadership situations. Watch what leaders actually do or what advice they provide to others. Think about outcomes and whether the crucible of leadership was the principal determinant of how things turned out—or whether even larger forces were at work and determined the outcome, regardless of the quality of leadership. And watch for failure, which can be just as valuable as success in teaching us lessons about leadership.

Very important, as you read to lead, talk to others about the book you are reading. The more conversations you can have with others about the book itself, the leadership lessons you think you are learning from it, or the life experiences of a more senior leader that relate to the content of the book, the better. When I was preparing to become a ship captain for the first time in my mid-thirties, I spent a great deal of time reading books about sea captains—everyone from Jack Aubrey in the novels of Patrick O'Brian to Ulysses in *The Odyssey* to the unnamed commanding officer of the ship in C. S. Forester's magnificent World War II novel, *The Ship*. Reading those books was helpful; but the real payout was discussing them with more senior officers who had already been through the crucible of command.

Should you form a book club? Not a bad idea. While these small organizations are often the preserve of those living in suburban neighborhoods, the fundamental idea is a very good one. How about a book club in your circle of friends and colleagues with a focus on the lessons of leadership? By exchanging ideas with others interested in leadership, you can compare your impressions, lessons, and ideas about applying what you have learned with others. No one of us is as smart as all of us thinking together are—these sorts of study and conversation groups can be immensely useful when given structure and purpose.

As you work through the fifty books that follow, you will find many leadership lessons. We have tried to illuminate them in short essays about each of the books, as well as providing a bit of background on the author. We have also indicated which of the many four-star officers we interviewed recommended the book and included something about that officer's own career. And at the bottom of each essay are a few small lessons of leadership that stood out to us about that particular book.

In subsequent chapters we will discuss other aspects of the reading life—but the heart of this book is the fifty classics that follow.

THREE

THE LEADER'S BOOKSHELF "TOP 50"

Adm. James Stavridis and R. Manning Ancell

The best guide to books is a book itself. It clasps hands with a thousand other books.

—Maurice Francis Egan

This chapter—the heart of the book—presents the fifty books that stood out most in our interviews with top military leaders. There are books from a variety of genres: novels, history, historical fiction, biographies and memoirs, and books about war, leadership, and ethics. Each book is presented in an essay that includes a summary of the work's high points, the name and affiliation of the flag or general officer who recommended it, and a synopsis of the leadership lessons that can be derived from reading it.

The books are presented in descending order of the number of mentions each received from the four-star officers we interviewed for the project. Rather than being a highly personal and subjective list that the two of us put together, this is truly the product of the nearly two hundred interviews conducted with four-star officers over several years. While not scientific or definitive, it provides a coherent way to think about the books that are truly important to this community of highly regarded leaders. While many of the books on the list were recommended by multiple flag and general officers, we single out one four-star for each book who most strongly sang that book's praise.

It is worth pointing out that although this is a list recommended by senior military leaders, the leadership lessons that emerge are applicable in virtually all walks of life. Military leaders face many of the same stresses and challenges that leaders in business, government, academia, medicine, the law, and sciences do: creating effective strategies, inspiring subordinates, distributing scarce resources, communicating effectively, building collaborative teams, and developing innovative solutions to seemingly intractable problems. These are universally applicable books that reward their readers with rich lessons in the kind of leadership we all need to exercise successfully in life, whatever our profession or level.

1 ⟿ *The Killer Angels*
by Michael Shaara (David McKay, 1974)

Recommended by Adm. Thad W. Allen, 23rd Commandant of the U.S. Coast Guard 2006–10

In creating a fictional account of the Battle of Gettysburg, Michael Shaara is able to extract and depict the humanity of the participants so we can experience the crushing pressure of responsibility and the need to make decisions that leaders face. From Chamberlain at Little Round Top to Pickett's failed charge, we can envision how the leaders coped with circumstances and made decisions that charted the course of our nation. I have always been intrigued by Longstreet's role and his failed attempt to influence Lee's decisions. There is a lesson there in speaking truth to power and understanding the truth.

Quote from the book "General, soldiering has one great trap: to be a good soldier you must love the army. To be a good commander, you must be willing to order the death of the thing you love. We do not fear our own death you and I. But there comes a time we are never quite prepared for so many to die. Oh, we do expect the occasional empty chair. A salute to fallen comrades. But this war goes on and on and the men die and the price gets ever higher. We are prepared to lose some of us, but we are never prepared to lose all of us. And there is the great trap, General. When you attack, you must hold nothing back. You must commit yourself totally. We are adrift here in a sea of blood and I want it to end. I want this to be the final battle" (Robert E. Lee to Lt. Gen. James Longstreet during the Battle of Gettysburg).

About the Author

Michael Shaara was born on June 23, 1928, in Jersey City. His father was an immigrant from Italy, his mother a longtime resident of Georgia. He served as a sergeant in the 82nd Airborne Division prior to the Korean War, graduated from Rutgers in 1951, and pursued a career writing science fiction while employed as a police officer and amateur boxer throughout the 1950s. In a widely circulated quote of uncertain origins Shaara is reported to have said, "I wrote only what came to mind, with no goal and little income," adding "always for the joy of it, and it has been a great joy."

Despite multiple rejections *The Killer Angels* was finally published in 1974 and was awarded a Pulitzer Prize the following year. Five years after Shaara's death in 1988 his signature book was transformed into the hit movie *Gettysburg*. His son Jeff has picked up the mantle from his father and writes bestselling novels about the Civil War.

About the Book

Killer Angels is the acknowledged flagship of a new fleet of memorable and meaningful works of historical fiction. The novel covers in great detail the four days when the armies of the North and South clashed at the small community of Gettysburg in central Pennsylvania on the last day of June and the first three days of July 1863. The beauty of *The Killer Angels* is Michael Shaara's ability to take an event of epic proportions and reduce it to a handful of characters who tell the story of the battle in individual terms that the reader can understand and relate to. Shaara's uncanny ability to remain completely objective draws the reader into the story. Whether you have sympathy for the Blue or the Gray, you are compelled to build empathy for both sides, and with it an understanding not easily gained in the vast majority of books about battle.

The book focuses on Gen. Robert E. Lee, commander of the Army of Northern Virginia, who believed it was necessary to take a stand against the solidly entrenched Union forces his army stumbled upon near Gettysburg. Lee's trusted subordinate Lt. Gen. James Longstreet is portrayed correctly as a loyal and obedient commander who is twisted by indecision on the part of his commander and yet resolves to put his forces in harm's way in a battle he feels is not winnable. A few lesser Confederate characters such as Brig. Gen. Lewis Armistead, Maj. Gen. George Pickett, and the actor Henry Harrison—who is an effective spy for Longstreet—add pathos and sympathy to the challenges presented as the battle unfolds. On the Union side we learn about Maj. Gen. George Meade's leadership of the Army of the Potomac through the eyes of Brig. Gen. John Buford, Col. Joshua L. Chamberlain—commander of the 20th Maine—his brother, Lt. Thomas Chamberlain, and one of the few fictional personalities, Sgt. Buster Kilrain, a close advisor and friend of Chamberlain as the battle unfolds at Little Round Top.

The defining moment of the book, as well as the movie, which faithfully follows the storyline, is when Colonel Chamberlain and Sergeant Kilrain—a "tough old Mick" from Ireland—are sitting beneath a tree discussing the battle unfolding around them.

"Tell me something, Buster," Chamberlain says. "What do you think of Negroes?"

"Well, if you mean the race, I don't really know," replies Buster. "This is not a thing to be ashamed of. The thing is, you cannot judge a race. Any man who judges by the group is a pea-wit. You take men one at a time."

Chamberlain pauses to reflect. "You see, to me there was never any difference."

"None at all?"

"None at all. Of course, I haven't known that many freedmen, but those I knew in Bangor, Portland . . . You look in the eye, there was a man. There was a 'divine spark,' as my mother used to call it. That is all there is to it. Races are men. What a piece of work is man. How infinite in faculties and form, and movement. How express and admirable. In action how like an angel."

A serious, contemplative look comes over the face of the Irish sergeant, who replies,

Well, if he's an angel, all right then, but he damn well must be a killer angel. Colonel, darling, you're a lovely man. I see a vast great difference between us, yet I admire you, lad. You're an idealist, praise be. The truth is, Colonel, there is no "divine spark." There's many a man alive no more of value than a dead dog. Believe me. When you've seen them hang each other the way I have back in the Old Country. Equality? What I'm fighting for is to prove I'm a better man than many of them. Where have you seen this "divine spark" in operation, Colonel? Where have you noted this magnificent equality? No two things on Earth are equal or have an equal chance. Not a leaf, not a tree. There's many a man worse than me, and some better, but I don't think race or country matters a damn. What matters, Colonel, is justice—which is why I'm here. I'll be treated as I deserve, not as my father deserved. I'm Kilrain, and I damn all gentlemen. There is only one aristocracy and that is right here.

Buster pauses momentarily and taps his head. "And that's why we've got to win this war."

The Killer Angels is widely acclaimed for its character development and concentration on the foibles and challenges of command on the battlefield, as well as the intricacies of decision making. It is most definitely a page-turner, although that is the least of its many attributes. The book is a beautiful portrait of grace under extreme pressure that depicts leadership in the crucible of battle better than virtually any other.

Leadership Lessons Summarized

There are many leadership lessons in Shaara's book, and they all revolve around the tyranny of command in combat—the requirement to send men to die in a higher cause. Each of the characters—mostly leaders of combat troops—brings to the fight a deep understanding of the geography of the battlefield, a sense of the need for effective gathering of intelligence, and an intuitive understanding of the enemy's moves. Most of the characters, to their great advantage, had exceptionally well-qualified, tenacious subordinates working for them. The best leaders trusted their subordinates to make the right decisions in the heat of battle; the subordinates trusted the senior leaders to let them make those decisions without undue speculation or interference. In the simplest terms it is called "teamwork up and down the chain of command"; and it is vital in any organization.

Although a bit further down the leadership ladder—mostly at the level of captains and lieutenants—Chamberlain had a team within the 20th Maine on the crucial battlefield of Little Round Top. When Chamberlain surmised that ammunition would not hold out and the Confederate forces would attack yet again, he instinctively thought "outside the box" of traditional infantry tactics and ordered an attack with fixed bayonets. There was no hesitation on the part of his junior officers, and that innovative decision saved the day and perhaps the war.

Thus, the key lessons for leaders from *Killer Angels* are to delegate, to trust and have confidence in the team, to know the battlefield, to collect intelligence, to innovate under extreme pressure, and to follow intuition when metrics and facts are insufficient.

— *R. Manning Ancell*

2 ⚔ *Once an Eagle*
by Anton Myrer (HarperTorch, 1968)

Recommended by Gen. Peter J. Schoomaker, USA (Ret.), commander in chief U.S. Special Operations Command 1997–2000, chief of staff U.S. Army 2003–7

Throughout my more than three decades of military service, professional reading has been the most important source of leadership preparation—second only to personal experience in training and combat. In all of my commands I have maintained an active professional reading list for my subordinates. I believe this practice to be quite widespread because most of my seniors and mentors over the years did the same, as do most of my peers today.

Without question, the most important—and most treasured—book in my personal library is *Once an Eagle* by Anton Myrer. I read it as a young officer and have never found a more complete combat leadership primer in print. It's the first book I tell leaders to read, and I refer to it often. It has also served as a potential leader assessment tool for me. I have noticed that "pretenders" don't relate well to the book, while "warriors" do. Having grown up in an Army family and having "experienced" much of my father's thirty-two-year career—including aspects of World War II, the Korea conflict, Vietnam, and the Cold War—as well as my own, *Once an Eagle* depicts real life challenges of military leadership sans political correctness.

Quote from the book "Massengale will never make an enemy and he'll never have a friend" (Sam Damon, hero of *Once an Eagle*, on his lifelong antagonist).

About the Author

Like his fellow novelists William Manchester and James Jones, who also served in combat in World War II, Anton O. Myrer quit his studies at Harvard to join the Marine Corps in 1942. Discharged as a corporal in 1947, he returned to college and graduated magna cum laude that summer. His first novel was published in 1951; others followed with moderate success, but not until 1968—at the height of the Vietnam War—did his most successful book, *Once an Eagle*, begin to receive the acclaim it deserved. Myrer died of leukemia on January 19, 1996.

About the Book

Reading a book the size of *Once an Eagle* (900 pages) is akin to tackling Tolstoy's *War and Peace*. Critics early on panned Myrer's masterpiece as being too "gray" rather than "black and white" and containing wooden characters. Historian Matt Gallagher came to Myrer's defense in his *Battleland* blog on August 29, 2011. Myrer's book has two characters—both Army officers—at the opposite ends of the spectrum of human personality and leadership: a sincere, dedicated man of immense integrity named Sam Damon; and a reprehensible opportunist named Courtney Massengale. Gray does not play well here; black and white dominate because the main characters are so polarized. "This is a book of consequence," Gallagher notes; "it is both historically intriguing and forward-looking in its vision. . . . It's a hero's epic set during the American Century and chronicles the life of its protagonist Sam Damon."[1]

Gallagher identifies Massengale as a "snake" who dodges combat assignments and moves up the ranks on the basis of favoritism and politics. The reader is forced to take sides early on because in the end there is no reasonable compromise between these characters who represent the two extremes of a military professional's life and career: selflessness and selfishness. Take a poll among today's career officers (and indeed in civilian professions as well) and there will be confirmation that there are Damons and Massengales everywhere and at many levels.

The novel follows both protagonists through their long lives as active-duty Army officers. Both rise through the ranks to become general officers and serve in World War I and World War II, and both end their careers in a thinly disguised Vietnam. Their personal lives are deeply intertwined, as is the case for many military officers. The combat sequences in the book are brilliantly realized, and the quiet heroism of Damon is consistently contrasted with the obsequious toadyism of Massengale.

New readers of *Once an Eagle* would be correct in assuming that delving into the lives and careers of two totally different officers who lived and served yesterday will accurately provide a portrait of the contrasts between warriors and staff officers of today. What has changed, however, is that our armed forces today are indelibly "purple"—a popular euphemism for "joint," or multiservice; officers cannot progress beyond the rank of major or lieutenant commander without having served in a joint environment involving the U.S. Army, U.S. Air Force, U.S. Navy, and U.S. Marine Corps. Officers serving today may wear different uniforms, but their mindset is purple, and the kind of inner society within the U.S. Army depicted in the novel is now diluted by mandatory staff assignments for all officers. Damon and Massengale grew up in an Army insulated from the rest of American society, a peacetime organization hindered by its small size and structure, which were dictated by meager appropriations in the midst of the Depression. Up until the early months of World War II promotions came by seniority, not achievement, which meant that the people ahead of an officer on the promotion list would have to be promoted, retire, or die. The higher up the structure, the less likely was further advancement. Other factors often played a role, however, and in this regard it is worth examining the careers of two iconic officers who actually lived and served during the times of the fictional Damon and Massengale: George C. Marshall and Douglas MacArthur.

Marshall and MacArthur were born months apart in 1880. MacArthur went to West Point, Marshall to VMI. MacArthur, whose father was a lieutenant general and Medal of Honor recipient, graduated first in his class in 1903. In World War I Marshall performed brilliantly as a trainer and planner and rose to the rank of colonel. Most important, he gained the trust of Gen. John J. Pershing, who became his mentor and friend. MacArthur came to the war as chief of staff of the 42nd ("Rainbow") Division and became a brigadier general on June 25, 1918, at the age of thirty-eight.

When the war ended, Marshall was a colonel, but he reverted to major, served as aide-de-camp to General Pershing, and served in a variety of staff and command positions as a lieutenant colonel and colonel. MacArthur retained his star and went on to be the youngest superintendent at West Point, then chief of staff of the Army. After retirement he returned to the Philippines to live and was appointed a field marshal in the Philippine army. Characteristically, he flew a flag with six stars. Meanwhile, Marshall crept up the promotion ladder and with significant encouragement and support from General Pershing became chief of staff of the Army when Gen. Malin Craig retired in 1939.

Years later, while appearing on *The Dick Cavett Show*, the eminent actor Orson Welles said, "Marshall is the greatest man I ever met. . . . He was a tremendous gentleman, an old-fashioned institution which isn't with us anymore."[2] MacArthur, in the meantime, had been relieved from command of United Nations forces in Korea by President Truman, who had nothing but disdain for this egotistical but successful leader.

Readers can draw their own conclusions about who might be the Damon or the Massengale in this clash of titans, or if Damon and Massengale models even existed. Obviously, real life is more "shades of gray" than black and white. But the contrast between the "E Ring Ballerinas" (those serving in the Pentagon on staffs along the all-important E Ring of the building) and the warriors who have spent much of their lives in combat continues as a central tension in the armed forces. It exists as well in big businesses, the tech industry, and any large bureaucracy where operators and staff personnel compete.

Leadership Lessons Summarized

Many lessons are written in the pages of Myrer's epic novel. As you consider them, keep in mind that the author intentionally crafts "two species of military man"—the combat leader and the staff officer—and acquaints us with the effect they have on those who enter their lives in war and peace.

At its heart, *Once an Eagle* is a parable with clearly defined characters representing two sides of the human spirit and two distinct styles of leadership. In one sense, Myrer looks at life as a poker game. Whatever hand you are dealt, you must play it; you can fold and wait for something better to come along, you can play the hand according to what the other players do, or you can bet "all in." Damon and Massengale were dealt different hands and played them differently. But the author clearly sets up Damon's moral and ethical leadership style as the right way to play the hand. "That's the whole challenge of life—to act with honor and hope and generosity, no matter what you've drawn," Myrer opines. "You can't help when or what you were born, you may not be able to help how you die; but you can—and you should—try to pass the days between as a good man." In that sense, this is a book about the choices leaders are offered and how they decide their path. Choosing courage, honor, and commitment to those you lead—the leader as servant—is the highest good. There is no better book to illustrate that principle than *Once an Eagle*.

— *R. Manning Ancell*

3   The Holy Bible
by multiple authors; according to both Christians and Jews, inspired by God

Recommended by Gen. Charles C. Krulak, USMC (Ret.), 31st Commandant of the Marine Corps 1995–99

Quote from the book   "Also I heard the voice of the Lord, saying, Whom shall I send, and who will go for us? Then said I, Here *am* I; send me" (Isaiah 6:8).

About the Authors

The "authorship" of the Bible has been debated for millennia. Many, many Jews and Christians view it as inspired and essentially authored by God, working through the writing of the prophets and the apostles. In most liturgies, after a reading from the Bible the lector intones, "The word of the Lord." Throughout some of the Old Testament books there are words that either state or strongly imply God, or Yahweh, as the actual author directing the hand of a prophet. Most of the books of the New Testament can be attributed to various human authors, many of them apostles. Some scholars and believers think God actually "dictated" the words (Orthodox Jews believe that in regard to the Torah), while others (a majority one would think in surveying both the scholarly and the ecclesiastical literature) believe that the Bible was "inspired" by the Lord but not literally dictated. Additionally, there have been countless translations over the years, further diluting the various theories of authorship.

No it is NOT!

About the Book

If there is a book that needs no introduction, especially to a Western audience, it is the Holy Bible, a sweeping work of literature full of dramatic moments, high emotion, desperate violence, winners and losers, spiritual philosophy, epic history, and all of the other things that make it perhaps the best-selling work of literature in the world. But at its heart, the Bible is a book about how to live a life—and therefore in a very real sense is a book for leaders. It offers practical lessons—thousands of them—in the form of parables, anecdotes, direct discussions, and living examples. And it certainly has a fair share of leadership lessons embedded in its many pages.

Perhaps the most iconic leadership book in the Bible is Isaiah. Two of the best verses in the book deal with how leaders behave in moments that test them. The first has to do with exhaustion and the renewing power of believing in something bigger than yourself: "But they that wait upon the LORD shall renew *their* strength; they shall mount up with wings as eagles; they shall run, and not be weary; *and* they shall walk, and not faint" (Isaiah 40:31). This means that leaders can—and must—dip into the ultimate reserves of their strength. The second is about leaders being the first to volunteer, the first to take the hard task: "Also I heard the voice of the Lord, saying, Whom shall I send, and who will go for us? Then said I, Here *am* I; send me" (Isaiah 6:8). Often referred to as "Isaiah's Commission," these words are the epitome of leadership.

Another powerful leadership lesson comes from Noah's experiences in the face of the Great Flood. In the book of Genesis, Noah is the leader who is willing to risk all on an utterly unconventional course of action. His energy, zeal, innovation, love of family, and commitment to fulfilling a deeply disturbing and fundamentally odd mission allow him to survive along with his family and most of the animal kingdom. Leaders are often called upon to take a path that may appear not to make sense.

Certainly one of the most famous leadership stories from the Bible is that of David and Goliath. In the book of Samuel we learn the story of the young shepherd boy who cannot wear the armor provided for him because it is far too big. Armed with nothing deadlier than a slingshot, he faces a nine-foot giant, Goliath, who is fully armed and armored. As everyone knows, David defeats Goliath through the power of innovation, the courage to believe in his own attributes and faith, and the spirituality provided by his unshakable belief in a higher power. All of these are gifts for a leader.

Countless other stories from the Bible shine a light on leadership in very practical ways—Abraham and Moses are often cited, as are Joshua and David of the lion's den; the passion of Peter and Paul shines through the many centuries since they walked the earth and led the early Christians in the face of brutal persecution. But, of course, the principal story of leadership in the Bible is provided by Jesus: the leader as servant, washing the feet of all who present themselves; the determination and charisma of Jesus as he sweeps the temple clean of moneylenders; the leader as merciful judge; and—above all—the leader who will sacrifice himself in the highest cause. Leaving aside any belief in his

[handwritten note at top: Jesus is the ultimately penultimate LEADER for Isl is God incarnate. Note Israel surpass God at all in heaven or earth!]

deity, Jesus is a "hands on" leader who demonstrates a wide variety of leadership skills in the New Testament.

Another broad leadership element in the Bible is found in the stories of the geopolitics of the era it describes. The tyranny of various harsh regimes—from the Egyptians to the Romans, and many more ancient ones as well—is fully documented. Throughout the Bible, leaders are men and women of principle who are willing to sacrifice themselves in the face of death, torture, pain, and sacrifice. The central story of the New Testament, that of Jesus of Nazareth, is the most obvious and iconic example of this. But there are many others through both the New and Old Testaments. This theme of heroic self-sacrifice on behalf of geopolitical ends—defeating an unjust regime—runs throughout the work.

There is also a continuing thread of "leader as servant" throughout much of the Bible. Again, Jesus kneeling to wash the feet of his disciples is the most familiar example of this. But there are many other leaders in the Bible who are willing to put the interests and needs of their followers ahead of their own ambitions and personal comfort, including Moses, Elijah, Gideon, and many others. Today we often try to find and overcome the "toxic leader." In the Bible we find many examples of the "supporting leader."

Overall, there is a leadership lesson every few pages in the Bible. Regardless of the depth of your faith (or lack thereof) in organized religion, the Bible rewards focused reading with leadership in mind.

Leadership Lessons Summarized

There are far too many to name individually—but certainly high on the list are the vital necessity of the leader as servant; the notion of sacrifice in a high cause; the power of innovation to succeed against long odds; the fundamental need for a leader to demonstrate determination and personal example; the importance of endurance in the face of adversity; and the crucial belief in oneself. There are few lessons of leadership that cannot be illuminated by referring to the pages of the Bible.

— Adm. J. Stavridis

4 *Team of Rivals: The Political Genius of Abraham Lincoln*

by Doris Kearns Goodwin (Simon and Schuster, 2006)

Recommended by Gen. Victor E. Renuart, USAF, commander U.S. Northern Command 2007–10

You know, *Team of Rivals* is really an extraordinary book. It describes how Lincoln was a coalition builder. He understood who his rivals were in politics and he did what masterful leaders have done in the past, and that is to say, "OK, fine, they're going to be part of my team, and we'll figure this out"; and he was able to craft them from being rivals into being teammates. That's always been a fascinating model to me, and so that's a book I've read two or three times, and I go back to it quite a bit because it's a great example of how you can deal in a very difficult set of circumstances with difficult partners and figure out how to succeed.

Quote from the book "Washington was a typical American. Napoleon was a typical Frenchman, but Lincoln was a humanitarian as broad as the world. He was bigger than his country—bigger than all the Presidents together" (Doris Kearns Goodwin).

About the Author

A native of New York, Doris Kearns Goodwin distinguished herself at Colby College in Maine by graduating magna cum laude in 1964, then attended Harvard University, where she earned a PhD in government. She served two years as an intern in the Johnson administration despite her opposition to the Vietnam War and an article she published in the *New Republic* titled "How to Dump Lyndon Johnson." Reportedly LBJ commented, "Oh, bring her down here for a year and if I can't win her over, no one can." She came; he didn't succeed.

Goodwin published her first book, *Lyndon Johnson and the American Dream*, while teaching at Harvard. Her book *No Ordinary Time—Franklin and Eleanor Roosevelt: The Home Front during World War II* was a bestseller when it was published in 1994 and earned her the Pulitzer Prize for History the following year.

About the Book

Goodwin's magnificent *Team of Rivals* is about character and leadership in facing the biggest events, not about the events themselves. It joined a crowded field when it was published, with historian James M. McPherson accurately noting in his *New York Times* review that "more books about Abraham Lincoln line the shelves of libraries than about any other American." One can imagine her publisher groaning "Not another book about Lincoln" when her proposal arrived. But the book was a huge commercial and critical success, with reviewers consistently writing that it is not only a powerful new look at Lincoln as a leader but also an extraordinary view into the second-tier characters who make up his story.

Indeed, *Team of Rivals* offers readers a unique, fresh perspective on a story that has been told countless times: the presidency of Abraham Lincoln. This view from inside the administration and the cabinet relates how Lincoln selected, balanced, and even manipulated the men (and they were all men in those days) who constituted his leadership team during the Civil War. The biographical sketches of these men form the backbone of the book: their roots, education, families, beliefs, politics, and relationships. But the narrative becomes a vastly larger sum than its parts individually.

Edwin M. Stanton was offered the post of secretary of war in spite of his visible contempt for the president. Born to Quaker parents in Steubenville, Ohio, on December 19, 1814, Stanton was given a privileged private education; at the age of ten he studied Latin, Greek, and classical history. He became an attorney and settled in Washington, D.C. When Daniel Sickles shot and killed Philip B. Key—son of Francis Scott Key—on February 27, 1859, for having an affair with Sickles' daughter, Stanton was recruited to join the team representing Sickles. His impassioned plea to the jury for the sanctity of marriage won Sickles a not guilty verdict.

When the first shots of the Civil War were fired on April 12, 1861, Stanton was serving as attorney general. Later, when Confederate and Union forces clashed in the First Battle of Bull Run (also known as the Battle of Manassas) on July 21, 1861, on the outskirts of Washington, Stanton wrote to former president James Buchanan: "The dreadful disaster of Sunday can scarcely be mentioned. The imbecility of this administration has culminated in that catastrophe, and irretrievable misfortune and national disgrace are to be added to the ruin of all peaceful pursuits and national bankruptcy as the result of Lincoln's 'manning the madness' for five months."[3]

Stanton stayed on after Lincoln's untimely death but continued to be vehemently opposed to conciliatory moves to bring the former Confederacy back into mainstream America. He was nominated by President Grant, who succeeded President Johnson, for a seat on the Supreme Court, and it was approved by the Senate, but Stanton died suddenly four days later at the age of fifty-five.

A nationally prominent Republican second only to William H. Seward, Salmon P. Chase, one of ten children, was born on January 13, 1808, in Cornish, New Hampshire. His father died suddenly when he was nine, and he went to live with his uncle, Bishop Philander Chase of the Protestant Episcopal Church. Chase graduated from Dartmouth and studied law in Washington, D.C. Elected to the Senate in 1849 as an active member of the Free Soil movement, which opposed the spread of slavery, he served until 1855, when he became the first Republican governor of Ohio. At the expiration of his term he ran for the Republican nomination for president but lost to Abraham Lincoln. He was reelected to the Senate but resigned three days after taking office to accept Lincoln's appointment as secretary of the treasury. Chase had a superior term as head of the Treasury Department and earned the great respect of President Lincoln. When Chief Justice Roger B. Taney died in October 1864 Lincoln nominated Chase as his replacement, and Chase served until his death in 1873. He was a talented public servant who served his president and his country with distinction.

William H. Seward, also a senator and governor, was the leading candidate at the Republican National Convention in 1860, but his support of parochial schools was his downfall. Appointed secretary of state by Lincoln, he came into the administration "condescending and skeptical" of the president, but over time a sincere affection developed between the two. William O. Stoddard notes in his biography of Lincoln that

> conferences between Mr. Seward and Mr. Lincoln were almost of daily occurrence, and the iron hand discernible in the conduct of our foreign affairs was not solely that of the shrewd and able head of the State Department. These conferences were generally held at the White House, to and from which Mr. Seward went and came with the easy familiarity of a household intimate rather than with any observance of useless etiquette. It was not at all uncommon, however, for Mr. Lincoln to walk over to the State Department, in the daytime, or to Mr. Seward's house, in the evening, with or without an attending private secretary to carry papers.[4]

Seward was criticized for advocating the purchase of Alaska from Russia—known at the time as "Seward's Icebox" or "Seward's Folly"—yet today it is recognized as a master stroke in the consolidation of the nation in the High North.

The fourth individual profiled in Goodwin's book, Edward Bates, is much less known than the others. "A small, white haired man, not noticeable in appearance, with a good head, sharp features, and pleasant face well fringed with gray whiskers," journalist Noah Brooks described him at the time. "He is not meddlesome in public affairs, lives retired, and next to Montgomery Blair, is the least influential man in the cabinet."[5] Although a respected and experienced statesman, Bates' service as attorney general went largely unnoticed by the public.

All of these men considered themselves political rivals of the newly elected Lincoln. They were unimpressed by what they knew of him, and several were close to being hostile. Goodwin sets out to explain why Lincoln selected these particular people—who differed from him in culture, education, personality, and experience—to become part of his inner circle, the cabinet; how they responded; and how he worked to manage them into a high-performing team. How he cultivated their respect, loyalty, and friendship is a fascinating study in leadership. "He never lost sight of the intricate task he faced in building a Cabinet that would preserve the integrity of the Republication Party in the North, while providing the fairest possible representation to the South," Goodwin notes.[6]

Each of Lincoln's rivals was sure the wrong man had been elected president. When asked by Joseph Medill of the *Chicago Tribune* why he had chosen a cabinet made up of enemies and opponents, Lincoln replied, "We needed the strongest men of the party in the Cabinet. . . . I concluded that these were the very strongest men. I had no right to deprive the country of their services." He worked hard to balance this team of rivals and consolidate his leadership.

The book is full of stories from diaries and private conversations detailing how Lincoln kept his team moving forward, and the author explores how the president maneuvered his path through this minefield of egos, scheming, and distrust. Goodwin masterfully illuminates a formerly dark corner of the behind-the-scenes machinations of wartime politics and highly skilled politicians.

Leadership Lessons Summarized

This book is a case study in a leadership challenge that the vast majority of leaders will face at some point in their careers: managing a high-strung, intensely talented, and very headstrong team. The key to understanding Lincoln's brilliance in this situation is knowing that these men were not only rivals with each other, but also at one time or another rivals with their boss. And of course all of it took place amid the tumultuous events of the time when the future of the nation literally hung in the balance.

In approaching this precarious situation Lincoln set out several crucial operating principles; all of them are relatively easy to articulate but very difficult to inculcate into day-to-day interactions.

Give offense to no one. Lincoln, being presented with frequent good reason to lose his temper and lash out, realized that he always had to be "the adult in the room." Ensuring that he at least avoided offending his prideful teammates was the first order of the day.

Take personal responsibility. Lincoln often declared that he, and not his cabinet, was at fault for errors imputed to them. The press and the public were, naturally enough, in a constant state of concern verging on hysteria. The tabloid papers of the day spewed constant criticism of all decisions, many of which had disastrous consequences, especially in the early days of the war. Lincoln always took responsibility for the broad actions of his administration, and his team—gradually perceiving the altruism of his approach—responded over time.

Develop real human relationships. Despite their initial political animosity, Lincoln kept his rivals close both to him and to each other. He took the time to know each of them as individuals, to understand their families and finances, and he used his keen sense of compassion and good humor to make real friendships, and it paid enormous dividends over time. He treated people with dignity and respect and found a path to friendship with each of them.

Know when to delegate. Lincoln was at pains to protect the integrity and autonomy of the cabinet, realizing that he could not do everything himself, despite his incredible talent and capacity. He ensured that tasks that rightly fell to individual agencies of government were conducted there and avoided the natural temptation to take matters into the White House. If there was ever a president who could have become a benevolent dictator, it was Lincoln. His leadership of this "team of rivals"—and especially his ability to appropriately delegate to them—helped ensure that never happened.

—R. Manning Ancell

5   The Art of War
by Sun Tzu (first published in 513 BC)

Recommended by Gen. Alfred M. Gray Jr., USMC (Ret.), 29th Commandant of the Marine Corps 1987–91

I was always interested in the whole idea of maneuvering as opposed to a "hi-diddle-diddle straight up the middle" kind of thing. Early on I became quite a student of Sun Tzu and the Eastern philosophy. I favored maneuver and "go where they aren't" as opposed to the dictums that came out of my readings of Clausewitz. I've read everything there is about Sun Tzu as well as Timor and Tamerlane. I kind of gravitated in later years to that side of the world, since in my first twenty-two years as a Marine most of my time was in the Pacific and the Far East. I learned so much. Pick any one of the books. All these great leaders had that faculty for, if there was a crisis or a serious situation, they had that faculty for showing up, for being there, and they had that faculty for calming everything down, and they all were courageous and brave. They're all different but they all had those traits, and they believed in their people.

A lot of people talk a good game, and they have these sixteen traits of leadership or their ten things you must know, and all that, but that's all recipe-type stuff. It has to come from the heart. You know that. They had that faculty and they were intensely loyal to those they had served with. Not to a fault, but they believed in them, they looked after them, and most of the great leaders that I associated with did not care about the credit for anything. They wanted to share, they wanted others to get the credit, but all of them would take the responsibility, and they would stand up and be counted when the chips were down. Those kinds of ideas or those kinds of traits you can get from books if you read the right books, like The Art of War.

Quote from the book "There are three ways in which a ruler can bring misfortune: By commanding the army to advance or to retreat, being ignorant of the fact that it cannot obey. By attempting to govern an army in the same way as he administers a kingdom, being ignorant of the conditions which obtain in an army. This causes restlessness in the soldiers' minds. By employing the officers of his army without discrimination, through ignorance of adaptation to circumstances. This shakes the confidence of the soldiers" (Sun Tzu).

About the Author

The noted philosopher and novelist Ayn Rand begins her groundbreaking book *Atlas Shrugged* with a simple question: "Who is John Galt?" It can be argued that *The Art of War* could legitimately begin with "Who is Sun Tzu?" The elusive Chinese military strategist and Taoist philosopher, whose name translates as Master Sun, was a general who lived in the sixth century BC. It was a time when the Zhou kingdom had greatly expanded and created numerous states that were beginning to show prosperity. It was the age of Confucius.

Historians are uncertain exactly when Sun Tzu lived and when he wrote *The Art of War*, also known as *The Thirteen Chapters*. There are those who question whether he actually wrote the book, suggesting that the content could well have been provided by an understudy or aide in much the same way that those studying under great masters created paintings credited to them. Such is ever the fate of master artists from Shakespeare to Rembrandt, because there are always doubters that "one man" could have created so much perfection. We are unlikely ever to know the precise nature of Sun Tzu, but the book reads collectively as though a single individual wrote it all, not like a patchwork of ideas.

About the Book

For many centuries, warfare in ancient China was practiced by the ruling class as a kind of sport in which "chivalry prevailed and rules were not to be bent or broken." Sun Tzu put his thoughts on paper and then proved their validity in battle, and as a result, the nature and practice of war gradually changed. In 2002 Peter Mackay wrote a thought-provoking review of *The Art of War* that reaches into the essence of what this book is all about. "War is ugly, dirty, brutal, wasteful and expensive," he says. "That is the reality of it. Let's not pretend otherwise. Having said that, the ancient Chinese master strips away all the familiar trappings of war—the warriors, weapons, forts and tactics—to reveal the essence of conflict and how to win. His lessons are as valid here and now as they were in an empire a long time ago and far, far away. It simply does not matter how you are fighting, what you are fighting over, or even why you are fighting."[7]

In the course of the book, which is quite short, two ideas appear again and again and are central to good leadership. The first is, as General Gray suggested, the vital importance of maneuver. The best battle is the one that the leader never actually has to fight and is won through a combination of maneuver, intimidation, deterrence, and clever use of balance in the approach to actual combat. The second overarching message in the book is the importance of the leader's determination, because followers will quickly recognize indecision, fear, and a wavering set of objectives. Sun Tzu tells us "when on death ground, fight," meaning that all the maneuver in the world may win the battle, but in the end it is our determination and courage that must carry the day if we arrive on the field of death itself.

Leadership Lessons Summarized

Sun Tzu is among the most quotable of all leadership writers, and a powerful and simple way to summarize the key lessons is simply to list them here.

Keep your enemy off balance. "If your enemy is secure at all points, be prepared for him. If he is in superior strength, evade him. If your opponent is temperamental, seek to irritate him. Pretend to be weak, that he may grow arrogant. If he is taking his ease, give him no rest. If his forces are united, separate them. If sovereign and subject are in accord, put division between them. Attack him where he is unprepared, appear where you are not expected."

Intelligence is vital. "Keep your friends close and your enemies closer."

Keys to victory. "Thus we may know that there are five essentials for victory: (1) He will win who knows when to fight and when not to fight. (2) He will win who knows how to handle both superior and inferior forces. (3) He will win whose army is animated by the same spirit throughout all its ranks. (4) He will win who, prepared himself, waits to take the enemy unprepared. (5) He will win who has military capacity and is not interfered with by the sovereign."

Confidence is a force multiplier. "Opportunities multiply as they are seized."

Simplicity matters when plans are assembled. "There are not more than five musical notes, yet the combinations of these five give rise to more melodies than can ever be heard. There are not more than five primary colors, yet in combination they produce more hues than can ever been seen. There are not more than five cardinal tastes, yet combinations of them yield more flavors than can ever be tasted."

Lead as servant and protector. "Treat your men as you would your own beloved sons and they will follow you into the deepest valley. Engage people with what they expect; it is what they are able to discern and confirms their projections. It settles them into predictable patterns of response, occupying their minds while you wait for the extraordinary moment—that which they cannot anticipate."

Dream. "Can you imagine what I would do if I could do all I can?" Every leader should have that aphorism taped above his or her desk.

〜— R. Manning Ancell

6 *The Face of Battle: A Study of Agincourt, Waterloo and the Somme*
by Sir John Keegan (Viking Press, 1976)

Recommended by Gen. Alexander M. Haig Jr., USA, vice chief of staff U.S. Army, then supreme allied commander Europe 1974–79

I think John Keegan's *The Face of Battle* is a wonderful book because it goes through the ages of the great battles and humanizes them. That's a very important book for what makes the world go round. I've read everything [about the great battles] ever written, I guess, especially when I was young. Hans Morgenthau and all of the writers that emerged after the Second War, with the nuclear age, I call them deterrence-related books. Again, as you get old you get a little stale, but I can pick out what I think is worth reading.

You live your profession through reading. It's the most important crutch you have. My only complaint is I've been such an operational guy and an activist that I have never had a chance to read everything. I just moved into my home in Virginia and I've got more books than I have house to hold them. I don't want to ever throw one away because if I haven't read it from cover to cover, I don't like that. I don't mean that I'm that kind of a scholar, I'm not. I'm more of an activist, but maybe that's why I'm thirsty for it.

Quote from the book "There are certain wicked people in the world that you can't deal with except by force" (John Keegan).

About the Author
Sir John Keegan was born on May 15, 1934, in London. He was a lecturer in military history at Sandhurst, the Royal Military Academy, for twenty-six years. *The Face of Battle* is the fourth of twenty-six books

published during his distinguished career. Following his experience at Sandhurst, Keegan joined the *Daily Telegraph* as a defense correspondent and remained there until his death on August 2, 2012.

About the Book

In the nearly four decades after Keegan published his revolutionary *The Face of Battle*, he forged a worldwide reputation as a military historian despite his lack of a combat background or experience. "I have not been in a battle," he writes, "not near one, not heard one, nor heard one from afar, nor seen the aftermath." Nevertheless, as attested to by many who have had deep personal experience on the battlefield, he manages to capture the emotion and misery of the individual soldier on the battlefield as if he *had* been there. "The book is an attempt to examine three historical battles from the point of view of the participants," notes Patrick Shrier in his review. Three famous battles are examined: Agincourt in 1415, Waterloo four hundred years later in 1815, and the Somme in 1916. Shrier points out that "there has not been enough attention paid to the individual and their experiences in war" and offers Keegan's book as a dynamic new benchmark.[8] It is also a powerful book about leadership under extreme stress.

One particularly interesting thread that Keegan discusses is the evolution of the weapons and tactics soldiers employed in the three historical battles. At Agincourt, the forces of France and England met face-to-face in northern France in yet another of many such encounters during the Hundred Years' War. Later, at Waterloo, the newer weapons permitted killing at great distance as well as within arm's reach. In World War I, advanced artillery and aircraft bombardment increased the range of engagement, although individuals still fought at close quarters as well. The face of battle does morph as technology changes, and that narrative is powerfully explored throughout this magnificent book.

The clash of forces essentially involved three separate technological matchups: archers versus infantry and cavalry; cavalry versus infantry; and infantry versus infantry. Given that gunpowder was just coming into use in medieval Europe (although invented by the Chinese in the ninth century) there were no sounds of weapons except the barely perceptible whine of arrows zooming through the air. Early fighting was done in very personal and close ways, and the sounds and smell of battlefields reflected that.

Technology had advanced to such a degree by 1815 that the forces of Napoleon and Wellington at Waterloo went into battle well aware that projectiles of various sizes and types would strike them from all angles and directions. Unlike Agincourt, where battlefield encounters "generally occurred between dismounted men," at Waterloo many of those soldiers went into battle astride horses, and paintings of the battle depict masses of cavalry slamming into one another at high speed. "Give me the boys who will go at a swinging gallop for the last seventy yards," a senior officer in the Light Dragoons says, "applying both spurs when you come within six yards. Then if you don't go through them I am much mistaken."

At the Battle of Waterloo, which took place on Sunday, June 18, 1815, about nine and a half miles south of Brussels and a mile or so from the town of Waterloo, Napoleon faced a force of British, Prussian, Belgian, and Dutch soldiers—23,000 British under the command of the Duke of Wellington and roughly 44,000 troops commanded by the aged Generalfeldmarschall Gebhard Leberecht von Blücher, who had earned the nickname Marschall Vorwärts (Marshal Forward) because of his "aggressive approach to warfare."

Napoleon had escaped from his exile on the island of Elba the previous year and returned to retake his crown in France. The countries that opposed his rule formed the Seventh Coalition, which was prepared to eliminate him for good at Waterloo. The French forces were somewhat superior, employing 74,000 troops and 250 cannons. In addition to cavalry battling cavalry, the French and Allied forces faced artillery as well as infantry. Infantry battled infantry, of course, and also artillery. Infantry troops were compelled to stand still rather than seek cover during an artillery barrage from the enemy, Keegan explains, "for the whole purpose of enemy artillery fire was to make men break formation. When, out of self-preservation, they did, it could have disastrous results." In the end the Allied forces were victorious and the rule of Napoleon was halted forever.

The third conflict Keegan analyzes is the Battle of the Somme, which began on July 1, 1916, and involved the British Expeditionary Force, "one of the most remarkable and admirable military formations ever to have taken the field, and the Fourth and Third Armies, which were to attack the Somme, provided a perfect cross-section of the sort of units which composed it." It was very much a mixed bag on the first day of the battle. The French Sixth Army and the British Fourth Army successfully drove the entrenched German Second Army about six miles back into German territory, but it was at the same time the worst day in history for British forces. On the front between the Albert–Bapaume Road and Gommecourt the British suffered 60,000 casualties. Only a small number of British troops reached the German front line.

Of the thirteen attacking divisions involved in the Somme engagement, four were composed entirely of regulars—"long-service volunteer soldiers." Also involved in the engagement were British "pals battalions," groups of young men from the same area who enlisted together and served together. The pals, Keegan says, were a "spontaneous and genuinely popular mass movement which has no counterpart in the modern, English-speaking world and could have none outside its own time and place: a time of intense, almost mystical patriotism."

The Battle of the Somme saw the first use of airpower and tanks. To this day the engagement continues to be controversial "over its necessity, significance and effect."

Keegan weaves extraordinary detail and insight throughout this marvelous book. Every page bristles with the energy and danger of battle, and as a portrait of the universal challenge leaders face—bringing order out of extreme chaos—there is no better preparation than to read Keegan, no matter what the situation or business of a leader.

Leadership Lessons Summarized

The Face of Battle is not a book about leadership per se but rather an examination of human nature in three distinctly unique battles of Western history. Keegan presents persuasive evidence of the vital importance of the relationship between officers and soldiers from the age of knights and chivalry to the first modern global war, saying, "The personal bond between leader and follower lies at the root of all explanations of what does and does not happen in battle."

This is not a book that provides individual leadership lessons in the way Sun Tzu constantly does. *The Face of Battle* can best be appreciated as a sweeping canvas of crisis, allowing those studying and learning about leadership to think about how to handle the maximum level of stress. Its companion book by Sir John Keegan, *The Mask of Command*, can be profitably read alongside *The Face of Battle*, but it is the latter book that provides the best understanding of the heart of stress that leaders all must face.

— R. Manning Ancell

7 ⌒ *We Were Soldiers Once . . . and Young*
by Lt. Gen. Harold G. Moore (Ret.) and Joseph L. Galloway
(Random House, 1992)

Recommended by Gen. John H. Tilelli Jr., USA, vice chief of staff U.S. Army, commander U.S. Army Forces Command, and later commander U.S. Forces in Korea 1994–2000

We Were Soldiers Once . . . and Young by Hal Moore and photojournalist Joe Galloway tells the story of the battle of Ia Drang Valley in Vietnam. Hal Moore led the 1st Battalion of the 7th Cavalry Regiment, which was the unit I commanded in Desert Shield/Desert Storm (and Lt. Col. George Armstrong Custer took into the massacre at Little Big Horn June 25–26, 1876). Moore and Galloway's book is about the valor of a unit and the absolute role that a leader plays in cohesion in making a unit either strong or weak. That's a book that I keep and use when I'm giving speeches about the sacrifice of war and when I talk about Vietnam, because Vietnam is looked upon as being one of those places that the American Army and the armed forces didn't essentially do very well.

Quote from the book "There were two great tragedies in the twentieth century. One was the decline in morality in our country. The second was the war in Vietnam. It was an unnecessary war" (Lt. Gen. Harold G. Moore).

About the Authors

Harold G. Moore was born and raised in Georgia and graduated from West Point in 1945. He saw combat in Korea, taught infantry tactics at West Point—where one of his students was Cadet Norman Schwarzkopf—and was a battalion commander in the early days of the Vietnam War. He retired as a lieutenant general.

Joe Galloway grew up in a family of soldiers but opted to pursue a career as a journalist. General Schwarzkopf called him the "finest combat correspondent of our generation."

About the Book

If you have not read this incredible book—or watched the memorable movie starring Mel Gibson as Lt. Col. Hal Moore—we hope this brief review will inspire either a reading or a viewing of this heroic tale. We suggest beginning with the book.

There was an old saying in Vietnam that "he who controls the Central Highlands controls South Vietnam." That was certainly brought home on May 7, 1954, when a large detachment of French soldiers was outfought and defeated by Viet Minh communist troops at Dien

Bien Phu. This incident ultimately convinced the French government to give up its occupation goals in Indochina and bolstered Ho Chi Minh's expansionist vision of a consolidated North and South Vietnam. The United States, somewhat reluctantly, stepped into the breach, responding to the so-called domino theory that postulated a complete collapse of Southeast Asia into communism if South Vietnam were to fall.

Of note, revolutionaries worth their salt don't wear wristwatches or mark dates on calendars. As the Taliban have said in Afghanistan, "The Americans have all the watches, but we have all the time." Ho Chi Minh and his able military commander, General Vo Nguyen Giap, certainly felt that way; time was on their side, and what they hoped for most was a striking defeat of the U.S. Army forces that would break the will of the American people. On November 14, 1965, they had that chance. The North Vietnamese had three crack regiments "within walking distance" of a football-field-shaped clearing in the Ia Drang Valley in central South Vietnam, within shouting distance of the Cambodian border directly to the west. That small natural clearing was bounded on the north by open woodland and elephant grass, on the northeast and west by dry ravines; due west was a series of foothills known as the Chu Pong Massif. That mostly barren plot of land became Landing Zone X-Ray, where American troops, heavily outnumbered but with the support of UH-1B Huey helicopters, landed and began the first clash of what would become known as the Vietnam War.

There were several key players in the drama that unfolded that day. Lt. Col. Hal Moore was the forty-two-year-old commander of the 1st Battalion, 7th Cavalry Regiment. His men revered him for his quiet belief in their character and capability, and his willingness to take on any challenge alongside them. He was in the first helicopter to land at X-Ray.

Moore's right-hand man was forty-five-year-old Sgt. Maj. Basil Plumley, a veteran of the four major jumps with the 82nd Airborne in World War II. "The sergeant major was a no-bullshit guy," Moore says, "who believed, as I did, in tough training, tough discipline, and tough physical conditioning. To this day there are veterans of the battalion who are convinced that God may look like Sergeant Major Basil Plumley, but He isn't nearly as tough as the sergeant major on sins small or large. Privately, I thanked my lucky stars that I had inherited such a treasure. I told Sergeant Major Plumley that he had unrestricted access to me at any time, on any subject he wished to raise."

The 7th Cavalry was a key unit of the 1st Cavalry Division, commanded by Maj. Gen. Harry Kinnard, age fifty, one of the architects of the airmobile concept that brought together helicopters and infantry—described by a journalist as the "sky cavalry." Kinnard ensured his place in history during the siege of Bastogne in the Battle of the Bulge. Asked by his immediate boss, Brig. Gen. Anthony C. McAuliffe, for a response to the demand for surrender from the German commander whose forces completely surrounded the 101st Airborne, Kinnard said one word would suffice: "Nuts." (The Germans were initially bewildered but quickly got the idea.)

Coauthor Joe Galloway, who turned twenty-four two days before the opening hours at X-Ray, was a combat reporter and photographer for United Press International. He hitched a ride into the battle and recorded the historic event with his camera and notebook.

Maj. Bruce "Snake" Crandall, age thirty-two, and Capt. Ed "Too Tall" Freeman, age thirty-seven, were helicopter pilots who continued to fly into the killing zone when pilots of all the other choppers stayed away because of the increased danger. Their heroism saved lives and helped turn a calamity into a victory.

Finally, we can't overlook Nguyen Huu An, the thirty-nine-year-old commander of North Vietnamese forces who pressed hard at the battle but met his match in Lieutenant Colonel Moore, who anticipated his every move. An commanded Regiment 174, which overran the French forces at Dien Bien Phu on May 7, 1954.

Fought over a four-day period and centered on two landing zones near the Drang River, the battle was bloody in the context of the period. The U.S. forces suffered more than 250 killed—shocking to the American public—and the Vietnamese (both regular North Vietnamese troops and Viet Cong guerrillas) lost more than 1,000. While the battle could be viewed as a tactical draw, Galloway said later that it was the battle that convinced Ho that he could fight, kill, and triumph over regular U.S. soldiers. Despite a great deal of American heroism on the battlefield that day, the ultimate winners were probably the North Vietnamese.

Leadership Lessons Summarized

We Were Soldiers Once is full of examples of extraordinary personal heroism and leadership, but three in particular stand out. First, Lt. Col. Hal Moore's standard of personal engagement in the heart of the fighting. He took his battalion to the Ia Drang Valley, reconnoitered the area, set up a defensive perimeter, and prepared his men for the real possibility of a clash with North Vietnamese regulars. As the hours ticked off and skirmishes turned into battles, he rallied his badly outnumbered troops. His personal determination and courage were the inspirational keys for his men.

The only way to get in and out of the valley was by helicopter, and the chopper pilots constantly dodged enemy fire to bring in replacements, supplies, and ammunition critical to the survival of the battalion, "without which they would almost surely have gone down with much greater loss of life." As the intensity of battle increased, the medical evacuation helicopter pilots refused to fly any additional dangerous missions to take the wounded—and the dead, for the Army's pledge was "no man left behind"—back to Plei Me. Captain Freeman and Major Crandall took up the slack and flew additional critical missions. "We desperately needed ammunition and water and medical supplies— and Crandall's Hueys brought them to us," Moore remembers. "Our wounded, screaming in pain or moaning quietly in shock, had to be evacuated, or they would die where they lay, on their ponchos behind the termite hill." For their courage and selflessness both pilots were awarded the Medal of Honor. The lesson is that logistics matter, and a leader must be aware of the flow of resources to the battlefield.

Finally, mention must be made of Julie Moore, the consummate "den mother" back home who provided the glue that kept together the wives of the officers and soldiers who were fighting and dying at Ia Drang. This was leadership of a different sort, but representative of how families and friends—who may be very distant from the field of conflict—are an enormous part of all that occurs.

—R. Manning Ancell

8 ⟶ Dereliction of Duty: Lyndon Johnson, Robert McNamara, the Joint Chiefs of Staff, and the Lies That Led to Vietnam
by H. R. McMaster (Harper, 1997)

Recommended by Gen. John "Jack" Sheehan, USMC, former commander in chief U.S. Atlantic Command

Quote from the book "Military operations alone cannot defeat an insurgency because only economic development and political action can address most sources of disaffection. If military operations are not conducted consistent with political objectives or occur without economic development, they are certain to alienate the population further, reduce the amount of intelligence available to security forces, and strengthen rather than weaken the enemy" (H. R. McMaster).

About the Author
H. R. McMaster was born in Philadelphia in 1962 and went to West Point, where he was a standout student and athlete. His career has featured superb performances in combat, including leading a tank formation in the First Gulf War that resulted in his receiving the Silver Star. Lieutenant General McMaster also led his unit in combat in Iraq and served as a task force commander in Afghanistan. He has repeatedly been called one of the leading "warrior-thinkers" of his generation of

military officers. While in graduate school at the University of North Carolina at Chapel Hill in the mid-1990s he wrote *Dereliction of Duty*, widely regarded as a classic study of civil-military relations under stress—in this case the controversial war in Vietnam.

As a maverick who has consistently "bucked the system," he was passed over several times for promotion to both brigadier and major general. It took personal engagement by the secretary of the Army to ensure that the composition of the selection board included senior officers capable of understanding and appreciating the extraordinary courage and value of his (and others similarly gifted but bureaucratically challenged) record—including in the case of McMaster his intellectual contributions in addition to his extraordinary combat record.

During his service in Afghanistan he was deliberately placed in the most demanding and nontraditional role imaginable: countering corruption. His work there was particularly noteworthy, not only for the results it achieved but for the creative and energetic way in which he approached it—as the NATO supreme allied commander at the time, I witnessed his work firsthand. He is simply extraordinary. Now a three-star lieutenant general in the U.S. Army, he is leading the effort to reshape that most traditional of organizations and bring it into the twenty-first century.

About the Book

This is a searing book that points a finger squarely at the uniformed U.S. military for not being fully truthful with their civilian leaders in the days leading up to the full combat deployments to Vietnam. In addition to the senior military figures of that time, the book additionally takes to task the civilian staffs at the Pentagon and the White House who likewise failed to develop any coherent plan to deal with the expanding crisis in Vietnam. As lies stacked upon the initial lies, the "system" failed to produce either a plan to defeat the North Vietnamese army and combat capability *or* to address the virulent insurgency led by the Viet Cong.

McMaster focuses on the period from November 1963 to July 1965, when the most disastrous decisions were made in a war that would ultimately cost 58,000 American lives. His cogent and dispassionate analysis of both the policy and the military decisions is masterful and full of (mostly negative) leadership lessons as well. It was a challenging period: the Johnson administration's Department of Defense, led by Secretary of Defense Robert McNamara, was dominated by the "whiz kids" out of the Ivy League (see David Halberstam's seminal book about the senior personalities in the Kennedy and Johnson administrations, *The Best and the Brightest*). Given the slow bureaucratic pace of the military, McNamara quickly lost faith and broke his relationships with his uniformed subordinates. McMaster says the chiefs "were unable to respond to McNamara's demands fast enough, and their cumbersome administrative system exacerbated the administration's unfavorable opinion of them." The book is powered by meticulous, original, and truly scholarly research conducted by McMaster using newly declassified documents and official reports on the war.

The book also details an approach on the part of the administration that centered on the domestic politics of the war rather than on the tactical, operational, or strategic goals and objectives. There was a sense that first and foremost, actions should be passed through a filter of "how will the newspapers and television networks cover this?" And above all, "how will this work for us in terms of possible reelection?" As domestic politics poisoned the center of the Vietnam debate, the administration tried to straddle a difficult line between "soft on communism" and avoiding the "domino theory," on one hand, and dealing with the outcry about an increasingly unpopular war on the domestic front—with combat deaths of draftees building weekly and protests sprouting across the United States—on the other.

The basic failures that provide lessons to leaders are straightforward. First, "wanting to please the boss" on the part of the military caused subordinates to shade the truth. Additionally, there was an inability to use the military instrument—admittedly a blunt force tool—effectively in creating appropriate objectives. All of this led to a failure to measure honestly the factors against which progress (or failure) could be determined. Finally, and most fundamental of all, the military simply failed to conduct effective operations in the field. While General McMaster finds the most fault with the uniformed military, he has significant criticism for civilian leaders and their staffs as well.

Leadership Lessons Summarized

Strong leaders must follow the truth wherever it leads. Nothing is more dangerous than a subordinate who will shade or alter the truth in order to curry favor or impress the boss. Leadership must be built on teamwork, mutual respect, and above all a shared sense of a common objective.

— Adm. J. Stavridis

9 *On War*

by Carl von Clausewitz
(published in numerous versions and many languages)

Recommended by Gen. Barry R. McCaffrey, USA, commander U.S. Southern Command 1994–96

If you wish to understand war, you must master the concepts contained in *On War*. It will take a month of intense part-time study to complete this complex work. Pulling your thoughts together in an essay will help. The payoff for understanding Clausewitz will be enormous.

I read the Hardy Boys and the Tom Swift series as a little kid, but I read military history or history in general nonstop from the time I was about seven on. I think I finally cracked when I was a battalion commander, because it was killing me; I was reading two, three, four books a week. It was such a demanding job that I'd be reading from ten o'clock at night until two o'clock in the morning, and that's when I started to back off to a book or two a week. That was really the way I was raised. I remember my aunt saying, "Oh my God, should he be reading that?" Whatever "that" was.

> *Quote from the book* "The aim of war should be the defeat of the enemy. But what constitutes defeat? The conquest of his whole territory is not always necessary, and total occupation of his territory may not be enough" (Carl von Clausewitz).

About the Author

Carl Philipp Gottfried von Clausewitz was born in Prussia to a middle-class family on June 1, 1780. At the age of twelve or thirteen he joined the Prussian army as a *Fahnenjunker*, or cadet, fought in the war with France in 1793–94, and was promoted to lieutenant at the age of fifteen. Six years later Clausewitz was admitted to the War Academy in Berlin and attended classes taught by forty-five-year-old Oberstleutnant (lieutenant colonel) Gerhard von Scharnhorst, an officer whose reputation was most definitely on the ascendancy. Clausewitz met Marie von Brühl during his time at the academy, and they married six years after his graduation in 1804. His marriage into an aristocratic family in Berlin permitted him to move at the highest levels of society and contributed in great measure to his promotion at a young age to major general. His book *Vom Kriege* (*On War*) was unfinished on his death in 1831 from cholera and was completed and published by his widow. She writes, "It goes without saying that I have no intention whatever of regarding myself as the true editor of a work that is far beyond my intellectual horizon."

About the Book

"When you were given a particular assignment, that was the primary way that you had books brought to your attention," Gen. John H. Tilelli recalled in our interview with him. "If it wasn't part of a curriculum or a program of instruction, you'd have in fact peers or seniors say that you ought to read that book, it's a great book for self-development, plus they knew what the time constraints were and whether the book was an easy read or a difficult read. For example, at the War College we all had to read Clausewitz's *On War*. Well, I can tell you that's a hard book to read, so you don't want to read that book for entertainment. But there are a lot of lessons learned out of *On War* that are applicable to the political-military situation that not only our current forces are in, but also our nation. So in a lot of cases you'd have individuals making recommendations to you, and in other cases you'd have instructional requirements. Reading was a part of self-development but it was also part of unit development."

So, what is there in this book that is "must" reading? Clausewitz is best known by his most famous declaration that "war is merely a continuation of politics [by other means]." A relevant question, given the dense, academic nature of this book, is why it has stood the test of two centuries to remain a cornerstone of the military profession. The most often cited explanation for its popularity is its rigorous analysis of how wars are won, which so often results not simply from what happens on a battlefield but rather from the effect achieved in the mind of an opponent. This deceptively simple premise has echoes for leaders at every level and in virtually every profession—and has kept the book at the heart of the leadership canon. The key to understanding and applying the insights of the book is in a close reading of the text, participation in open discussion comparing views on it, and in consciously applying its various concepts—rendering it perfect for leadership seminars.

Clausewitz's masterpiece is actually a compendium of eight books: *On the Nature of War*; *On the Theory of War*; *On Strategy in General*; *The Engagement*; *Military Forces*; *Defense*; *The Attack*; and *War Plans*. Altogether there are 732 pages of often intricate instruction and insights into the major factors of warfare in the very early nineteenth century. Naturally, the nature of war and the societies that spawned it in succeeding generations have gone through marked changes.

Renowned military strategist Bernard Brodie provides a detailed "Guide to the Reading of *On War*" in the latest edition of Clausewitz's book, but with definite caveats. He writes that "the main purpose of this guide is to enhance the reader's comprehension of the text at first reading. If he finds it failing in that purpose, or not sufficiently succeeding in it to be worth the time, he should avail himself of the nearest exit, which is as close as the next comma or period."

Finally, *On War* contains many of the so-called principles of war that have evolved over the ages and are still memorized by military officers today. While Clausewitz does not explicitly list them, the general thrust of the list is contained in his work, and the fundamental idea of using them when thinking through planning is of great use to leaders. The list currently in use by the U.S. military, taken from Field Manual 3-0,[9] has nine principles:

1. *Objective*. Direct every military operation toward a clearly defined, decisive, and attainable objective. The ultimate military purpose of war is the destruction of the enemy's ability to fight and will to fight.

2. *Offensive*. Seize, retain, and exploit the initiative. Offensive action is the most effective and decisive way to attain a clearly defined common objective. Offensive operations are the means by which a military force seizes and holds the initiative while maintaining freedom of action and achieving decisive results. This is fundamentally true across all levels of war.

3. *Mass*. Mass the effects of overwhelming combat power at the decisive place and time. Synchronizing all the elements of combat power where they will have decisive effect on an enemy force in a short period of time is to achieve mass. Massing effects, rather than concentrating forces, can enable numerically inferior forces to achieve decisive results while limiting exposure to enemy fire.

4. *Economy of force*. Employ all combat power available in the most effective way possible; allocate minimum essential combat power to secondary efforts. Economy of force is the judicious employment and distribution of forces. No part of the force should ever be left

without purpose. The allocation of available combat power to such tasks as limited attacks, defense, delays, deception, or even retrograde operations is measured in order to achieve mass elsewhere at the decisive point and time on the battlefield.

5. *Maneuver*. Place the enemy in a position of disadvantage through the flexible application of combat power. Maneuver is the movement of forces in relation to the enemy to gain positional advantage. Effective maneuver keeps the enemy off balance and protects the force. It is used to exploit successes, to preserve freedom of action, and to reduce vulnerability. It continually poses new problems for the enemy by rendering his actions ineffective, eventually leading to defeat.

6. *Unity of command*. For every objective, seek unity of command and unity of effort. At all levels of war, employment of military forces in a manner that masses combat power toward a common objective requires unity of command and unity of effort. Unity of command means that all the forces are under one responsible commander. It requires a single commander with the requisite authority to direct all forces in pursuit of a unified purpose.

7. *Security*. Never permit the enemy to acquire an unexpected advantage. Security enhances freedom of action by reducing vulnerability to hostile acts, influence, or surprise. Security results from the measures taken by a commander to protect his or her forces. Knowledge and understanding of enemy strategy, tactics, doctrine, and staff planning improve the detailed planning of adequate security measures.

8. *Surprise*. Strike the enemy at a time or place or in a manner for which he is unprepared. Surprise can decisively shift the balance of combat power. By seeking surprise, forces can achieve success well out of proportion to the effort expended. Surprise can be in tempo, size of force, direction or location of the main effort, and timing. Deception can aid the probability of achieving surprise.

9. *Simplicity*. Prepare clear, uncomplicated plans and concise orders to ensure thorough understanding. Everything in war is very simple,

but simplicity is difficult. Simplicity contributes to successful operations. Simple plans and clear, concise orders minimize misunderstanding and confusion. Other factors being equal, parsimony is to be preferred.

Leadership Lessons Summarized

As was pointed out earlier, many people over the years have declared that Clausewitz designed his book so that the reader must actually *read* the book and not expect to understand what he presents in it by the use of abbreviated reviews. Therefore, much as was the case with Sun Tzu (with whom Clausewitz is often contrasted) we present a handful of cogent quotes that we trust will encourage you, the reader, to tackle the book in its entirety.

Good leaders can never rest on their laurels. "There is only one decisive victory: the last." In the surface Navy, this is often translated to: "You are only as good as your last sea detail," meaning each time you take the ship into danger of any kind, your reputation is on the line. So be it.

Leaders reach for the stars. "If the leader is filled with high ambition and if he pursues his aims with audacity and strength of will, he will reach them in spite of all obstacles." And "Never forget that no military leader has ever become great without audacity."

Delegation is crucial. "We must, therefore, be confident that the general measures we have adopted will produce the results we expect. Most important in this connection is the trust that we must have in our lieutenants. Consequently, it is important to choose men on whom we can rely and to put aside all other considerations. If we have made appropriate preparations, taking into account all possible misfortunes, so that we shall not be lost immediately if they occur, we must boldly advance into the shadows of uncertainty."

Focus on objective. "Pursue one great decisive aim with force and determination."

"No one starts a war—or rather, no one in his senses ought to do so—without first being clear in his mind what he intends to achieve by that war and how he intends to conduct it."

Leaders must be determined. "After we have thought out everything carefully in advance and have sought and found without prejudice the most plausible plan, we must not be ready to abandon it at the slightest provocation. Should the certainty be lacking, we must tell ourselves that nothing is accomplished in warfare without daring, that the nature of war certainly does not let us see at all times where we are going; that what is probable will always be probable though at the moment it may not seem so, and finally, that we cannot be readily ruined in a single error, if we have made reasonable preparations."

And most iconically: "The best form of defense is attack."

— *R. Manning Ancell*

10 — *Nimitz*
by E. B. Potter (Naval Institute Press, 1976)

Recommended by Adm. Thomas B. Hayward, USN, commander in chief U.S. Pacific Fleet 1976–78, Chief of Naval Operations 1978–82

While I may wish it were otherwise, I never became an avid reader of books in my earlier years. Perhaps that is why both of my daughters have such a consuming habit today. As for books that did have a profound impact on my career I would put biographies and Pacific World War II books high on my list. I especially focused on John Paul Jones, Admiral Nimitz, and Admiral Spruance. Their willingness to "go in harm's way," to be contrasted with today's "risk free" philosophy, provided the underpinning direction of the Sea Strike maritime strategy that I and my advisors followed during my tenure as CINCPACFLT and CNO.

I'm ninety years old. I try to go back that far and it's a long ways. I can't remember how they fit into why I read them and why it was important—it was just good history that I wanted to know. I don't think that I could say I read those kinds of books because I expected something specific. It was just a matter of our naval profession that it was important to know. What you get out of those things . . . is leadership decisions that were made, good and bad, that you walk away with.

Quote from the book "God grant me the courage not to give up what I think is right even though I think it is hopeless" (Fleet Adm. Chester W. Nimitz).

About the Author

E. B. "Ned" Potter was born in Norfolk, Virginia, two days after Christmas in 1908. From an early age he had a penchant for history. He earned a BA from the University of Richmond in 1929, taught history in a high school, and received an MA in history from the University of Chicago in 1940. The following year he joined the Navy Reserve and was assigned to the U.S. Naval Academy to teach history. Except for three years of active duty during World War II Potter remained at Annapolis until his retirement in 1977, publishing eight books along the way.

About the Book

Capt. Ken White is a historian and former Coast Guard officer with special insights into the complex career that propelled Admiral Nimitz into the hallowed halls of naval history along with John Paul Jones, David Farragut, and a few others. In our interview White told me: "To me this is really several books in one because it speaks to so many topics: naval asset and operations development prior to World War II.

They include naval organization and strategy prior to and during World War II; theory and conduct of naval operations prior to and during World War II; establishment of relationships among numerous now-famous political and military personages prior to World War II and the results of these relationships during World War II; national and military service politics during conduct of the Pacific war; strategic conduct of the Pacific war itself; conduct of Pacific war battles and lessons learned; and more, such as taking the fight to the enemy. But what impressed me the most in my reading of the book, and from which I suggest lessons can be learned, is the conduct, personality, and style of this man Chester Nimitz."

An early event in his career set the stage: young Ensign Nimitz, fresh out of Annapolis, ran the destroyer *Decatur* aground entering Batangas Harbor south of Manila. He was court-martialed, found guilty of neglect of duty, and received (only) a public reprimand for his failure. He was given a second chance and all during his career exercised great personnel management skill by giving second chances to others who had "failed" in their assignments. Rather than trashing their careers, he attempted to place them in assignments that matched their skills and tendencies to maximize their possibility of future success. He was widely known for delegating to staff, and for using his homespun Texas upbringing to soberly recognize and transfer those who didn't measure up. He saved many an officer.

As a rear admiral Nimitz was offered the position as commander in chief Pacific but asked to be excused, reasoning that such a hard job would be even harder given the resentment he could expect when he was selected for the job over flag officers senior to him. It was early 1941, and the assignment went to a more senior officer: Rear Adm. Husband E. Kimmel. Kimmel was thus in command at Pearl Harbor when the Japanese attacked on December 7. Nimitz was assigned to relieve Kimmel and then conducted the Pacific war from Pearl Harbor, initially (and surprisingly) keeping Kimmel's staff as his own because they were informed and in place.

Six days before taking command—on Christmas Day 1941—Admiral Nimitz took a boat tour of Pearl Harbor. It was a sobering sight, to say the least. As the tour boat returned to the dock, the young helmsman of the boat asked, "Well, Admiral, what do you think after seeing all this destruction?" Admiral Nimitz replied in a steady voice, "The Japanese made three of the biggest mistakes an attack force could ever make or God was taking care of America. Which do you think it was?" The young helmsman replied, "What do you mean by saying the Japanese made the three biggest mistakes an attack force ever made?" Nimitz explained.

Mistake number one: the Japanese attacked on Sunday morning. Nine out of every ten crewmen of those ships were ashore on leave. If those same ships had been lured to sea and been sunk, we would have lost 38,000 men instead of 3,800. Mistake number two: when the Japanese saw all those battleships lined in a row, they got so carried away sinking those battleships, they never once bombed our dry docks opposite those ships. If they had destroyed our dry docks, we would have had to tow every one of those ships to America to be repaired. As it is now, the ships are in shallow water and can be raised. One tug can pull them over to the dry docks, and we can have them repaired and at sea by the time we could have towed them to America. And I already have crews ashore anxious to man those ships. Mistake number three: every drop of fuel in the Pacific theater of war is in top of the ground storage tanks five miles away over that hill. One attack plane could have strafed those tanks and destroyed our fuel supply. That's why I say the Japanese made three of the biggest mistakes an attack force could make or God was taking care of America.[10]

Nimitz ended his active naval career as the Chief of Naval Operations, the most senior job in the Navy. Afterward, he did some work for the United Nations, spoke against unifying the armed forces, and accepted appointments to a presidential commission as a counter to the McCarthy hearings and as a regent of the University of California. He never took advantage of his fame or positions and in general avoided the public eye. He lived his life as himself.

Leadership Lessons Summarized

As is the case in many biographies, the leadership lessons are built into the narrative of Nimitz's extraordinary life. Two powerful lessons for leaders emerge: innovate to succeed, and when pushed to a conflict, go straight at an opponent.

Nimitz was a relentless innovator who throughout his life and career sought the nontraditional solution. Early in his career and as a result of commanding the submarines *Plunger*, *Snapper*, *Narwhal*, and *Skipjack*, he campaigned against gasoline engines in submarines and became an expert in diesel engines, advocating them for naval use. During 1912 he lectured at the War College and published on diesel engines in *Proceedings*. He experienced a problem and advocated an innovative solution, becoming a technical expert in the process.

In April 1917, as the executive officer of the oiler *Maumee* (the first Navy surface ship powered by diesel engines), he became the co-inventor of refueling at sea. By July of that year, *Maumee* had refueled thirty-four destroyers at sea, demonstrating the feasibility of the process.

Assigned to the War College as a student in 1922, Commander Nimitz wrote his thesis on the 1916 naval battle engagement off Jutland and studied the advantages of the circle formation with Cdr. Roscoe C. MacFall, the formation's innovator. Later, Nimitz introduced the circle formation to the fleet while serving as the aide, assistant chief of staff, and tactical officer to the commander in chief of the battle fleet on board the battleship *California* in San Pedro. While in this assignment he also exercised the Navy's lone aircraft carrier, the *Langley*, at the center of the circle formation and urged that she (and her under-construction sisters, *Saratoga* and *Lexington*) be integrated into the fleet. That concept is still in use today in the Navy's powerful carrier strike groups.

Selected from the fleet in 1926, Commander Nimitz was one of six officers assigned to establish the university-based Naval Reserve Officers' Training Corps (NROTC) and to teach at the University of California at Berkeley. The NROTC provides the Navy and Marine Corps today with a sizable percentage of their officers and strengthens the civil-military bonds in the nation powerfully.

The other significant lesson from his life and career was his straightforward approach to facing up to conflict. Like Lord Nelson of the previous century, Nimitz thought that direct action was often the solution, and his legacy as a leader burns brightly today: taking the fight to the enemy is now standard in naval policy and plans. Indeed, Admiral Hayward noted that Potter's discussion of Nimitz's letter of instruction to Spruance for the Battle of Midway (ordering Spruance to take the fight to the enemy) had a great influence on him in the creation of global maritime strategy when he was assigned as commander in chief of the Pacific Fleet and through his tour as the Chief of Naval Operations.

— R. Manning Ancell

11   *Personal Memoirs of Ulysses S. Grant*
by Ulysses S. Grant (C. L. Webster, 1885)

Recommended by Gen. Edwin H. Burba Jr., USA, commander U.S. Army Forces Command 1989–93

I believe that *Personal Memoirs of U. S. Grant* makes a clear case for the importance of clarity of thought and expression, personal "follow-me" courage, calm demeanor, and perseverance in the heat of battle. Leadership involves as much knowing what to do as inspiring others to do it. There are impressively good leaders who have intrinsic persuasive and inspirational charisma who don't read much, but they limit their potential substantially, and as a result, they never become truly great leaders. Others with average charisma, but who read and think while they read, learn how to inspire individuals and small or large groups through their reading as well as to comprehend what to do better than anyone, and they become great leaders.

Quote from the book "Although frequently urged by friends to write my memoirs I had determined never to do so" (Ulysses S. Grant).

About the Author

Ulysses S. Grant's life was as unpredictable as a ride blindfolded on a brand-new roller coaster. Born Hiram Ulysses Grant in 1822 in Point Pleasant, Ohio, he grew up in Georgetown, Ohio, where his father owned and operated a tannery. He attended West Point, served under Zachary Taylor and Winfield Scott in the war with Mexico, but declared during that time that "a military life had no charms for me." This from the man who would win the Civil War for the Union and, of course, eventually become America's eighteenth president purely on the strength of his military portfolio. Grant became disaffected with Army life while he was stationed alone at Fort Vancouver in Washington and began drinking to excess, which led to disciplinary issues and his resignation in April 1854.

The next seven years were difficult for the young Grant family. They moved to Missouri and farmed land given them by Julia Grant's father. When that venture failed, they moved to St. Louis in 1857, and then to Galena, Illinois, a short time later in order to work in the elder Grant's leather goods shop. Grant was seemingly on the road to oblivion when the Civil War erupted. Based on his prior military experience and West Point degree, he was appointed a colonel in the Union Army in 1861.

Grant won one of the first Union victories of the war, at Fort Donelson, repulsed a surprise attack by the Confederates at the Battle of Shiloh in Tennessee—where Gen. Albert S. Johnston was mortally wounded—and clinched the Union's victory with an ingenious attack on Vicksburg, breaking the Confederacy's stranglehold on that key city and the Mississippi River. As his star and reputation rose, he was named lieutenant general in command of all Union troops by President Lincoln and took the fight directly to the Confederate armies in the field. He eventually accepted the surrender of enemy forces by his opposite number, Gen. Robert E. Lee, at Appomattox Court House, was named a four-star general, and in 1868 was elected president of the United States.

About the Book

Grant's memoirs are not in any sense a complete autobiography. They cover essentially his military service, including the Mexican-American War and, of course, the Civil War. There is virtually nothing in them about his early life or his time as president. This allows a very crisp focus on the leadership lessons and challenges Grant faced, as well as striking portraits of the military leaders he encountered.

Within the four-star community there is near unanimity that General Grant's *Personal Memoirs* is unequaled in its detail, humility, candor, and honesty. "In a race against throat cancer, Grant wrote what would become the paragon for a general's memoir," observes Gen. Stanley McChrystal, who commanded the International Security Force in Afghanistan. "Reading it in the West Point library, I was drawn to his candor, plain leadership lessons, and humility. Grant's tenacity and a lifetime of writing clear orders are evident in his lean phrases, while his bedrock humanity produces rich portraits of a gruesome war."[11]

To comprehend and understand the importance of Grant's *Memoirs* one must recognize that its author was a man of immense resoluteness, talent, and resourcefulness balanced with exceptional humility. In his memoirs, Grant said, "Although frequently urged by friends to write my memoirs I had determined never to do so, nor to write anything for publication." Thank heaven Grant changed his mind in the twilight years of his life as he battled terminal cancer—taking up the pen strictly to generate resources to support his family after his impending death. He completed the final editing of his book the day before he died, and his friend Mark Twain was largely responsible for its exceptional success in the marketplace.

Grant's description of the Battle of Vicksburg exemplifies his vision and leadership:

On the 14th General Parke arrived with two divisions of Burnside's corps, and was immediately dispatched to Haines' Bluff. These latter troops—Herron's and Parke's—were the reinforcements already spoken of sent by Halleck in anticipation of their being needed. They arrived none too soon.

I now had about seventy-one thousand men. More than half disposed across the peninsula, between the Yazoo at Haines' Bluff and the Big Black, with the division of Osterhaus watching the crossings of the latter river farther south and west from the crossing of the Jackson road to Baldwin's ferry and below.

There were eight roads leading into Vicksburg, along which and their immediate sides, our work was specially pushed and batteries advanced, but no commanding point within range of the enemy was neglected.

On the 17th I received a letter from General Sherman and one on the 18th from General McPherson, saying that their respective commands had complained to them of a fulsome, congratulatory order published by General McClernand to the 13th corps, which did great injustice to the other troops engaged in the campaign. This order had been sent North and published, and now papers containing it had reached our camps. The order had not been heard of by me, and certainly not by troops outside of McClernand's command until brought in this way. I at once wrote to McClernand, directing him to send me a copy of this order. He did so, and I at once relieved him from the command of the 13th army corps and ordered him back to Springfield, Illinois. The publication of his order in the press was in violation of War Department orders and also of mine.

As an example of Grant's observations and acuity, it is hard to top this passage from his encounter with Robert E. Lee at Appomattox Court House at the end of the war:

> What General Lee's feelings were I do not know. As he was a man of much dignity, with an impassible face, it was impossible to say whether he felt inwardly glad that the end had finally come, or felt sad over the result, and was too manly to show it. Whatever his feelings, they were entirely concealed from my observation; but my own feelings, which had been quite jubilant on the receipt of his letter, were sad and depressed. I felt like anything rather than rejoicing at the downfall of a foe who had fought so long and valiantly, and had suffered so much for a cause, though that cause was, I believe, one of the worst for which a people ever fought, and one for which there was the least excuse. I do not question, however, the sincerity of the great mass of those who were opposed to us.

The book truly stands out as a vibrant memoir full of leadership lessons won through the hardest of passages.

Leadership Lessons Summarized

Three key lessons emerge from Grant's memoirs for leaders today. First was his determination to succeed at a task no matter what the challenges. Lincoln searched long and hard to find the right general who could go directly at the enemy and win battles. Grant shows again and again the resolute determination of a true leader. Second, Grant was a master communicator and delegator. When a subordinate commander received one of Grant's handwritten orders, there was no question what Grant expected of him. As a result, Grant's relationship with his senior commanders—particularly Sherman—was one of unconditional trust and closeness. The war likely would not have been won by Union forces had this intimacy with key subordinates not existed. Third, Grant's memoir shows us again and again the value of humility in a senior leader.

Much of the affection Grant gained from his troops throughout his long military career was a direct result of his modest personal style. He was able to see himself clearly and never tried to elevate himself over the men who followed him from battle to terrible battle; despite all the losses, his inner moral compass was evident to his men, and they cherished his leadership.

— R. Manning Ancell

12 *Crusade in Europe*
by Dwight D. Eisenhower (Doubleday, 1948)

Recommended by Gen. George Joulwan, USA (Ret.), supreme allied commander, Europe at NATO, and commander in chief U.S. Southern Command

When preparing to take on the responsibilities of supreme allied commander in Europe, I often turned to the memoirs of the first SACEUR, General Eisenhower. Time and time again, his humility and intelligence solved the hardest problems.

Quote from the book "In preparing for battle I have always found that plans are useless, but planning is indispensable" (Dwight D. Eisenhower).

About the Author
Dwight David Eisenhower was born in Denison, Texas, in 1890, although he moved at the age of two to Kansas and always considered that his home. After attending West Point and graduating in the middle of his class, he launched a long and distinguished career in the U.S. Army, culminating in assignments as the supreme allied commander in the European theater (SACEUR) in World War II and then as chief of staff of the U.S. Army. He served on the staff of Gen. Douglas

MacArthur as a senior military aide in Washington, D.C., and later in the Philippines, part of the long, slow slog up the command chain of the interwar Army that included his remaining a major for sixteen years. He showed great promise throughout this period and remained loyal to the Army when many of his contemporaries abandoned it for the business world.

After Pearl Harbor his career accelerated with blinding speed. By 1942 he was a major general and was at the heart of operational planning to defeat both Germany and Japan. His operational activity began with leading Operation Torch in North Africa, and then the follow-on invasion of Sicily. This led directly to his appointment as SACEUR in December 1943—a job his mentor Gen. George Marshall coveted but would not be given because President Roosevelt was reluctant to let Marshall leave Washington.

As SACEUR Eisenhower planned and led Operation Overlord, the successful Normandy invasion, and the forces under his command went on to achieve total victory over Germany. This campaign is the heart of *Crusade in Europe*, his memoir of that time. Eisenhower was appointed military governor of Germany, then chief of staff of the U.S. Army. After his initial retirement from the Army he served briefly as president of Colombia University in New York before being asked to return to full-time active duty in Europe as the first supreme allied commander, Europe of the newly formed North Atlantic Treaty Organization.

After successfully standing up NATO, Eisenhower returned to the United States and twice ran successfully as the Republican candidate for president of the United States. After retiring he pursued his hobbies of golfing and oil painting until his death in 1969 at the age of seventy-eight. At his death, former president Richard Nixon said, "Some men are considered great because they lead great armies or they lead powerful nations. For eight years now, Dwight Eisenhower has neither commanded an army nor led a nation; and yet he remained through his final days the world's most admired and respected man, truly the first citizen of the world." He led an extraordinary life in every regard.

About the Book

This 550-plus-page memoir, full of maps and charts, is crisply written and full of facts and anecdotes that paint a vivid picture for the reader. It begins immediately after Pearl Harbor as Eisenhower is called to the Pentagon to work on war plans to protect the Philippines, a region he knew well from his time there with General MacArthur. His work is brilliant, and he is shifted to working on the plans to defeat Germany. Marshall, knowing both his qualities and his ability to plan, shifts Eisenhower to full command of the initial campaign to retake Europe, beginning with North Africa, then through Sicily and into Italy.

After some controversy and disagreement with Marshall, Eisenhower is made the supreme commander for Operation Overlord. The book then follows the complex campaigns that smashed the Nazi war machine and liberated France. The "crusade in Europe" continues until Germany falls, and the reader stands alongside the supreme commander through this turbulent period.

Several themes run through the book and are germane to leadership. The first is the idea that planning matters deeply. No leader can be effective unless he or she is an effective planner. That is not to say that every plan will be successful, or even executed as envisioned. But the process of planning becomes the basis for action, resilience, teamwork, creativity, and execution. To paraphrase the Eisenhower quote above, *planning* is everything, but the *plan* is nothing. Good leaders are good planners, but they are not tied to their plan as though it were an anchor—leaders know that no plan will survive contact with the enemy fully intact.

A second key idea is that an effective leader must be a coalition builder. To bring together such disparate commanders as Patton, Montgomery, Bradley, De Gaulle, and many others required a light touch, an iron will, a sense of humor, flexibility, and the nicest sense of emotional intelligence. Ike could alternatively charm, bully, agree, hire, or fire with lightning speed; and his instincts about people were nearly always right. His team recognized those qualities and responded in kind, despite the occasional internal firefight.

Third, good leaders are logisticians. As the old military saying goes, "Amateurs think tactics, professionals think logistics." Eisenhower was a detail-oriented professional when it came to logistics. He forced his team to focus on the enormity of their commands, knowing that the ability to move millions of soldiers with all their equipment and supplies, supported by endless bombers and fighters, and often at sea, would be crucial to the crusade.

Written in 1948 reportedly without the assistance of a ghostwriter (although he was helped by military historians and researchers), *Crusade in Europe* has a light, breezy, and personal style. It compares well with Churchill's classic *The Second World War*, but is of course more focused on the arena of Europe. This is a book full of leadership lessons on virtually every page, and the man who would go on to become president is clear and transparent to the reader.

Leadership Lessons Summarized

Good leaders above all build teams, even when the participants come from vastly different cultures and have strikingly unmatched personalities. Leaders are both detail oriented and capable of seeing and executing the big strategic picture. And leaders must be very capable planners with the ability to deviate from the plan in the heat of execution without losing sight of the big objectives.

— Adm. J. Stavridis

13   *Men against Fire: The Problem of Battle Command in Future War*
by S. L. A. Marshall (William M. Morrow, 1947)

Recommended by Gen. Paul F. Gorman, USA, commander U.S. Southern Command 1983–85

In 1867 the Army had acted on the recommendation of Maj. Gen. Emory Upton that it designate as its basic unit a "pair of fours"—eight soldiers—and to train how to fight with these as its smallest tactical element (the basic unit of the Roman legion was the eight-man mess, the *contubernia*). For the next hundred years the Army continued to adjust the basic size of the small tactical unit. Most of the changes added either (1) more powerful weapons or (2) higher rank for squad NCOs. This turbulence is convincing evidence that the Army sensed something was not right with its "basic combat unit," and that something badly needed fixing.[12]

I have often reflected that Brig. Gen. S. L. A. Marshall's death was untimely. Part of his life's work came to fruition in the Army's National Training Center, and it is sad that he never had a chance to join troops exercising there. Those of us who laid out the concept for such a facility and first described the training techniques it would use were students of his. Surely he would have rejoiced in the opportunities the NTC provides to assert in the training of line battalions, better than ever before, those enduring verities of human nature that govern the soldier in battle far more than weapons, or doctrine, or time or clime.

Quote from the book "In the military services, though there are riches for the pedant, character is at all times at least as vital as intellect, and the main rewards go to him who can make other men feel toughened as well as elevated" (S. L. A. Marshall).

About the Author

Known as "SLAM," Samuel Lyman Atwood Marshall was born in Catskill, New York, in 1900 and raised in the West. At the age of seventeen he enlisted in the Army and fought against Pancho Villa's rebels on the Mexican border and then served in an engineering battalion at Saint-Mihiel and the Meuse-Argonne in World War I. He received his commission in 1919 at the age of nineteen. Between the wars Marshall earned a degree from the Texas School of Mines, now the University of Texas at El Paso. He gravitated into newspaper reporting and published his first book, *Blitzkrieg: Armies on Wheels*, in 1940. In World War II and again in Korea Marshall acquired firsthand insights on battle in the front lines by gathering "surviving members" and conducting a group interview a few days after the battle. Despite some criticisms about his research methods, he left an impressive list of books at his death in 1977, the most famous being *Pork Chop Hill*.

About the Book

Marshall created something of a sensation as a military analyst and historian in World War II—and again in the Korean War—when he went onto battlefields and interviewed surviving members of units who had recently been embroiled in combat. "In a squad of 10 men, on average fewer than three ever fired their weapons in combat," Russell W. Glenn notes in *Vietnam* magazine. "Day in, day out—it did not matter how long they had been soldiers, how many months of combat they had seen, or even that the enemy was about to overrun their position. This was what the highly regarded Brigadier General Samuel Lyman Atwood Marshall, better known as S. L. A. Marshall, or 'SLAM,' concluded in a series of military journal articles and in his book *Men against Fire,* about America's World War II soldiers."[13]

Marshall observes that the American fighting man was ingrained with the belief that the "taking of life is prohibited and unacceptable" in American society. The "fear of aggression has been expressed to him so strongly and absorbed by him so deeply and pervadingly—practically with his mother's milk—that it is part of the normal man's emotional makeup. This is the great handicap when he enters combat. It stays his trigger even though he is hardly conscious that it is a restraint upon him." Frontline soldiers in small units who do not fire their weapons significantly degrade the effectiveness of that unit and the parent units. In his book Marshall presents his findings from hundreds of interviews straightforwardly and succinctly and makes it possible for readers to draw their own conclusions.

General Gorman pointed out that Marshall "warned against misreading the import of a bloodletting like the 28th Infantry at Cantigny."

The brief battle of Cantigny, from May 28 to May 30, 1918, was the first engagement of the AEF on European soil. It was designed to test the regiment's effectiveness in an offensive engagement but cost 1,603 casualties, including 199 killed in action.

Marshall explains that the people

> who write of war tend to use loosely the expression "battle-seasoned troops" as if there were a kind of mental toughening which comes from experience under fire. The idea is wholly misleading; it mistakes the shadow for the substance. One of the effects of the shock of engagement is that it shakes the weakest files out of the organization. But as for the veterans who remain, they do not grow more callous to danger as they meet it increasingly nor do they ever become more eager for the contest. . . . Since troops do not conquer the fear of death and wounds, it is idle to think of any such basis for the establishment of a combat discipline. The latter is simply the reflection of the growth of unit confidence that comes of increased awareness of [the unit's] own resources under conditions, which at first seem extraordinary but gradually become familiar. Until that kind of confidence is born, there can be no effective action. . . . With the growth of experience, troops learn to apply the lessons of contact and communicating, and out of these things comes the tactical cohesion which enables a group of individuals to make the most of their united strength and stand steady in the face of sudden emergency.

A variety of criticisms have been leveled against Marshall over the decades since the book appeared, ranging from whether or not he inflated his own combat record to controversy over the number of interviews he conducted. But the core of his work remains readable, valuable, and applicable to any leader attempting to lead a small unit into chaotic conditions. The book provides much-needed insight into the long-standing challenge of bringing a very high percentage of infantry soldiers (or any actor in a chaotic environment) effectively into battle at crucial moments. It involves much more than the innate characteristics of the American soldier; more important, it also describes leadership at several levels as well as the tactics and techniques of fighting on lethal and sometimes intimidating battlefields.

Leadership Lessons Summarized

Leadership is an activity that occurs across a wide variety of levels, from the extraordinary demands on a senior leader trying to synchronize the actions of hundreds of thousands of troops to the challenges of a very junior person with responsibility for a dozen men and women. The value of *Men against Fire* is that it provides leadership lessons for those at the smallest scale of leadership. Thus it focuses on understanding the dynamics of the small unit, integrating the individuals into it so that they gain confidence in each other, inculcating affection and admiration between teammates, outlining the tasks ahead in a personal and convincing way, and directing individual elements of the squad in chaotic situations. These are lessons for young leaders in any organization, and they ring true across the decades since this seminal work appeared. Simply put, you should read *Men against Fire* for its insights on leadership in small units—which is the heart of leadership.

— R. Manning Ancell

14 *The Last Lion—Winston Spencer Churchill: Defender of the Realm, 1940–1965*
by William Manchester and Paul Reid (Little, Brown, 2012)

Recommended by Adm. Ronald J. Zlatoper, USN, commander U.S. Pacific Fleet 1994–96

I've gone through the trilogy [by Manchester that covers the entire life of Churchill], but the one that I really paid most attention to was *The Last Lion*. Jim [Stavridis] and I were both military assistants to the secretary of defense. I was military assistant when Caspar Weinberger was the secretary of defense, 1983–85. He was a gigantic aficionado of Winston Churchill. I mean, he's a Churchill-lite beyond. One day or another he had a new novel or historic bio or whatever about Churchill, and I admired him greatly, so that's what triggered me to labor my way through the first two just because it was important. Then I picked up and read *The Last Lion*. To me, it was a celebration, a guide in a time when the history was sort of passé (and I'm not sure it still isn't that way). Here was a guy that changed the world. Many failures, but always rising up.

It is said that it's not how many times you get knocked down, it's how many times you get up. Right? It's how many times you get back up and strive. There was no question in my mind that Manchester and Reid both admired Churchill, but they still didn't make him a God-like figure. Yeah, he was brilliant, but he was flawed. He was dynamic, and he was also a person that was willing to do things, to jump in and do things.

I thought Manchester did a wonderful job in taking a human who was brilliant, active, but flawed, dynamic, kept on, turned around, came back, lost, came back, lost, came back.

Quote from the book "Power is the one thing that has fascinated me ever since I was a kid in Springfield, Mass. . . . How do some people get it and others miss it entirely?" (William Manchester).

About the Authors
Despite the popularity of his eighteen books, which include *The Last Lion* trilogy, *Death of a President* (about John F. Kennedy's assassination), *The Arms of Krupp*, and *American Caesar* (a biography of Douglas MacArthur), surprisingly William Manchester never won a National Book Award, Pulitzer Prize, or Nobel Prize. Born and raised

in Springfield, Massachusetts, he followed in his father's footsteps and enlisted in the Marine Corps at the beginning of World War II. He saw action in the Pacific and was awarded a Purple Heart at Okinawa in June 1945. Manchester returned to college after the war and settled into a career as a journalist and academician. By 1998 he had suffered two debilitating strokes and was forced to give up writing. "Language for me came as easily as breathing for fifty years," he said, "and I can't do it anymore."

Eight months before he died, in 2003, Manchester asked Paul Reid, a onetime feature writer for the *Palm Beach Post*, who had never written a book, to complete the third volume of *The Last Lion*. Reid and Manchester had met through military circles and shared a passion for the Boston Red Sox. When he was asked to work on the final volume, Reid wasn't quite sure how much of the final task would be his, given Manchester's declining health. Fortunately their styles mesh perfectly, and the result is a seamless masterpiece. Reid brings the necessary balance and objectivity while maintaining an arm's-length relationship with Churchill's bigger-than-life career and personality. "The gravity of his role was obvious, yet though all saw him, all did not see him alike," Reid writes. "He was a multifarious individual, including within one man a whole troupe of characters, some of them subversive of one another and none feigned."

About the Book

Churchill was born to Lord Randolph Churchill and his American wife, Jennie Jerome, on November 30, 1874. He grew up accustomed to the perquisites of privilege and with a desire to be a public servant. Throughout his life he transitioned with ease from government service to private pursuits. Reid observes that Churchill's

> character had been fully formed at the turn of the century, as an officer in Victoria's imperial army, as a war correspondent, and as a young MP under the Old Queen. . . . In many ways Churchill remained a nineteenth century man, and by no means

a common man. He fit the mold of what Henry James called in *English Hours* "persons for whom the private machinery of ease has been made to work with extraordinary smoothness." . . . He had never ridden a bus. The only time he availed himself of the London Underground was during the general strike in 1926. . . . In the years before he became prime minister, even his train tickets were bought for him. As befitted a man of his class and stature, he never prepared a meal in his life. . . . To the British public he had become the ultimate Englishman, an embodiment of the bulldog breed, with the pugnacious set of his jaw, the challenging tilt of his cigar, his stovepipe hat, his pronouncements that "foreign names were made for Englishmen, not Englishmen for foreign names." . . . He himself had always ignored dietary rules and rarely paid a penalty for it, and he drank whatever he wanted, usually alcohol, whenever he wanted, which was often.

We are reminded that Churchill had a reputation for drinking much like Grant. "Clearly he was blessed with a remarkable constitution, one which disposed of alcohol with exceptional efficiency," notes Reid. "Despite his prolonged, consistent, and prodigious consumption of alcohol, Churchill was not a drunk. But neither was he a moderate social drinker, as some of the memoirs and protestations of his close friends and private secretaries maintain." Late in the war Field Marshal Sir Alan Brooke, the chief of the Imperial General Staff, "was summoned by Churchill in the middle of the day. Brooke, who often noted Churchill's prodigious intake of alcohol, that night told his diary, 'I found him very much worse for wear for evidently having consumed several glasses of brandy at lunch.' Such slides into outright drunkenness were exceedingly rare for Churchill, but they occurred."

Given Manchester's penchant for research, coupled with Reid's editing skill and fondness for details, it should come as no surprise that anyone with even the remotest interest in Churchill will find a tangential connection with events or individuals that crossed Churchill's path. Of course the major figures in the war on both sides appear, plus Edward VIII, John Keegan, Edward R. Murrow, Vinegar Joe Stilwell—the list is diverse, long, and broad.

Churchill and General Eisenhower were chummy partly because the British had control of North Africa while Ike was overall commander of Torch. Manchester writes: "Cunningham directing the efforts at sea, Tedder in the air, and Alexander on the ground . . . Churchill had gained everything he sought while giving Roosevelt what he wanted, an American commander."

Churchill was known to "truly like and admire Eisenhower," but his relationship with Ike put a strain on the general. "Before he left London to command Torch, he [Ike] and Churchill had instituted regular Tuesday luncheons and frequently took their business to Chequers on weekends, where, given Churchill's work habits and absurdly late hours, Eisenhower often found himself having to stay overnight. Ike knew to expect late nights and long dinners upon Churchill's arrival, and dreaded it."

Leadership Lessons Summarized

We will not repeat the many stories that are woven into the fabric of *The Last Lion* and urge you instead to discover them as you make your way through the book. You will find story after story that provides leadership lessons both positive and negative. Perhaps the easiest way to capture the essence of Churchill's leadership style is to read the words of the man himself:

Planning matters, but so does luck. "It is a mistake to try to look too far ahead. The chain of destiny can only be grasped one link at a time." And "Politics is the ability to foretell what is going to happen tomorrow, next week, next month, and next year. And to have the ability to explain why it didn't happen."

Keep a sense of humor about yourself. "All I can say is that I have taken more out of alcohol than alcohol has taken out of me." And "It is a good thing for an uneducated man to read books of quotations."

Determination and grit are the ultimate tools of a leader. "I have nothing to offer but blood, toil, tears and sweat." And "We shall defend our island, whatever the cost may be; we shall fight on the beaches, we shall fight on the landing grounds, we shall fight in the fields and in the streets, we shall fight in the hills; we shall never surrender."

Keep good records. "History will be kind to me for I intend to write it."

— *R. Manning Ancell*

15 — *Truman*
by David McCullough (Touchstone, 1992)

Recommended by Gen. Stephen R. Lorenz, USAF, commander Air Education and Training Command 2008–10

I believe reading biographies and having a sense of history make you a better leader. Reading about other leaders who have gone before you puts your life and trials and tribulations in perspective and shows you the ways others have persevered and succeeded.

Quote from the book "I am here to make decisions, and whether they prove right or wrong, I am going to make them" (President Harry S. Truman).

About the Author

Born and raised in Pittsburgh of affluent Scots-Irish parents and grandparents, who taught him at an early age the intrinsic value of reading, David McCullough has long possessed an interest in the relationship between history and people, believing that history is the story of people. Therein lies the yardstick by which his works have been measured, well received, and richly rewarded, including two Pulitzer Prizes.

About the Book

America's thirty-third president came from humble roots in the heartland. He was a college dropout with poor eyesight and slight stature. He read avidly and favored his piano lessons over sports. Truman joined the Missouri National Guard in 1917 as a private, but the men in his artillery battery elected him to lead them; he went on to command the battery in combat in France. Lt. Col. James R. Groves has studied Truman extensively and remembers that he "learned the rewards and satisfaction of hard work by farming with his father, and never lost the farm habit of early rising. He experienced failure as a small businessman, but was soon drawn to local politics and public service." With the support of the Democratic Kansas City political machine (run by Tom Pendergast) Truman was elected to the U.S. Senate in 1934, where some called him "the Senator from Pendergast."

Truman gained national attention by vigorously attacking corruption in military procurement during World War II, and a committee of Democrats chose him to replace Vice President Henry A. Wallace as the running mate for ailing President Franklin Roosevelt in the 1944 elections. The burdens of the presidency descended upon his shoulders when FDR died on April 12, 1945.

An incident that occurred shortly after he became the new commander in chief told the American people what they could expect from him. A matter of days after moving into the White House, Truman was on his "morning constitutional"—his brisk two-mile walk before breakfast—when an Army captain approached from the opposite direction, rendered a perfect salute, and said, "Good morning, Mr. President." Truman stopped, returned the salute, and addressed the startled officer. "Son, you are the first son of a bitch to salute me since I became president, and I want you and your family to have dinner with me and Mrs. Truman."

As president, Truman was immediately faced with major decisions on winding down the war, using the new weapon of mass destruction, rebuilding Europe and Japan, forming the United Nations and a

European alliance, and recognizing the state of Israel, among other international issues. At home, the economy had to return to peacetime pursuits. The Central Intelligence Agency, the National Security Administration, and the Department of Defense emerged during his administration in much the same form they have today. Labor unrest was accommodated and racial integration of the armed forces was begun. As the Cold War heated up, Truman was confronted with the Berlin Blockade and Airlift and the Korean War, where his relief of General of the Army MacArthur energized his political opponents. "I am here to make decisions," he said, "and whether they prove right or wrong, I am going to make them."

Leadership Lessons Summarized

All good leaders know the value of crisp decision making, and President Harry Truman is a classic example of a tough-minded and pragmatic decision maker. Anyone given the opportunity to visit the Oval Office during his time as president would have been reminded of that by the plaque resting prominently on his desk that read: "The buck stops here." The essential leadership lesson from this marvelous biography is the need to make hard decisions that are not going to please everyone.

Two key decisions he made during the war had a great and lasting effect on world history. Truman signed the order that authorized dropping an atomic bomb on Hiroshima and another on Nagasaki if the Japanese government did not surrender unconditionally after the first attack. On August 6, 1945, the *Enola Gay*, a B-29 bomber piloted by Col. Paul Tibbets, dropped the world's first deployed atomic bomb over the center of Hiroshima, wiping out 90 percent of the city and instantly vaporizing 70,000–80,000 Japanese citizens. Three days later a second bomb devastated Nagasaki, killing 40,000 people. President Truman, asked about the difficulty he encountered in making this momentous decision, replied: "The atom bomb was no 'great decision.' It was merely another powerful weapon in the arsenal of righteousness." Pragmatism and realism carried the day.

A second highly pragmatic (and at the time unpopular) decision was the firing of Gen. Douglas MacArthur. President Truman and General MacArthur had never liked one another. MacArthur held Truman in disdain, and the president was taken aback by the monumental size of MacArthur's ego. The two met on Wake Island, a seven-thousand-mile trip from Washington. MacArthur was still basking in the glory of his successful landing at Inchon the previous month, and the president felt it necessary to reinforce the long-standing rules that policy decisions would be made in Washington, not in Tokyo. In particular, there was considerable talk about the possible use of atomic bombs against the 260,000 Chinese forces that had stormed across the Yalu River on June 24, 1950, much to MacArthur's surprise. Truman wanted to ensure that MacArthur fully understood that American forces were prohibited from moving north of the thirty-eighth parallel.

The situation with MacArthur worsened in the early months of 1951 and finally came to a head on April 11 when the White House announced at a press briefing that President Truman had relieved MacArthur of command. "I fired MacArthur because he wouldn't respect the authority of the president," Truman later said. "I didn't fire him because he was a dumb son of a bitch, although he was."

Truman's exceptional leadership was based on a sound sense of morality and solid Christian principles: "I do not believe there is a problem in this country or the world today which could not be settled if approached through the teaching of the Sermon on the Mount."

— R. Manning Ancell

16 ⚔ Infantry Attacks
by Erwin Rommel (Ludwig Voggenreiter Verlag, 1937)

Recommended by Gen. Richard E. Cavazos, USA, commander U.S. Army Forces Command 1982–84

One's ability to plan is greatly influenced by the ability to look analytically at numerous courses of action. So often only one or two are ever examined, probably because it's all that comes to mind, or influenced by the persuasive hip shooter. Most fights begin with the idea of promoting maneuver to destroy the enemy. Attrition warfare is somewhere at the beginning or at the end when the fight degenerates into a slugging match. History, of course, but with the view to broaden one's perspective. *Infantry Attacks* by Rommel explores the impact of reconnaissance, a lost art, and boldness in war at the battalion level. This is a basic, must read primer.

Quote from the book "In a man-to-man fight, the winner is he who has one more round in his magazine" (Generalfeldmarschall Erwin Rommel).

About the Author

Born on November 15, 1891, in Heidenheim an der Brenz, Germany, Erwin Rommel spent his adult life in service to his country. Decorated for bravery in World War I, he commanded the 7th Panzer Division in the invasion of France in 1940, earned a worldwide reputation as the "Desert Fox" while leading the Afrika Korps in North Africa, and was handpicked by Hitler to head German defenses as the Allies prepared for the invasion of Normandy. Rommel supported the unsuccessful attempt to assassinate Hitler on July 20, 1944. When confronted and offered a choice between suicide and trial and execution for treason, he took poison on October 14, 1944. Following a state funeral, he was buried at Ulm, Germany.

About the Book

In a scene from the popular movie *Patton* depicting the Battle of El Guettar in southern Tunisia in late March 1943, elements of Lt. Gen. George Patton's II Corps have dug in and await the arrival of fifty tanks of the 10th Panzers and supporting infantry. The U.S. forces had earlier intercepted a message that Rommel would be leading this force in a surprise attack. The Germans were totally surprised. According to some accounts (which have been disputed) Patton watched the battle unfold through his binoculars and declared triumphantly, "Rommel, you magnificent bastard, I read your book."

Rommel's *Infantry Attacks* was compiled from copious and highly detailed notes he kept during combat in World War I augmented by his exceptionally vivid memory. Rommel's recollections are invaluable reading for those who have responsibilities for others on the field of battle. Here is a snapshot of a typical chapter and the "observations" Rommel draws to explain what happened in his own terms and viewpoint:

> I assumed command of about two hundred bearded warriors and a 440-yard company sector of the front line. A French reception committee greeted me with a concentration of "Whiz Bangs." The position consisted of a continuous trench reinforced by numerous breastworks. . . . My first order was that whenever artillery opened on us, all dugouts would be vacated and the men would take cover in the trench proper. I also issued orders that the dugout roofs would be strengthened so that they could at least withstand field artillery fire.

You are drawn here into the intimacy of warfare through the eyes of young Lieutenant Rommel, and his observations are spot on:

> The attack on January 29, 1915, showed the superiority of the German infantry. The attack of the 9th Company was no surprise and it is difficult to understand why the French infantry lost its nerve and abandoned a well-prepared defensive position lavishly protected by wire, three lines deep, and well-studded with machine guns. The enemy knew the attack was coming and had tried to stop it by means of heavy interdiction fire. The

fact that we were able to resort to offensive action and break from the encircled Labordaire position is ample proof of the combat capabilities of our troops.

Each chapter is a nitty-gritty play-by-play from the point of view of a young officer in charge of well-trained troops in combat. Part 1, "The War of Movement, Belgium and Northern France, 1914," consists of three chapters describing small-unit encounters early in the war. Part 2, "Trench Warfare in the Argonne and High Vosges," also has three chapters. You cannot help but appreciate the resiliency of the troops on both sides who endured month after month of deprivation and bombardment by artillery missiles. The seven chapters in part 3, "Open Warfare in Rumania and the Carpathians, 1917," cover entirely different ground. By the time you have finished chapter 13, the final chapter, you will have gained—if nothing else—an appreciation for Rommel's observations and insights. We recommend reading *Infantry Attacks* equipped with a highlighter and red pencil, for there is much in the book that requires serious thought and rereading.

Leadership Lessons Summarized

Above all, leaders are good observers. We often think of communication as consisting largely of transmitting ideas, as though its essence could be summed up by a megaphone. But the heart of leadership is two-way communication that begins with being an observer—of human nature, terrain, technology, and all the other things that surround us. This book is a good lesson in observation because Rommel relied on reconnaissance throughout his distinguished career.

During the war's early days when the Afrika Korps reigned supreme, Rommel constantly made "personal reconnaissance in North Africa by station wagon, armored car, or Storch observation plane. His troops called him 'the General of the Highway.'" He often boasted that he knew more about the enemy than they knew about him. "The swiftness with which the Afrika Korps switched from armored attack to antitank defense," notes Major DeWeerd in the *Infantry Journal* in early 1944, "showed that he remembered the lessons of 1914–18." As leaders, we have to look, listen, and feel the environment around us— Rommel illustrates that perfectly in this absorbing book.

— R. Manning Ancell

17 — *The 7 Habits of Highly Effective People*
by Stephen R. Covey (Simon and Schuster, 1989)

Recommended by Gen. Greg "Speedy" Martin, USAF, commander U.S. Air Forces, Europe and commander U.S. Air Forces Material Command 2000–2005

I recommended this book often to the junior officers working for me, especially on the Joint Staff. It is a terrific way to apply many of the principles of leadership from the business world to broader tasks of leadership.

Quote from the book "Most people do not listen with the intent to understand; they listen with the intent to reply" (Stephen R. Covey).

About the Author
Stephen Covey (1932–2012) was a very well regarded and nationally recognized author, businessman, speaker, and educator. He wrote a series of extraordinarily popular books based on a very simple principle: by identifying the characteristics (he called them habits) of very successful people, one can derive life lessons that will ultimately help anyone become more effective. His most popular book by far was *The Seven Habits of Highly Effective People*, although he produced many others—including *The Eighth Habit* and *The Seven Habits of Highly Effective Families*. A Mormon, he attended the University of

Utah, Harvard Business School, and Brigham Young University; he was awarded ten honorary doctorates. He was the father of nine children and the grandfather of fifty-two, something about which he was extremely proud. He died of complications from a biking accident at the age of seventy-nine.

About the Book
The Seven Habits of Highly Effective People has sold more than thirty million copies worldwide and has been translated into dozens of languages. Deceptively simple, it is centered on seven key characteristics that Covey identifies as tightly correlated with success in life:

Habit 1: Be Proactive. Especially in your relationships. Reach out constantly to the world around you, especially the people in it. Follow up on meetings, return phone calls, engage in conversation, and always be seeking to build relationships. This really opens up one of the top skills of any leader, which is "active listening." To do this right, you must NOT be formulating your next questions, observation, or objection while a person is speaking; indeed, your next correct move is to repeat back what you have heard to make sure that you understand it and that your interlocutor perceives that you are hearing him or her. The proactive part begins with this and moves forward in a way that respects and indeed takes joy in others in all their diversity and complexity.

Habit 2: Begin with the End in Mind. Have a plan that moves things in a positive direction. If there is a single quality that distinguishes the truly top leaders, it is strategic thinking. Leaders have to rise above the mundane (even as they handle details when necessary) but truly look to the horizon and inspire an organization to sail the furthest.

Habit 3: Put First Things First. Take charge of your personal situation. No good leader can succeed if he or she is burdened with difficult, ignored, complicated, or destructive personal situations. This applies across the range of relationships, marriages, children, parents, medical concerns, personal finances, and all the other individual elements that make up our lives.

Habit 4: Think Win/Win. Collaborate wherever possible. Collaboration has emerged as THE twenty-first-century leadership skill, overtaking many other more traditional qualities. This book was among the first to champion this approach and does so in vivid and convincing ways. Think of a peloton of bicycle riders—they have to work together to achieve both team and individual success.

Habit 5: Seek First to Understand, Then to Be Understood. Empathy and understanding of others is key. This of course relates well to the idea of "active listening" above, but it is more than that. It is truly the idea that there are other ideas than your own—and they may be BETTER than whatever you have come up with. Listening with a truly open mind is key to that.

Habit 6: Synergize. Seek to find ways that the sum can be greater than the addition of the parts. Very related to the idea of the "win/win" outcome, the power of synergy is undeniable. The book provides many lessons that are very convincing, but the best proof is in our personal lives and careers. Synergy occurs when you add an element to a mix and suddenly there is an explosion of energy, talent, and determination.

Habit 7: Sharpen the Saw. Constantly improve, continue your self-education, focus on expanding your knowledge of the world. Education is a lifelong process, both formally and informally. If you are not constantly learning a new language, reading both fiction and nonfiction, taking courses, going to workshops, listening to speakers, and tapping the vast resource that is represented by the Internet, then you are stagnating. Massive open online courses (MOOCs) are prime places to energize lifelong learning.

While each of these admonitions is simple in isolation, in the aggregate they are very powerful. Many are based on long-standing Christian (and other world religions') beliefs. Throughout the book, Covey provides very specific examples of individuals who choose to follow some aspect of the seven habits and prosper as a result. The entire work is extremely practical and easy to read, as the very best leadership texts are.

In the end, this is a book about the human condition, comparable to the great series of novellas and stories by Honoré de Balzac in *The Human Comedy* of the nineteenth century. Covey uses anecdotes and storytelling to compress the essentials of leadership into very tight lessons that are approachable and remarkable in their simplicity. Above all, this is not a "checklist," but rather a guidebook to a journey that a young leader should willingly and easily embark upon. Covey is a believer in building bridges wherever possible, saying, "When the trust account is high, communication is easy, instant, and effective." One of the books by his son Stephen M. R. Covey, *The Speed of Trust*, is built on this idea.

In summary, one of the truly "great habits" is to ask daily whether you are embodying the principles of Stephen Covey—kindness, empathy, listening, planning, and pursuing self-education. A huge part of the message of the book is taking responsibility for who you are as a leader. As Steve Covey says early in the book, until a person can say deeply and honestly, "I am what I am today because of the choices I made yesterday," that person cannot say, "I choose otherwise."

Leadership Lessons Summarized

Above all, listen before you speak. Spend time trying to understand the other person, and specifically seek win/win outcomes in any discussion or negotiation. Build coalitions. A leader is constantly seeking to learn and improve every single day of her or his life.

—Adm. J. Stavridis

18 *From Beirut to Jerusalem*
by Thomas L. Friedman (Farrar, Straus and Giroux, 1989)

Recommended by Adm. Michael G. Mullen, USN, Vice Chief of Naval Operations 2003–4, commander in chief U.S. Naval Forces, Europe and commander Allied Joint Force Command 2004–5, 28th Chief of Naval Operations 2005–7, and chairman of the Joint Chiefs of Staff 2007–11

The war in Iraq began on March 19, 2003, and I became VCNO that August. About six months into my watch I came home one night and my wife, Deborah, was reading Tom Friedman's book *From Beirut to Jerusalem*. She looked at me and said, "Has anyone in a position of responsibility read this?" She finished it quickly and soon afterward I read it thoroughly. I felt he made the case that we didn't understand much about the Middle East. In ways it became a devastating indictment of our decision to go to war in the Middle East.

I love New York City. It's one of several "electric cities" that have a cross-section of people with backgrounds of different ethnicities living there. Other electric cities include Dubai, Hong Kong, Istanbul, and Beirut. Tom reveals the heart and soul of Beirut at a troubling time.

Quote from the book "What the Americans did not understand in December 1982 was that while they were making Lebanon an extension of what they knew, the Lebanese were doing the same thing in reverse. In order to handle the Americans, to digest them, to make them fit into their tiny land, they made the Marines an extension of what they knew, and what they knew was the feud. President Gemayel, instead of using the Marines as a crutch began to use them as a club to beat his Muslim opponents."

About the Author

Friedman was born into a Jewish family in Minneapolis, Minnesota, on July 20, 1953. His father died when Tom was nineteen and attending the University of Minnesota. He later transferred to Brandeis University and graduated summa cum laude in 1975. From there he attended St. Anthony's College, Oxford, where he earned a master's degree in Middle Eastern studies. Following graduation from St. Anthony's Friedman joined United Press International and lived in Beirut from June

1979 to May 1981. Friedman joined the *New York Times* in 1981 and today writes a weekly column for the paper from his home in suburban Washington, D.C.

Friedman has published six books. *From Beirut to Jerusalem*, his first, won the National Book Award. Ten years later came *The Lexus and the Olive Tree*, followed by *Longitudes and Attitudes: Exploring the World after September 11* (2002); *The World Is Flat: A Brief History of the Twenty-First Century* (2005); *Hot, Flat and Crowded: Why We Need a Green Revolution—and How It Can Renew America* (2008); and *That Used to Be Us: How America Fell behind in the World It Invented and How We Can Come Back*, co-written with Michael Mandelbaum (2011).

A three-time recipient of the Pulitzer Prize, Friedman won the prestigious award in 1983 for his coverage of the tragic war in Lebanon, in 1988 for his coverage of Israel in international affairs, and in 2002 for his writings on the worldwide terrorist threat.

About the Book

From Beirut to Jerusalem draws on Friedman's experiences and observations in Beirut to describe the resiliency of the five-thousand-year-old city, using examples such as the venerable American University of Beirut—independent, secular, and marvelously scholarly—and the magnificent Phoenicia Intercontinental Hotel in the heart of Beirut overlooking the Mediterranean Sea. The hotel opened two days before Christmas 1961 and became an instant success. Expansion brought in record numbers of guests until 1975–76, when the "Battle of the Hotels" turned the Phoenicia into a battleground and left the popular hotel a burning and discarded hulk. After nearly a quarter century the hotel was renovated and reopened in the spring of 2000, only to be severely damaged following the bombing assassination of Rafik Hariri nearby. Once again refurbished and reborn, it opened three months later and today is a jewel in the city known as "the Paris of the East."

Beirut during the time Friedman was there was the picture of survivability tempered by adaptability. My favorite example of the resilience of the Lebanese in Beirut is one that Friedman shares in his book:

Beirut was Goodies Supermarket—the gourmet food store that offered a cornucopia of foodstuffs ranging from quail eggs to foie gras flown in daily from Paris. Amine Halwany, Goodies' unflappable and ever upbeat owner, used to tell me that his was the ideal business for a city like Beirut, because he had products to offer people under any and all conditions. "In times of crisis," explained Amine, "everyone wants bread, water and canned food—things that are easy to prepare and won't need much refrigeration. People go back to a very primitive style of cooking. They also buy a lot of sweets and nuts during the troubles—nervous food they can pop in their mouths while sitting at home. But as soon as things calm down for a few days, the high-class customers are back buying caviar and smoked salmon." . . . Legend has it that one day a disheveled young man entered Goodies, walked up to the cash register with a rifle, and demanded all the money. Within seconds three different women drew pistols out of their Gucci handbags, pumped a flurry of bullets into the thief, and then continued pushing their shopping carts down the bountiful aisles.

The beauty of Friedman's book is in his descriptions of everyday life in Beirut during the worst of times and the occasional best of times. Goodies today is popular as ever and a must see for visitors. People routinely book a stay at the Phoenicia Hotel at reasonable prices. Sure, the government is not ideal and class warfare still simmers just beneath the surface, but there is hope in a continuation of Christian and Muslim cooperation and civility that goes back decades to before the time of Camille Chamoun.

Friedman goes on with his reporter's journey to look at Jerusalem, a patchwork quilt of multicultural, national, and religious neighborhoods and sympathies. Taken together, his comparison of the Arab world of Beirut with the deep historical significance of Jerusalem provides a lesson in how to approach one of the most challenging and difficult areas of the world.

Leadership Lessons Summarized

Two of the most important skills for any leader are cultural understanding and creative solution making. This brilliant book of reportage provides a case study in both. Friedman's keen eye for observation shows again and again how important knowledge of the history and culture of any region is to finding solutions. He also provides creative thoughts about how to solve seemingly intractable challenges through the application of both pragmatic reasoning and deep empathetic understanding. Both are essential skills for any leader.

— R. Manning Ancell

19 — *The Second World War*
by Sir Winston Churchill (Houghton Mifflin, 1948–53)

Recommended by Adm. Jonathan T. Howe, former deputy national security advisor, former commander in chief Allied Forces Southern Europe

Winston Churchill's six-volume series on World War II is a revealing and still relevant story of the challenges he faced as a leader in the war. He describes the "moral of the work" as "In War: Resolution, In Defeat: Defiance, In Victory: Magnanimity, In Peace: Good Will." It is an invaluable reference.

Quote from the book "I felt as if I were walking with destiny, and that all my past life had been but a preparation for this hour and for this trial. . . . I thought I knew a good deal about it all, I was sure I should not fail" (Winston Churchill).

About the Author

To say that Sir Winston Churchill needs no introduction may be the understatement of the century. His biography by William Manchester (in three volumes, with a focus on the third, *The Last Lion*) appears elsewhere on this list, and he is widely regarded as one of the iconic leaders of the twentieth century. During his long, distinguished, and varied career he was a soldier and cavalry officer, a journalist, a cabinet official, a lecturer, and above all prime minister of his country during its greatest period of modern crisis. Along the way he was awarded a Nobel Prize in Literature and was made the first "honorary citizen" of the United States (his mother, Jennie Jerome, a famous beauty, was born an American). His determination came to represent the indomitable spirit of the British Empire. Tragically, in his view, he was also present at the breakup and dissolution of that empire, and was turned out of office at the end of World War II by a British population that was simply exhausted with war and deeply tired of the burden of empire. Upon his death at the age of ninety in 1964, Queen Elizabeth II granted him the high honor of a state funeral.

About the Book

This monumental work in six volumes is certainly the best-*written* history of World War II, and it won a well-deserved Nobel Prize in Literature for the author. Winston Churchill's magnificent prose rolls along like thunder and lightning. Reading his description of events is like opening the King James Bible and listening to the epic story of the creation of the world. Distinctive in voice and full of anecdotes, this is a long but rewarding journey through the most important set of events in the twentieth century. So often we tend to think of history as somehow predetermined—as though it was inevitable that fascism and in particular Nazism would fail; that Hitler would overplay his hand in invading Russia and declaring war on the United States; that the United States would ultimately enter the war and provide the men and material to overcome the Axis. None of those things was inevitable, and with a few small twists in history the world might be vastly different from the world we know today. Churchill's brilliant exposition is the most readable version of those events and manages to suffuse the tale with real suspense.

In terms of leadership, the book provides numerous examples of how leadership works (and fails) in the real world. The portraits of Churchill's extraordinary cast of fellow leaders are in themselves a leadership laboratory for the ages (see Churchill's companion work, *Great Contemporaries*, for detailed looks at each of them). Across the stage strut Hitler, Stalin, Roosevelt, Mussolini, De Gaulle, Eisenhower, and their myriad supporting casts. And at the center, of course, is Sir Winston—providing wide-ranging and constantly running color commentary of what works and what does not for each of these leaders. Churchill was again and again able to motivate the people of Great Britain, even when all seemed lost. He used his considerable communication skills brilliantly as well as his own personal example in facing up to danger and risk with them. All of the leadership gifts he inherited and the "tricks of the trade" he developed over his long and varied career are thoroughly on display through *The Second World War*. As he said, "Courage is what it takes to stand up and speak; it is also what it takes to sit down and listen." Churchill also radiates his desire to serve, to be part of something larger than himself. This is a fundamental lesson for all leaders, captured in his comment "We make a living by what we get, but we make a life by what we give." No one gave more to his nation than Winston Churchill in the twentieth century.

Leadership Lessons Summarized

Determination is at the heart of any leader's skills set. As Churchill said, "Success is not final, and failure is not fatal: it is the courage to continue that counts." Additionally, creativity and imagination set a leader apart from others. Leaders in nondemocratic situations can bring greater authority to bear more swiftly, but a skillful leader in a democratic setting can win others to his or her cause using reason, logic, interpersonal skills, rhetoric, and emotion.

—Adm. J. Stavridis

20 ⁓ In Love and War: The Story of a Family's Ordeal and Sacrifice during the Vietnam Years
by Jim and Sybil Stockdale (Harper and Row, 1984)

Recommended by Adm. William McRaven, USN (Ret.), commander Joint Special Operations Command and commander U.S. Special Operations Command 2009–14

This is a love story that is also full of the lessons that leaders must apply: courage under extreme adversity and how important a loving marriage can be in sustaining all of us through the darkest times.

Quote from the book "You must never confuse faith that you will prevail in the end—which you can never afford to lose—with the discipline to confront the most brutal facts of your current reality, whatever they might be" (Vice Adm. James Stockdale).

About the Authors

Vice Adm. James Bond Stockdale (1923–2005) graduated from the U.S. Naval Academy and became a fighter pilot. His career followed the normal trajectory for a successful naval aviator with the striking exception that he developed a deep appreciation and understanding of the classics of Greek philosophy, through both self-study and formal classwork. In 1964 he was a mid-grade officer in command of a fighter squadron leading strikes from the USS *Ticonderoga* during the well-known Gulf of Tonkin incident off the coast of Vietnam. He survived that dangerous combat tour and redeployed in command of a wing of carrier-based aircraft the following year. On that subsequent deployment in 1965, as commander of Carrier Air Wing 16 flying from the USS *Oriskany*, he was shot down over North Vietnam and captured—becoming one of the most senior prisoners of war in the Vietnam conflict.

Throughout a particularly brutal captivity he behaved with extreme heroism while enduring seven and a half years in the infamous "Hanoi Hilton" prison in North Vietnam. Eventually he received the Medal of Honor and twenty-five other combat decorations, including four Silver Stars. Throughout his time in captivity he led an internal resistance to the harsh interrogations and torture that all of the prisoners suffered. The lessons of the Greek Stoic philosophers in particular were of extreme value to him throughout that challenging period.

As a result of his conduct during the Vietnam War, Vice Admiral Stockdale was among the most decorated admirals in modern U.S. Navy history. After Vietnam he became the president of the U.S. Naval War College while on active duty, and following his retirement the president of the Citadel in Charleston, South Carolina. He eventually became a Distinguished Fellow at the Hoover Institution at Stanford University in Palo Alto, California. He wrote extensively throughout the remainder of his life, largely on the classics, ethics, and morality. Of note, he was a candidate for vice president of the United States on the controversial third-party ticket with Ross Perot (also a U.S. Naval Academy graduate) in 1992. That ticket received more votes than any third-party candidacy in American history. He died of Alzheimer's disease in 2005 and is buried at the U.S. Naval Academy in Annapolis, Maryland.

Mrs. Sybil Stockdale became well known during her husband's captivity through her work for prisoner-of-war issues. She was a cofounder and eventually national coordinator of the National League of Families, a nonprofit organization focused on working for prisoner-of-war and missing-in-action issues. Her efforts helped publicize the challenges faced by such families and eventually led to the award of the Navy Distinguished Public Service Award, among the highest civilian awards the Navy can bestow. She is the mother of four sons, all of whom have been involved in education. She holds a BA from Mount Holyoke and an MA from Stanford University.

About the Book

In alternating chapters, *In Love and War* portrays Vice Admiral Stockdale's life in captivity in Vietnam and the life and work on the home front of Mrs. Stockdale and their four children. It is a superb depiction of strong individuals facing the most rigorous of life's challenges. We see in vivid prose the story of a spouse and children dealing with immense difficulties while a family member forward deploys into combat and ultimately faces the worst and most dangerous circumstances short of death a military professional can face: lengthy incarceration and awful torture.

The book is also a vivid and highly accurate description of military family life generally. The early chapters portray the Stockdale family in the early days of their marriage, the ascent up the slow career ladder of Navy life, and ultimately their joy and excitement at Vice Admiral Stockdale's selection for command of a carrier air wing, the most senior flying job in the U.S. Navy. All of this comes crashing to a halt when he is shot down and captured, and the alternating chapters begin, conveying the brutality of Admiral Stockdale's treatment in prison side-by-side with the sadness and the determination of Mrs. Stockdale on the home front.

Above all, the leadership lessons both Admiral and Mrs. Stockdale bring to bear in their respective venues are timeless and profoundly well illustrated. Vice Admiral Stockdale, as the senior Navy officer in the prison, had to demonstrate personally his determination to overcome the harsh conditions and the brutal torture. His fierce resolve not to give an inch to an implacable enemy determined to use him as a tool of propaganda led eventually to him beating himself in the face with a stool so he could not be photographed during one particular propaganda session. He earned enormous respect from his men for his calm, stoic acceptance of the awful surroundings, often commenting that they had all been dropped into a medieval world of pain and deprivation, and their only hope was to endure and overcome.

We also see how Admiral Stockdale organized the resistance in the prison using a wide variety of leadership techniques. First among them was personal example, showing repeatedly that a true leader will undergo any hardship on behalf of his or her followers. Admiral Stockdale also personified the rock-hard determination a leader must demonstrate, especially when events seem hopeless. A third leadership technique was Admiral Stockdale's continuous use of communication, even when that was profoundly difficult given the separation in the prison. His innovative means of communicating, ranging from knocking on walls to dropping notes to using hand signals and gestures, is noteworthy. Fourth, we see a leader who helped his followers focus on the overall objective—resistance and honor, but with the ultimate goal of survival. As Admiral Stockdale says, "You must never confuse faith that you will prevail in the end—which you can never afford to lose—with the discipline to confront the most brutal facts of your current reality, whatever they might be."

Leadership Lessons Summarized

Determination in the face of harsh conditions is the first task of a leader. Creativity and imagination in overcoming opponents, even when facing overwhelming odds, is key. Love and family support are of enormous value to a leader.

— Adm. J. Stavridis

21 *Hell in a Very Small Place: The Siege of Dien Bien Phu*
by Bernard B. Fall (Harper & Row, 1967)

Recommended by Gen. Ronald H. Griffith, USA, vice chief of staff U.S. Army 1995–97

The U.S. Army has long held a philosophy that officers are developed professionally through (1) academic study at various schools, both professional military schools (branch advanced courses, Command and General Staff College, the War College) and advanced degree work in civilian colleges and universities; (2) experience gained in a variety of field and staff assignments; and (3) professional reading and study accomplished on one's personal time and throughout one's professional career. The latter of the three—personal reading and self-study—are the most difficult to adequately accomplish for a number of obvious reasons: demanding and time-consuming assignments, family responsibilities, deployments, and on and on. Nevertheless, some of the most valuable lessons and professional insights a committed military officer gains come through disciplined and rigorous self-study.

In 1964 I was placed on orders for Vietnam, where I was to serve all of 1965 as an advisor with the Army of the Republic of Vietnam. In preparation for this assignment I attended the Army's Special Warfare School at Fort Bragg, North Carolina. During our six weeks of training, one of our guest lecturers was a French gentleman by the name of Bernard Fall who had written a book on the French military's experience in Indochina titled *Street without Joy*. In the early years of the Vietnam conflict the book became one of the Army's principal references on counterinsurgency warfare. I personally carried this book in my backpack throughout my first year in Vietnam, and I drew lessons from it continuously. Later, Fall would write another book on the French experience in Vietnam. *Hell in a Very Small Place* tells the tragic story of the battle of Dien Bien Phu and the defeat that convinced the French that their colonial experience in Indochina was at an end. I think that today this book offers extraordinary lessons to young military leaders who are preparing themselves to lead soldiers in an uncertain future. Along with *Street without Joy*, it had a huge impact on me and on my contemporaries who fought, led, and advised during ten years of experience in Vietnam.

Quote from the book "Future historians will tell whether it was necessary for the West to suffer a defeat at Dien Bien Phu in 1954 in order not to have to face one in South Vietnam in 1967; or whether, had a decisive defeat at Dien Bien Phu been avoided in 1954, Vietnam's history would have taken a less troubled course" (Bernard B. Fall).

About the Author

Perhaps as instructive and interesting as the battle itself, Bernard Fall's own life ended in Vietnam in 1967 while he was traveling as a reporter with American Marines near Da Nang. Fall, the son of French Jews, whose mother died at Auschwitz and whose father was tortured and killed by the Nazis for his work with the Resistance, served as a teenager in the French Maquis (resistance fighters). His service both as an irregular and as a French soldier armed him with an incredible ability to capture the experience of combatants on both sides. Equally interesting is Fall's American postgraduate work and time as a college professor. His American wife kept his memory alive long after a "Bouncing Betty" mine robbed the world of this talented individual.

About the Book

Bernard Fall's description of the siege and fall of Dien Bien Phu in May 1954 is a historical masterpiece written with all the excitement and suspense of a thriller novel. Even knowing the outcome of the battle and the fate of the French defenders, the reader is drawn into the events as Fall unveils them in painstakingly researched detail. Indeed, Fall begins the saga with a preface describing the highlights of the fight for Dien Bien Phu, realistically describing its relatively insignificant numbers (compared with the siege of Stalingrad, for example). Yet he continues by describing this as not only a decisive battle but perhaps the most decisive battle of the twentieth century. Even after the Tet Offensive in Vietnam in 1968 and Saddam Hussein's decisive defeat and ejection from Kuwait in February 1991, Bernard Fall's placement of Dien Bien Phu in the hierarchy of modern battles is compelling. His description of the contest from both combatants' perspectives also ranks near the top of battle narratives.

Lt. Col. Terry Johnson (Ret.), a West Point–educated helicopter pilot, originally read Fall's book more than forty-five years ago and has studied that battle and many others since. Having fought in what Fall calls the Second Indochina War—America's ill-fated Vietnam experience—

Johnson experienced an epiphany of sorts in reframing this epic siege. His considered view is that while it is easy to question the selection of that particular difficult-to-defend valley by the French, the reality of the outcome had much less to do with the terrain than with underestimating the enemy. After serving two tours with the French army in France and having a French combat helicopter regiment under orders during Desert Storm, Johnson found that his study of the battle reinforced his profound respect for the French army. Whatever faults the French army had in 1954—and there were many—lack of courage and élan was not among them, and the defeated defenders preserved their honor to the end and beyond.

Fall overcame enormous research challenges in assembling this account, surprisingly more so on the French side than in communist North Vietnam. The North Vietnamese were, by his account, more than willing to provide details of their proud victory, but Fall was denied full access to the French archives until 1963. Fall also overcame a serious personal illness during the research and writing of this book, but persevered to write a small masterpiece.

The book ranges widely between the Hanoi headquarters of Major General Cogny to the chaos of Brigadier General De Castries' dug-in command post in Dien Bien Phu to the mobile command post of Viet Minh general Vo Nguyen Giap, the victorious commander in chief. It renders in chronological order the battle preparations of the French and Viet Minh as well as the events of the siege, naming key players on both sides and faithfully reconstructing the order of battle by unit for both attacker and defender.

Fall presents the perspective of the respective commanders from their own personal accounts. He tackles the controversy of responsibility for the defeat with both firsthand accounts of key players and comprehensive reviews of archived reports. His depiction of the crisis in command within the French compound during the peak of the battle presents an intriguing study of human behavior under duress and extraordinary courage and leadership by officers and noncommissioned officers often very junior in rank. At the same time Fall shows the strength and shortcomings of the French leadership as a combination of experience at lower levels and lack of experience in commanding large formations at higher levels. The tension between De Castries and Cogny, and the parallel tension between De Castries and his subordinate, Lieutenant Colonel Langlais, is almost a sidebar in this account but is an important study of personalities. Langlais became the de facto commander of Dien Bien Phu when De Castries suffered a well-hidden meltdown, only to become a better leader as a captive. Cogny, fighting the battle from Hanoi, never saw the importance of Dien Bien Phu either tactically or as a strategic fight. While he comes in for well-earned criticism in Fall's analysis, Cogny, like many other senior French officers, tried to save his men as the battle raged.

As a study of leadership, the most interesting question is why the seasoned professionals on the French side failed to best the citizen-soldier leaders of the Viet Minh. Arguably, Giap and his field commanders achieved an astonishing five-to-one ratio in fighters, which exceeded, as Fall notes, the three-to-one advantage military manuals recommend for the offensive to prevail. Yet it was not in the execution of the offense or the failure of the defense or in the relative numbers discrepancy that the French lost this battle. It was logistics. Despite heroic attempts to resupply the defenders by air and parachute, the equipment and supplies flown in on American aircraft could not meet the needs of the besieged French. In the end, the French fought valiantly down to virtually their last rounds, ending the battle with no serviceable artillery pieces to fire the few remaining shells.

On the Viet Minh side, four infantry divisions and one heavy division, armed with Soviet-provided as well as captured American weapons, encircled the French defenders and rained artillery and mortar shells for days on the bunkers and dugouts, reducing much of the region to a sea of mud. The Communists' air defenses effectively created curtains of flak and accurate gunfire that French and American pilots rated as far denser than anything they had faced in World War II or Korea. And all of this ordnance arrived in Soviet-built trucks on unimproved roads or, more often, by pushcarts and bicycles carrying up to four hundred pounds apiece. The French never expected such a deluge of mortars, rockets, and artillery.

The Viet Minh's trenching and tunneling efforts were equally impressive. Despite monsoon rains and deadly fires and counterattacks by the French, the communist soldiers dug trenches to within meters of the French positions. Viet Minh sappers also burrowed under the fortifications, driving the French defenders to distraction as they listened to the digging beneath them, before finally setting off tons of TNT under the French fortress.

The cost in casualties for both attackers and defenders was overwhelming. The Viet Minh endured massive losses, and just as they would in the follow-on fight against the Americans, dragged their dead and wounded away whenever possible. The French were able to evacuate the wounded in the beginning with helicopters and airplanes but lost that ability when air operations became impossible. French medical personnel cared for an ever-increasing number of wounded in underground bunkers in appalling conditions. The French casualties totaled more than 13,000, of whom 2,242 were killed. Viet Minh losses were estimated to be nearly 23,000, with 7,900 dead. At the battle's end on May 7, 1954, only 6,500 French remained, and all ended up as prisoners.

Fall's analysis of the geopolitical issues, particularly of the Americans' decision to avoid direct involvement, cites both the Truman and Eisenhower administrations' reluctance to get embroiled in Indochina. Nevertheless, Fall notes the enormous contribution of American material and supplies and the presence of American major general John "Iron Mike" O'Daniel in Dien Bien Phu before the battle. The reader will find more than enough material here to appreciate the irony of America's slow escalation that began ten years later. In fact, Bernard Fall published this book after the insertion of major U.S. combat forces in Vietnam.

Hell in a Very Small Place is a hard read full of French acronyms, countless names, unit designations, and place-names that even the most ardent reader will find challenging. The meticulous endnotes, detailed appendixes and index, and bibliography make up for this difficulty, especially for a dedicated researcher. Fall's *Street without Joy* may be an even better book and is better known, but his skill in describing the details of this siege make the reader almost taste the dust, wallow in the mud, and smell the cordite and dead and dying soldiers.

Leadership Lessons Summarized

For any leader, the ability to rally a force in crisis is crucial. This powerful book illustrates the ability of French leaders to motivate their forces even in extreme distress as ammunition and medical support were rapidly dwindling. The lessons include using heritage and tradition as a spur, communicating the battle plan openly and directly, using innovation to overcome material deficiencies, and accepting an inevitable outcome to cut losses in the face of certain defeat. The book also provides insight into the powerful role that national motivation (in this case demonstrated by the Viet Minh) can have in conventional conflict.

— *R. Manning Ancell*

22   *Lee's Lieutenants: A Study in Command* (3 vols.)
by Douglas Southall Freeman
(Charles Scribner's Sons, 1942, 1943, 1944)

Recommended by Gen. James T. Conway, USMC, 34th Commandant of the Marine Corps 2006–10

I think your premise is spot on with regard to the importance leaders—military leaders in particular—should place on understanding history. Of course, reading, even in this multimedia age, is still the best means for doing so. I have experienced, however, that my amount of professional/recreational reading was inversely proportional to the difficulty of the job I held—and to the number of children in the home. During my two years as the J-3 of the Joint Staff, for instance, I finished one book during the entire period.

I have enjoyed reading history, particularly military history, since my earliest years. My mother always said it was no surprise to her that I wound up a Marine. After a time I was captivated by the profiles in leadership, intensity, and innovation of the American Civil War. I consumed books that provided differing perspectives and over time became an ardent admirer of the tenacity and operational skills—though not necessarily the leadership—of Lt. Gen. Thomas "Stonewall" Jackson.

Somewhat interestingly, the first time I read *Lee's Lieutenants* I did so with great interest on maneuver and the operational art. The second time I read the volumes, I did so paying particular interest to the battlefield functions of intelligence and logistics. What a difference a few years make.

Quote from the book "We Virginians do not go to the storied shrines of the past to do worship, but rather to gain inspiration."

About the Author

Douglas Southall Freeman was a distinguished journalist and historian who was born and raised in Virginia. He moved with his family to Richmond in 1892 and earned a bachelor's degree from Richmond College in 1904 and a PhD from Johns Hopkins in Baltimore in 1908 at the age of twenty-two. He was unable to find an appropriate position in academia and instead secured a job as an editor at the *Richmond News Leader* in 1909, becoming editor in 1915 at age twenty-nine and staying there for thirty-four years. During his tenure as editor he became recognized as an expert on the history of the Civil War and wrote a number of definitive books. Of greatest note were the commentary and criticism that appeared year after year in the paper he edited. He died in 1953.

About the Book

This is the best book for leaders seeking to understand the qualities and characteristics of the South's leadership team in the Civil War. It is in a way a version of *Team of Rivals* set in a military key, with all the lessons inherent in building camaraderie in a diverse cluster of teammates, as Gen. Robert E. Lee was able to do. Across the pages of this three-volume classic (or even the one-volume abridged version, which is quite good) gallop and march the names that led the South through the war: Jackson, Longstreet, Ewell, Stuart, Bragg, Pickett, Johnston, Forrest, Hood, Hill, Mosby, Early, and others—all presided over by the quiet, almost enigmatic Lee.

The books have an insider quality that gives the reader the feeling of being next to the general officer at the most intimate of times. This is a reflection of the exhaustive research and the literary energy of the author, which allows the leadership lessons to flow naturally as the war unfolds. Freeman follows Lee's lieutenants from the heady days at the start of the war to Gettysburg (at the so-called high-water mark of the Confederacy) to the losses and the bitter ending at Appomattox Court House. It is a brilliantly realized work.

Freeman's retelling of one experience involving J. E. B. Stuart, the talented, narcissist upstart propelled to fame by the Civil War, exemplifies his style. After May 20, 1863,

> when Stuart moved his headquarters from Orange to Culpeper, he set his staff to work on plans for such a pageant as the continent never had witnessed. The stage for it fairly thrust itself upon him: It was a long wide field in the vicinity of Brandy Station, between Culpeper and the Rappahannock. At the ideal site on this field was a hillock no craftsman could have excelled in the design of a reviewing stand. To complete perfection, the field was so close to the Orange and Alexandria Railroad that a halted train would offer seats for spectators. Stuart pitched his

tents on nearby Fleetwood Hill, overlooking Brandy Station, to supervise everything, and he set June 5 as the date. Each staff officer must provide himself a new uniform and must see to it that mounts were flawless. A ball must be arranged in Culpeper the night before the review and, perhaps, another after the cavalry had shown its magnificence.

The reader can feel the immense sense of theater that drove Stuart, as well as the almost medieval quality of the Southern forces self-imbued with ideas of chivalry. This is an epic work that takes the reader deeply into the heart of leadership as practiced by an assorted group of capable generals, all in a cause that never deserved such effort.

Leadership Lessons Summarized

Like Lincoln on the other side of the Mason Dixon Line, Robert E. Lee had a very talented group of generals; but he desperately needed to meld them into a coherent force. One of the crucial lessons of *Lee's Lieutenants* is that merging a highly energetic and headstrong team will be difficult but achievable with the right mix of personality, discipline, and motivation.

Another key lesson is not to overdepend on any given subordinate. Lee lost Gen. Albert Sidney Johnston, a close friend since West Point days, at Shiloh and wondered aloud if he could win the war without him. Gen. Stonewall Jackson lost his left arm at Chancellorsville and died of complications on May 10, 1863. Freeman notes that "many theorists through the years have postulated that if Jackson had lived, Lee might have prevailed at Gettysburg." Even if you build a perfect team, recognize that there will be attrition and have a plan to fill in behind crucial teammates. Lee's failure to have that type of succession plan robbed him of several opportunities at pivotal moments in the Civil War.

— R. Manning Ancell

23 — *Gates of Fire*
by Steven Pressfield (Doubleday, 1998)

Recommended by Gen. John Allen, USMC (Ret.), deputy commander U.S. Central and commander of the International Security Assistance Force, Afghanistan

Gates of Fire is an epic of leadership and human endurance. It beautifully captures the warrior ethos on the battlefield and crystalizes what all leaders know: that the most important reason men and women perform under conditions of extreme stress is so often love for the person next to them. We have seen that again and again in the harsh crucible of combat—but it is a lesson that applies in every walk of life as well.

Quote from the book "You are the commanders, your men will look to you and act as you do. Let no officer keep to himself or his brother officers, but circulate daylong among his men. Let them see you and see you unafraid. Where there is work to do, turn your hand to it first; the men will follow. Some of you, I see, have erected tents. Strike them at once. We will all sleep as I do, in the open. Keep your men busy. If there is no work, make it up, for when soldiers have time to talk, their talk turns to fear. Action, on the other hand, produces the appetite for more action" (King Leonidas of Sparta).

About the Author
Of all the historical fiction depicting ground warfare, this brilliant novel may be the best—ironically, produced by an author with no combat experience drawing largely on ancient texts, telling the story of a lost battle that perhaps changed the course of history. Gen. Jim Mattis once asked Steven Pressfield, "How can you write so perfectly about men in

combat, never having fought yourself?" Pressfield replied, "That's why they call it fiction." Yet numerous generals and admirals admire this book deeply, recommend it incessantly, and insist on its place on command and service reading lists. It is taught at Annapolis, West Point, and the Marine Corps University in Quantico, Virginia—three of the leading centers of military theory and practice.

Steven Pressfield was born in Trinidad in 1943 while his father, an American sailor, was stationed there. He graduated from Duke University in 1963 and joined the Marine Corps Reserves. He was never called up to active duty, but clearly the military ethos took hold because the majority of his works are about combat operations in one era or another. He has written extensively both fiction and nonfiction, including historical fiction covering World War II (*Killing Rommel*), the Peloponnesian War (*Tides of War*), the campaigns of Alexander the Great (*The Afghan Campaign*), and the future of warfare and the use of mercenaries (*The Profession*).

About the Book

Set in 480 BC, *Gates of Fire* brilliantly imagines the world of the Greek city-states as they prepare to meet the overwhelming challenge of an invasion from the Persian Empire, ably led by the god-king Xerxes. While the fractious city-states can barely agree on how to mount their defenses, they all acknowledge that the incomparable Spartan army must hold the center of the effort on land. Pressfield spends a great deal of time in the novel explaining the essence of Spartan culture, how the Spartans conducted combat operations, and why their armies were so dominant in that period. He captures perfectly the essence of Spartan character, often through anecdote. When the Persians boast that their arrows will come so thickly that they will blot out the sun, the king of Sparta says, "So much the better: we will fight the battle in the shade." The Spartans can be killed, but their spirit cannot be defeated.

At the center of the novel is King Leonidas of Sparta, who goes to battle fully aware that he will in all likelihood never return. He personifies the Spartan motto passed from the women of Sparta to the warriors as they depart for war: "Come back in victory with your shield, or dead upon it." Leonidas hand-selects three hundred Spartans to join with a force of some four thousand Greeks who march to the narrow pass of Thermopylae (the Gates of Fire of the title) to try and hold off the million-man Persian army and give the rest of Greece time to mobilize the Athenian and allied fleets and raise a larger army. Their desperate efforts succeed in providing that time, but the entire force is destroyed after a traitor shows the Persians a hidden path that allows them to outflank the Greek force.

This is a particularly powerful book about leadership, and the constant example is King Leonidas. His harsh code of warrior ethic is perfectly balanced with his deep love for all under his command, and his respect is given to and received by each and every soldier. "A king does not abide within his tent while his men bleed and die upon the field," Leonidas says.

> A king does not dine while his men go hungry, nor sleep when they stand at watch upon the wall. A king does not command his men's loyalty through fear nor purchase it with gold; he earns their love by the sweat of his own back and the pains he endures for their sake. That which comprises the harshest burden, a king lifts first and sets down last. A king does not require service of those he leads but provides it to them. . . . A king does not expend his substance to enslave men, but by his conduct and example makes them free.

Above all, *Gates of Fire* is fundamentally about battle at ground level. This is not a book about the high art of geopolitics, or the brilliance of operational or tactical decisions, or how technology can determine the course of a battle. This is a book about what motivated men in ancient battles—and along the way it perfectly illuminates the great truth of combat, which is that men (and in today's world, women as well, of course) fight above all for the man or woman standing next to them. One of the characters says of men in battle that "the opposite of fear is not courage—it is love." He means the love of the fellow soldier.

Of ancient Sparta today, virtually nothing exists. Unlike the Athenians with their beautiful city and temples, the Spartans did not build big, glittering cities. All that they valued was held in the hearts of their citizens. Leonidas explains it perfectly:

A thousand years from now, two thousand, three thousand years hence, men a hundred generations yet unborn may, for their private purposes, make a journey to our country. They will come, scholars perhaps or travelers from beyond the sea, prompted by curiosity regarding the past or appetite for knowledge of the ancients. They will peer out across our plain and probe among the stone and rubble of our nation. What will they learn about us? Their shovels will unearth neither brilliant palaces nor temples. Their picks will prize forth no everlasting architecture or art. What will remain of the Spartans? Not monuments of marble or bronze, but this—what we do here today.

On the eve of the battle, he and his three hundred Spartans knew the value of what they were about to do. *Gates of Fire* is their memorial. As the story unfolds, we see the gritty courage of the Greeks on display again and again as they fight against impossible odds. At Thermopylae today there are two monuments. One has the verses well known through the legend of the three hundred Spartans:

> Go tell the Spartans, stranger passing by,
> That here, obedient to their laws, we lie.

The other is a simpler monument that carries the response of Leonidas when the Persian king offers the Spartans the chance to live if only they will lay down their arms. Leonidas says only two words: "*Molon labe*"—"Come and take them." The Greeks fought to the last man. Such is war, and there is no better book than this to allow a reader to understand the crucible of combat.

Leadership Lessons Summarized

Gates of Fire shows us a leader in extreme adversity and how he inspires subordinates in the face of overwhelmingly negative odds. It teaches us about the power of camaraderie on the literal and metaphorical battle-fields. And above all, it shows us the values that hold free societies together in the face of totalitarian challenge.

—*Adm. J. Stavridis*

24 ⁓ *Lincoln on Leadership: Executive Strategies for Tough Times*
by Donald T. Phillips (Warner Books, 1992)

Recommended by Gen. Howell M. Estes III, USAF, commander in chief North American Air Defense Command 1996–98

I'm the kind of guy who would not read books where the author does a clinical study of leadership. I'm calling it clinical because it's really hard to read and it's so in depth that you say, well, maybe somebody understands what this guy is talking about, but I don't. I have searched out books that, I'm not going to say make it easy, but put it in a language I can understand.

It's a great book. It's called *Lincoln on Leadership: Executive Strategies for Tough Times,* by Donald T. Phillips. What it does is develop at the end of each chapter a section called "Lincoln's Principles" that outlines maybe seven or eight principles, but in the chapter before that, he applies those principles to real-time things that affect people in current times. So it makes a direct connection and helps you understand what the principle meant because he fits it into a situation, and it's easy reading.

Quote from the book "Sir, my concern is not whether God is on our side; my greatest concern is to be on God's side, for God is always right" (Abraham Lincoln).

About the Author

Donald Phillips, born on March 10, 1952, is a business executive, motivational speaker, and three-term mayor of Fairview, Texas. He is also the author of more than twenty books, including his first, *Lincoln on Leadership*, published in 1992. He focuses on motivational leadership and the use of practical examples to illustrate key points for readers.

About the Book

In 2012 Ford's Theater—where John Wilkes Booth shot Abraham Lincoln—opened a display of books about Lincoln in the form of a "tower of books" 3 stories high and containing about 7,000 books. The director of Ford's Theater, Paul Tetreault, pointed out that more than 15,000 books have been written about Lincoln, second only to Jesus Christ.

"One key to writing a successful book is choosing a topic others have not," James G. Zumwalt, a retired Marine Corps lieutenant colonel, author, and son of the late CNO, told me. He is also a student of Lincoln. "Phillips has done a yeoman's job in describing and detailing Lincoln's ability in rising to the task of leading a divided nation back into being one again. He makes the book very entertaining by sharing Lincoln's humor and relating stories told as Lincoln endeavored to drive home to the listener a particular issue's importance. The author deservingly describes Lincoln as 'the essence of leadership'—a man who practiced all the 'revolutionary thinking' techniques a century before such thinking came into vogue."

Lincoln was driven by a passionate vision of preserving the Union at all costs. He clearly communicated this vision through consistent interactions with subordinates. He proved himself a skilled artisan in this regard, treating people as equals, soliciting their views, and when he disagreed, "stealthily" getting them to come around to his own viewpoint. His genius in doing so left listeners believing they had originated Lincoln's idea.

He spent about 75 percent of his time meeting with people—in the office (where the door was always open) and on the battlefield. Modern leadership experts call this "MBWA"—-Managing By Wandering Around—or "getting out of the ivory tower." This trait was critical for Lincoln, providing an essential building block for successful relationships: trust.

Lincoln's battlefield appearances were great motivators for the troops. He continued them throughout the war, even after nearly being hit by enemy fire. He visited the wounded in hospitals. He felt it imperative that his soldiers always knew that the nation was grateful for their sacrifices.

The president exuded confidence to his subordinates because he had confidence in himself. He sought to inject that same level of confidence in others, even—in the case of his generals—when battlefield failures occurred. He believed all of life's experiences, whether successful or not, become building blocks for the future.

In selecting his generals to lead the war effort Lincoln favored those willing to take the fight to the Confederates, and as one after another proved hesitant to do so, he moved them out of a power position into one better suited to their limited leadership skills. Lincoln went through nearly a baker's dozen generals before finding one who could win the war: Ulysses S. Grant.

"Lincoln's leadership legacy preceded his untimely 1865 death, as a *New York Herald* article noted in 1864," Jim Zumwalt said in our interview. "Plain common sense, a kindly disposition, a straightforward purpose, and a shrewd perception of the ins and outs of poor, weak human nature enabled him to master difficulties that would have swamped any other man."

Leadership Lessons Summarized

The leadership principles Lincoln embodied are timeless, and readers of *Lincoln on Leadership* will understand clearly why our sixteenth president is considered our greatest. Persuasion, rather than coercion, was one of his primary leadership strengths. "Dictatorship, force, coercion—all were characteristics of tyrants, despots, and oppressors in Lincoln's view," observes Phillips. "Lincoln learned, refined and mastered the art of persuasion during his early career. When he entered the political arena he used his ability to persuade as a bridge to the voting public."

President Lincoln seemed to have an endless supply of great thoughts on important subjects, but we have dredged through "Lincoln's Pond"—a source of wisdom similar to "Walden's Pond"—and offer these quotations for your contemplation.

On the power of books:
- My best friend is a person who will give me a book I have not read.
- Books serve to show a man that those original thoughts of his aren't very new after all.
- Get books, sit yourself down anywhere, and go to reading them yourself.
- All I have learned, I have learned from books.

On what matters in a life:
- Adhere to your purpose and you will soon feel as well you ever did. On the contrary, if you falter, and give up, you will lose the power of keeping any resolution, and regret it all your life.
- Courage is not the absence of fear. It is going forward in the face of fear.
- Be with a leader when he is right, stay with him when he is still right, but leave him when he is wrong.
- You cannot escape the responsibility of tomorrow by evading it today.
- Every man's happiness is his own responsibility.

On the political life:
- You can fool all the people some of the time, and some of the people all the time, but you cannot fool all the people all the time.
- No man is good enough to govern another man without the other's consent.

Nearly all men can stand adversity, but if you want to test a man's character, give him power.

With public sentiment, nothing can fail. Without it, nothing can succeed.

The best way to destroy an enemy is to make him a friend.

Those who deny freedom to others deserve it not for themselves.

Be sure you put your feet in the right place, then stand firm.

The best way to predict your future is to create it.

Lincoln was a quintessential American leader, and it is hard to imagine a better source for leaders than works on his life.

— R. Manning Ancell

25 *The Best and the Brightest*
by David Halberstam (Ballantine Books, 1969)

Recommended by Adm. James G. Stavridis, supreme allied commander NATO 2009–13

This is a terrific book that not only vividly illustrates how decisions get made (and not made) in large organizations like the U.S. government but also provides extraordinary insight into the culture that can pervade an administration and cause the best-laid plans of the best and brightest to sometimes go disastrously awry.

Quote from the book "The Marshall Plan had stopped the Communists, had brought the European nations back from destruction and decay, had performed an economic miracle; and there was, given the can-do nature of Americans, a tendency on their part to take perhaps more credit than might be proper for the actual operation of the Marshall Plan, a belief that *they* had done it and controlled it, rather than an admission that it had been the proper prescription for an economically weakened Europe and that it was the Europeans themselves who had worked the wonders" (David Halberstam).

About the Author

Halberstam, a classically trained scholar, historian, and journalist, was born in New York City on April 10, 1934. Halberstam edited the *Harvard Crimson* and always knew he wanted to be a writer—a goal he achieved with great success. He found numerous opportunities to exploit his position as a *New York Times* correspondent during the Vietnam War and early on earned a Pulitzer Prize for International Reporting in 1964. A remarkable retinue of subjects populates his twenty-two books, ranging from history and politics to the sports world. Tragically, he was killed in an automobile accident in California on April 23, 2007.

About the Book

This revealing and complex book is about the brilliant public servants in the Kennedy administration in the early 1960s who despite all of their abilities managed to stumble into the quagmire of Vietnam. It is perhaps best described by its author, who wrote that he spent two and a half years interviewing people—many at the "second, third and fourth tier" of government who could piece together "the men, the events, the decisions." Halberstam's lengthy book is so well structured that it can be read a bit at a time without having to go back and reread previously absorbed material.

"I set out to study the men and their decisions," he writes.

> What was it about the men, their attitudes, the country, its institutions and above all the era which had allowed this tragedy to take place? The question which intrigued me the most was *why*, why had it happened. So it became very not a book about Vietnam, but a book about America, and in particular about power and success in America, what the country was, who the leadership was, how they got ahead, what their perceptions were about themselves, about the country and about their mission. The men intrigued me because they were fascinating; they had been heralded as the ablest men to serve this country in this

century [the book was published in 1969]—certainly their biographies seemed to confirm that judgment—and yet very little had been written about them; the existing journalistic definition of them and what they represented was strikingly similar to their own definitions of themselves. So I felt that if I could learn something about them, I would learn something about the country, the era and about power in America.

The book is organized chronologically, which makes it easier to understand, with timelines and events and the people who populated them. He explains their place in history and how and why they got there. In addition to President Kennedy and Vice President Johnson, Halberstam illuminates the entire cabinet: Secretary of State Dean Rusk; Secretary of Defense Robert McNamara, the "whiz kid" president of Ford Motor Company; the president's brother Bobby, the attorney general—all have their moments on the stage along with countless others.

A great deal has been written about President Kennedy and his leadership, and of President Johnson as well. The nation's growing involvement with the Vietnam War affected their leadership, as it affected many up and down the chain of command, civilian and military. Halberstam gives us insight into how and why a good leader thrust into a difficult situation can attempt to prevail by applying lessons learned during a long career, amplified by attributes like character, honesty, and integrity—and find it all crashing down to defeat in the end. The title of the book is an ironic coda that seems to say, "If these really were the brightest and the best our nation had to offer, how did we stumble to defeat in Vietnam?"

Among those so affected was Gen. William C. Westmoreland, whose nickname, "Westy," was familiar to the public but seldom used by anyone but his closest friends—and there were few—and politicians. Halberstam correctly describes him as being "terrible at small talk, totally committed to his work, his job of being an inspiring commander." Indeed, Westmoreland was a picture-perfect general anointed for success at West Point, but he failed badly in leading the war in Vietnam.

At the apex of the war, Westmoreland returned to Washington to be chief of staff of the Army and his former classmate Creighton W. "Abe" Abrams took over as COMUSMACV—"the commander"—in Vietnam. Abrams and Westmoreland had never been close, and friction developed rather quickly between them. "Abrams came in when the war was very old and tried to hold it down under limited post-Tet resources," says Halberstam, "and suddenly he got all the good publicity when Westmoreland was getting all the bad publicity and somehow being blamed for Tet." Deeply depressed by the flow of events, Westmoreland wanted to go public and explain that many of the positive events taking place actually originated under his watch. "Friends had to take him aside and tell him that the last thing a very troubled United States Army could stand at that particular moment was a public split between Westmoreland and Abrams." This is but one of a thousand examples in this highly readable and still fascinating book about failure of leadership at the highest levels and the enormous cost.

Many of the same questions Halberstam asked about Vietnam can be asked today about the conflicts in Iraq and Afghanistan. The national security decision-making process in the 1960s and 1970s has striking relevance for today.

Leadership Lessons Summarized

Above all else, good leaders build teams. The failures of the Kennedy and Johnson administrations stemmed from the lack of effective teamwork. The ability to harness brilliant individuals into a coherent team is the essence of leadership. Lincoln succeeded masterfully; Lee did as well until his team was undone by attrition; here we see both Kennedy and Johnson failing.

Also, brilliance is necessary but not sufficient by itself—it is character that shapes the best leaders. Character is not just a luxury; it is mandatory in an effective and successful leader. This book illustrates the power of nineteenth-century German chancellor Otto von Bismarck's pointed aphorism: "Politics ruins character"; and he above all should know.

᠅— R. Manning Ancell

26 ~ *Ike the Soldier: As They Knew Him*
by Merle Miller (G. P. Putnam's Sons, 1987)

Recommended by Adm. James M. Loy, USCG, Commandant of the Coast Guard 1998–2003, deputy secretary of Homeland Security 2003–5

I have always been intrigued by the notion of leader development, and I never failed to encourage colleagues and subordinates alike to read biographies of great leaders. *Ike the Soldier* captured my imagination completely. Part of the capture was the author, Merle Miller. He was already renowned for his oral biographies of President Truman and President Johnson and was also a historical novelist with evidenced ability to tell a good story. The rest of the capture was all about simplicity and this ability to cut to the chase. I was reading *Ike the Soldier* in 1989 as a newly selected flag officer in the U.S. Coast Guard. I had commanded ships at sea and I'd been to war (USCG patrol boat commanding officer as a junior officer in Operation Market Time in Vietnam). I had already distilled my own leadership model to a succinct few words that I had used to focus staff and junior officers at sea and in staff positions on the beach. Those few words were "Preparation Equals Performance," and as I read every passing chapter of *Ike the Soldier*, that simple but understandable leadership model was reinforced. This book allowed me to observe the maturation process of one of our greatest soldiers from the frustration of staying at home during World War I to the undesirable joy of accomplishing his mission as supreme allied commander in 1945.

Along the way, *Ike the Soldier* is validated by extraordinary research by the author. That research then provides the ability to see Eisenhower through the eyes of an endless array of observers—from family members to five-star generals, from presidents to international heads of state, from frustrated subordinates to loyal members of his personal staff. Piecing that puzzle together both chronicles the life lived by a national hero and systematically describes the metamorphosis of Eisenhower's personal leadership model.

Many Eisenhower biographers have cited the oft-told examples of his capacity to lead. *Ike the Soldier* provides building blocks, one by one, to take the reader to an understanding of that leadership model such that it literally becomes available to the reader to use or modify or even discard. The life personifies the model with ringing success and for me cemented into place the picture of what's possible if one prepares well for any assignment or any occasion.

Ike the Soldier is immense—more than eight hundred pages of reflection about this American giant. What makes it simple and understandable is Eisenhower himself. As it related to one's personal responsibility to develop oneself as a leader, Eisenhower later said it was really about only three things: native ability, opportunity, and the knowledge of one's craft. To Eisenhower, native ability was a set of characteristics such as intelligence, self-confidence, risk taking, and embracing change that we are really born with and can't do much to change. Collectively, they sum to a capacity for leadership. He cited opportunity as being pretty serendipitous also—really mostly in the hands of others despite our desire to control it. Finally, he cites the knowledge of your craft as that area of choice in our lives where we can choose a profession and invest ourselves to get good at the things that constitute that work.

The real strength of this model and its ultimate simplicity is when you recognize that *if* you have invested properly in the knowledge of your craft, *when* your opportunity comes along, you will perform up to the full capacity of your native ability. *Ike the Soldier* reinforces that simple line of thinking by citing personal observations about Eisenhower on the Kansas farmyard, at West Point, at countless Army posts, in command posts in North Africa and

Malta, in the chamber of 10 Downing Street, and in that oval room in the White House. *Ike the Soldier* connects observations to the developed model and then suggests we can all learn from it and perform our own responsibilities better as a result.

Quote from the book "I never give up a battle until I am licked, completely, utterly, and destroyed, and I don't believe in giving up any battle as long as I have a chance to win" (General of the Army Dwight D. Eisenhower).

About the Author

Merle Miller was born on May 17, 1919. He attended the University of Iowa and served as a war correspondent and editor at *Yank* magazine during World War II. He continued his writing career after the war as editor of *Harper's Weekly* and *Time* magazine and as a book reviewer for the *Saturday Review of Literature*. His bestselling book *Plain Speaking*, based on hundreds of hours of conversations with President Harry Truman, came out in 1974. Miller died on June 10, 1986, before he could complete *Ike the President*, a sequel to *Ike the Soldier*.

About the Book

If you tackle this book with the intent of learning all there is to know about Dwight David Eisenhower, you will come pretty close to reaching that goal. Merle Miller treats us to facts and viewpoints that we likely wouldn't have found otherwise, snippets that reveal little-known facts about Ike. If you want to know how an obscure lieutenant colonel rose to be a five-star general and supreme allied commander of Allied forces in World War II, look to General of the Army George C. Marshall's influence on Eisenhower's career. It was Marshall who recognized Eisenhower's potential and gave him opportunities to prove himself—which he did.

The little details that Miller reveals about Eisenhower's life during World War II are what make this book a gem. For example, during stressful times when even close friends could not relieve the weight of the immense responsibility he carried, Ike turned to bridge. By immersing himself in that card game he could forget for a time the crushing doubt that arose in times of challenge and uncertainty. On New Year's Eve 1943 Eisenhower was a guest at a dinner party given by French brigadier Ian Jacob. "He finished the evening at 1:30 AM by calling and making a grand slam vulnerable, which put the seal on his happiness."

This book beautifully illuminates a complex, effective leader who struggled with his inner conflicts and managed to triumph over them. Miller shows us Ike with all his leadership skills on vivid display in the most challenging parts of his career.

Leadership Lessons Summarized

You will find a multitude of examples of Eisenhower's leadership in the book: his enormous emotional intelligence that permitted him to constantly put himself in the shoes of his teammates and use his understanding to motivate them; his ability to overcome his own huge temper by sheer dint of effort and will power; and his knowledge that everyone is looking at the commander and that he had to have his head up and his luminous smile on no matter how gloomy the outlook. Perhaps all of this is best summed up in the supreme allied commander's message to the troops on D-day as an enormous force prepared to invade France and begin the long march to Berlin:

> Soldiers, Sailors and Airmen of the Allied Expeditionary Force! You are about to embark upon the Great Crusade, toward which we have striven these many months. The eyes of the world are upon you. The hopes and prayers of liberty-loving people everywhere march with you. In company with our brave Allies and brothers-in-arms on other Fronts, you will bring about the destruction of the German war machine, the elimination of Nazi tyranny over the oppressed peoples of Europe, and

security for ourselves in a free world. Your task will not be an easy one. Your enemy is well trained, well equipped and battle hardened. He will fight savagely.

But this is the year 1944! Much has happened since the Nazi triumphs of 1940–41. The United Nations have inflicted upon the Germans great defeats, in open battle, man-to-man. Our air offensive has seriously reduced their strength in the air and their capacity to wage war on the ground. Our Home Fronts have given us an overwhelming superiority in weapons and munitions of war, and placed at our disposal great reserves of trained fighting men. The tide has turned! The free men of the world are marching together to Victory!

I have full confidence in your courage and devotion to duty and skill in battle. We will accept nothing less than full Victory! Good luck! And let us beseech the blessing of Almighty God upon this great and noble undertaking.

—R. Manning Ancell

27 ⌇ *Soldier, Statesman, Peacemaker: Leadership Lessons from George C. Marshall*
by Jack Uldrich (Amacom, 2005)

Recommended by Gen. Ray Odierno, chief of staff U.S. Army 2011–15, commander Joint Forces Command 2009–11

Leadership Lessons from George Marshall is full of practical ideas that leaders can put to use. It draws on the life and career of one of the most distinguished Americans of the twentieth century and offers powerful examples of integrity, humility, and creativity as applied to the biggest leadership challenges imaginable. A must read for leaders in any organization.

Quote from the book "He has been called the unknown famous American, but George C. Marshall is precisely the type of leader we need today. In an era when too many of our public and private leaders are more interested in serving themselves than society; more interested in short-term profits than long-term investments; and more interested in power than empowering others, it is useful—indeed necessary—to stop, study, and reflect upon those who have gone before us and lived a great and principled life" (Jack Uldrich).

About the Author

Jack Uldrich is best known for his work as a futurist and is well regarded as a motivational and leadership speaker. He is better positioned than most to think about what the future looks like; but he is also very accomplished at taking the basic ideas of leadership and conveying them simply and cleanly in the context of the life of an iconic American leader, Gen. George Marshall. In an interesting way, he applies his thinking about the need for great leaders in the future to mining the life of perhaps the greatest American leader of the twentieth century.

About the Book

It is important to understand the basic trajectory of General Marshall's life to appreciate the power of this book. In the sense of "where do the operating ideas of this book come from?" in many ways the author is General Marshall. What do we know of him? In very brief summary: he was a native Virginian who attended the Virginia Military Institute and always focused on a career in the military. He excelled at everything he attempted in a long and successful life. General Marshall served as chief of staff of the U.S. Army, in effect the senior military officer of the United States, throughout World War II. In that sense he was acting essentially as the first modern chairman of the Joint Chiefs of Staff. He then went on to serve as both the secretary of state and the secretary of defense in the postwar period, most notably creating and executing the world-changing Marshall Plan. His work in that regard rescued and reconstructed war-torn Europe to the powerful benefit of both Europe and the United States. General Marshall also served as the president of the Red Cross and was awarded a Nobel Peace Prize, the only career military officer in history to receive one.

Another towering twentieth-century figure, Prime Minister Winston Churchill, said of Marshall, "He was the noblest Roman of them all," stealing the line from Shakespeare's *Julius Caesar* (the sort of thing Sir Winston was prone to do).

This is a short, simple, very readable but powerfully constructed book that outlines the basic and timeless principles of leadership. These include:

1. Do the Right Thing—the principle of integrity. We see in George Marshall the endless determination to tell the truth and never to curry favor by thought, word, or deed. Every one of General Marshall's actions was grounded in the highest sense of integrity, honesty, and fair play.

2. Master the Situation—the principle of action. Here we see the classic "know your stuff and take appropriate action" principle of leadership coupled with a determination to drive events and not be driven by them. Marshall knew that given the enormous challenges of World War II followed by the turbulent postwar era, action would be the heart of his remit. And he was right.

3. Serve the Greater Good—the principle of selflessness. In George Marshall we see a leader who always asked himself, "What is the morally correct course of action that does the greatest good for the greatest number?" as opposed to the careerist leader who asks "What's in it for me?" and shades recommendations in a way that creates self-benefit.

4. Speak Your Mind—the principle of candor. Always happiest when speaking simple truth to power, General and Secretary Marshall never sugarcoated the message to the global leaders he served so well.

5. Lay the Groundwork—the principle of preparation. As is often said at the nation's service academies, know the six Ps: Prior Preparation Prevents Particularly Poor Performance.

6. Share Knowledge—the principle of learning and teaching. Like Larry Bird on a basketball court, George Marshall made everyone on his team look better by collaborating and sharing information.
7. Choose and Reward the Right People—the principle of fairness. Unbiased, color- and religion-blind, George Marshall simply picked the very best people.
8. Focus on the Big Picture—the principle of vision. Marshall always kept himself at the strategic level, content to delegate to subordinates when necessary.
9. Support the Troops—the principle of caring. Deeply involved in ensuring that the men and women under his command prospered, General and Secretary Marshall taught that if we are loyal down the chain of command, that loyalty will be repaid not only in kind but in operational outcomes as well.

Uldrich takes each of these simple ideas and illustrates them with multiple practical examples from the life of George Marshall. He then adds a handful of related examples from many impressive chief executive officers, most of whom were leading global corporations when the action described occurred. This creates a powerful mix of historical examples that neatly tie together military leadership and business leadership. Each of the principles "comes to life" in a very vivid way.

The Leader's Bookshelf recommends books about many subjects, not just leadership, but this is a superb example of a highly readable and practical book full of stories that aspiring leaders can draw upon. No wonder that Gen. Ray Odierno, a practical soldier in many ways, chose this book to highlight to us.

Leadership Lessons Summarized

The nine principles above are the simplest and most direct recitation of leadership itself in all of the forty books on this list. There are very few leadership challenges that would not be amenable to the principles described above.

— Adm. J. Stavridis

28   This Kind of War
by T. R. Fehrenbach (Macmillan, 1963)

Recommended by Gen. Dennis J. Reimer, USA, vice chief of staff U.S. Army 1991–93, commander U.S. Army Forces Command 1993–95, and chief of staff U.S. Army 1995–99

My father was a Chevrolet mechanic and my mother cooked at the school lunchroom. Early in life I didn't have a good background on the importance of reading books, particularly history. I really got my start at West Point, and as I went through my career I found that the books that were most meaningful to me were contemporary books based upon what I was doing at that particular time. A good example is Fehrenbach's *This Kind of War*. I got interested in that when I was in Korea under General Livsey and we asked Brad Smith to do a battlefield tour of Task Force Smith. He brought with him a little manual he put together after the Korean War. It was really about making training as realistic as possible, using as much live fire as you possibly can because it reflected his experiences when the North Koreans went through them like a hot knife through butter.

The thing about Fehrenbach is he talks about how you can bomb a nation into the Stone Age, but if you really want to save them and bring them back into civilization as a meaningful organization you have to do it like the Romans and put your troops in the mud. You read Fehrenbach and you learn we do need boots on the ground.

Quote from the book "To fail to prepare soldiers and citizens for limited, bloody ground action, and then to engage in it, is folly verging on the criminal" (T. R. Fehrenbach).

About the Author

Thomas R. Fehrenbach, a native Texan, wrote more than twenty books. He was born on January 12, 1925, and earned a degree from Princeton in 1947. He served as an Army officer in the Korean War and for nearly thirty years wrote a weekly column for the *San Antonio Express-News*. He died in San Antonio on December 1, 2013.

About the Book

History has demonstrated that it is the individual soldier, sailor, or marine, led and inspired by someone of slightly higher rank—a sergeant or a junior officer in some cases—who has most influenced the outcome of skirmishes, battles, and wars. Small-unit action is the genesis of success in battle, and Fehrenbach does a marvelous job of describing it in all its grittiness. With candor and some finger pointing he describes the laissez-faire attitude in the United States at the end of World War II brought about by the bombing of Hiroshima and Nagasaki. With the atom bomb in America's arsenal, many felt it was no longer necessary to commit ground troops in order to secure victory against an enemy anywhere in the world. "If the United States ground forces had not eventually held in Korea, Americans would have been faced with two choices," he explains, "holocaust or humiliation. General, atomic war, in a last desperate attempt to save the game, would have gained Americans none of the things they seek in this world; humiliating defeat and withdrawal from Korea would have inevitably surrendered Asia to a Communist surge, destroying forever American hopes for a free and ordered society across the world."

Be prepared for a retelling of the Korean War from the foxhole by a talented Army officer who led and observed troops who seem descended almost literally from Bill Mauldin's World War II sketchbook and were subjected to what a Korean American soldier described as "the factor of human suffering in war." Fehrenbach the Army officer and Fehrenbach the author merge to put a "historical human face" on those too-often-nameless soldiers who fought in frozen Korea. The book follows the course of the war in gravelly detail so vivid that you can feel the cold wind blowing from the Chosin reservoir. Indeed, the war in Korea was a nitty-gritty deal: bitter cold, a challenging mountainous terrain, and a merciless and well-trained enemy that often significantly outnumbered U.S. forces.

It all began on July 1, 1950, when Lt. Col. Charles B. Smith, commanding officer of the 1st Battalion, 21st Infantry, reported to his division commander, Maj. Gen. William F. Dean, at Itazuke Air Force Base. General MacArthur had ordered the 24th Division to leave Japan and come to Korea to "show the flag." Fehrenbach points out that the battalion, numbering some four hundred officers and enlisted men, "had been told that this was a police action." Furthermore, "it was not their fault that no one had told them that the real function of an army is to fight—and that a soldier's destiny—which few escape—is to suffer and if need be, to die."

Task Force Smith arrived in Korea five days later, dug in along the rolling hills adjacent to the highway between Suwon and Osan, and waited for the North Koreans. The disaster that unfolded was avoidable. Lieutenant Colonel Smith was a competent officer, but he was hamstrung by the lack of essentials for doing battle. Artillery could have smashed the advancing North Korean forces, but there was none of sufficient strength. Airpower could have made quick work of the enemy troops congregated along the highway, but there was none—the weather was uncooperative. Communication was hampered by outdated radios. And on and on. Fehrenbach hits the hammer on the nail when he insists that America had to "provide the bread-and-butter weapons that would permit its ground troops to live in battle. If it did not want to do so, it had no moral right to send its troops into battle."

By the end of 1950 the Eighth Army, commanded by Walton H. "Bulldog" Walker, had made a slow but measured withdrawal to the southern side of the thirty-eighth parallel, pursued by a strong enemy determined to annihilate the U.S. forces. Two days before Christmas Walker was traveling on a road near Uijeongbu when his jeep collided with a fast-moving civilian truck, killing the three-star general. Back in Washington, D.C., Lt. Gen. Matthew B. Ridgway was settling into the holiday spirit. There would be no holiday for him. Fehrenbach describes how Ridgway immediately began to turn around the demoralized Eighth Army and restore optimism and determination to the American forces by the sheer force of his leadership.

Leadership Lessons Summarized

Leaders must face the worst of situations with real grit and recognize that they can be thrust into the cauldron of action at any moment. The story of the Korean War is one of initial disaster followed by a long period of back-and-forth, and finally a negotiated settlement. The one constant throughout the roller-coaster ride was steady leadership at the mid-grade officer level up to the three-star grade, personified by Ridgway's turnaround of the Eighth Army. Leaders can make an enormous difference if they bring determination, optimism, and personal engagement even to a horrific conflict like the Korean War.

—R. Manning Ancell

29 A Connecticut Yankee in King Arthur's Court
by Mark Twain (Charles L. Webster, 1889)

Recommended by Gen. Stanley McChrystal, USA (Ret.), commander Joint Special Operations Command (JSOC) and commander International Security Assistance Force Afghanistan 2007–12

Mark Twain challenges the conventional, the expected, and more than anything, the idea of unchallenged tradition. In *A Connecticut Yankee in King Arthur's Court*, he leverages an unlikely hero in a tale of time travel, innovation, and ultimately commitment to the cause of opportunity for others. It's a surprisingly thoughtful message wrapped in an absolutely fun read.

Quote from the book "You can't depend on your eyes when your imagination is out of focus" (Hank Morgan).

About the Author

Samuel Clemens (1835–1910), better known as Mark Twain, is perhaps the most iconic American author in history. In addition to such classics as *The Adventures of Huckleberry Finn* and *The Adventures of Tom Sawyer*, Twain was a well-known political commentator and above all a satirist. *A Connecticut Yankee in King Arthur's Court* was inspired by a dream Twain had of himself struggling as a knight in the age of chivalry, nearly imprisoned in his suit of mail.

Born in Hannibal, Missouri, in 1835, he lived a long and highly productive literary life, finally passing away in 1910. His birth was marked by the appearance of Halley's comet, and he often said he would go out with it. He died the day after it returned seventy-five years later. He was worldly, well traveled, supremely and globally well connected, and he had an eye for irony and sarcasm second to none. While he made several small fortunes on his writing, he lost much of his money in mistimed and misplaced investments. William Faulkner, a highly acclaimed Nobel Prize–winning twentieth-century novelist, called Twain, "the Father of American literature."

About the Book

The Connecticut Yankee of the title is one Henry (Hank) Morgan, who lives in Twain's time—the mid to late 1800s—and suddenly finds himself back in the sixth-century court of King Arthur. Fortunately, he is skilled and knowledgeable in engineering, weapons, fortifications, and other aspects of "modern" technology. This allows him to become a sort of "magician" capable of deeply surprising the citizens of the early Middle Ages. The largely comedic novel follows the trials and tribulations—as well as the small triumphs and ultimate defeat—of Henry Morgan in a period markedly different from his own technologically.

After being captured by Sir Kay, a knight of the Round Table, at the start of the novel, Morgan quickly realizes that by definition he is the most technically advanced person on the planet and should be "running things." Before that can happen he must overcome a sentence of death—which he does by correctly predicting an eclipse of the sun (that he knew was coming from his earlier life). After this godlike moment he becomes de facto the second most powerful person in the kingdom after King Arthur. He learns to lead those around him by a combination of technology and optimism: "But it is a blessed provision of nature that at times like these, as soon as a man's mercury has got down to a certain point there comes a revulsion, and he rallies. Hope springs up, and cheerfulness along with it, and then he is in good shape to do something for himself, if anything can be done."

Hank continues to be challenged by others from Arthur's court, especially the "wizard" Merlin, whom Hank has supplanted as the king's chosen advisor and master of magic. Using gunpowder and a lightning rod, Hank destroys Merlin's tower, further cementing his reputation. He goes on to set up schools, teach others the key technologies, and generally work to improve conditions in the kingdom. He travels throughout the realm with King Arthur and, after they are accidentally enslaved, manages to rescue him with the help of Sir Lancelot and other knights who arrive on bicycles Hank had manufactured. He is a huge believer in the value of training: "Training is everything; training is all there is to a person. We speak of nature; it is folly; there is no such thing as nature; what we call by that misleading name is merely heredity and training. We have no thoughts of our own, no opinions of our own; they are transmitted to us, trained into us."

Further complications ensue as Hank marries and fathers a child, fights a series of knights who challenge him and his apprentices, and continues his conflict with Merlin. After a huge battle between a handful of Hank's trained apprentices and more than 30,000 knights organized by the Catholic Church (which has declared Hank and his knowledge forbidden), Hank is put into a long slumber by Merlin and awakens back in his own time.

The book is certainly Twain at his satiric best, laughing at the highly romantic idealization of the Middle Ages that was so popular in the nineteenth century. He was also railing against the kind of code of chivalry in battle that had led to massive slaughters in the Civil War. Above all, this is a book about leadership as we see an enlightened, technologically advanced commander trying to win over a society predisposed to believe in ancient (and incorrect) traditions. The climactic battle scene of thousands of knights charging against barbed and electrified wire and machine guns correctly presages the horrors of World War I. In a sense, the book is a long rant at the forces of conservatism and the opponents of imagination. At one point Hank says, "The only man who behaved sensibly was my tailor; he took my measurements anew every time he saw me, while all the rest went on with their old measurements and expected them to fit me." *A Connecticut Yankee in King Arthur's Court* is above all about seeing the world anew with all of its myriad possibilities: that is the role of the leader.

Leadership Lessons Summarized

Good leaders are masters of technology as well as optimists who can create an enlightened vision of the world. Sometimes a leader fails to overcome the entrenched interests of the day but continues the effort to do so against all odds. Small, elite forces—when well armed technologically and full of imagination—have immense power to shape events. As Twain puts it, speaking of his opponents, "Their very imagination was dead. When you can say that of a man, he has struck bottom. There is no lower deep for him." So true.

— Adm. J. Stavridis

30 *The Mask of Command*
by Sir John Keegan (Viking Press, 1987)

Recommended by Gen. Crosbie Saint, USA (Ret.), commander U.S. Army Command, Europe and commander NATO Central Army Group 1988–92

Quote from the book "The leader of men in warfare can show himself to his followers only through a mask, a mask that he must make for himself, but a mask made in such form as will mark him to men of his time and place as the leader they want and need. What they should know of him must be what they hope and require. What they should not know of him must be concealed at all cost" (John Keegan).

About the Author

Sir John Keegan (1934–2012) never served in the military, but his writing and analysis are highly regarded. He wrote more than two dozen books on military history, famous battles, leadership in combat, and many other military topics. He spent a quarter of a century as a distinguished professor at Sandhurst, the military academy of the United Kingdom, as well as serving for many years as the defense editor of the *Daily Telegraph*. His best-known works are *The Mask of Command* and *The Face of Battle* (no. 6 on our "Top 50"), as well as *A History of Warfare*.

About the Book

Throughout *The Mask of Command* runs the central idea of the commander as exemplar to his (and in today's world, her) troops. Keegan uses four famous generals to illustrate the differences of approach over the past 2,500 years.

Keegan categorizes Alexander the Great as the Heroic Leader. He leads from the front, suffers alongside his troops, and famously says to his army, "I have no part of my body, in front at least, that is left without scars; there is no weapon, used at close quarters, or hurled from afar, of which I do not carry the mark. I have been wounded by the sword, shot with arrows, struck from a catapult, smitten many times with stones and clubs—for you, for your glory, for your wealth." For the Heroic Leader, leading from the front at all times is crucial. But Keegan believes this is a failed model of leadership because it only destroys and does not build. As Keegan says in summarizing Alexander, "There is the nobility of self-forgetting in his life—danger forgotten, hunger and thirst forgotten, wounds forgotten. But they were forgotten with the amnesia of savagery, to which all who opposed his will were subject. His dreadful legacy was to ennoble savagery in the name of glory and to leave a model of command that far too many men of ambition sought to act out in the centuries to come."

Keegan sees the Duke of Wellington, the victor at Waterloo and later prime minister of the United Kingdom, as an example of the Antiheroic Leader. Cool and precise in his thinking, and always measured under pressure, Wellington said of his own mind, "There is a curious thing that one feels sometimes. When you are considering a subject, suddenly a whole train of reasoning comes before you like a flash of light. You see it all, yet it takes you perhaps two hours to put on paper all that has occurred to your mind in an instant. Every part of the subject, the bearings of all its parts upon each other, and all the consequences are there before you." Unlike Alexander, who always consciously strove to be the exemplar, Wellington was calculated and understated—anything but the preening hero. When asked after Waterloo if he was pleased to be mobbed by his thrilled countrymen celebrating his victory, he said, "If I had lost they would have shot me." He fought on thirty battlefields in the course of his career, risking his life on each, and always put duty ahead of glory.

Ulysses S. Grant, despite the implied glory of his first name, was what Keegan calls the Unheroic Leader. Grant experienced failure early and often in his life. Despite all of his achievements, he was plagued with alcoholism. He left the Army and worked as a mule driver between the Mexican-American War and the Civil War, and was plucked from obscurity to lead the Union Army. His presidency naturally followed but was tarnished by widely accepted allegations of corruption. Always wearing rough field clothes, he sought not to stand above his soldiers, perhaps considering in his heart that he did not deserve to do so. There was nothing heroic about Grant, but his drive and determination to win made him Lincoln's favorite general and helped hold his country together. Keegan says of him, "Grant knew, or was quickly to discover, that in a war of people against people, dispersed in a vast, rich but almost empty land, an army need have no permanent base at all. All that it required to operate was the ability to draw military supplies behind it by river and railroad, while it fed itself on the produce of the districts through which it marched. All that it then required to win was drill, discipline and belief in itself. Grant could supply all three." He was a straightforward leader and general who depended on the basics and hammered them home. Keegan summarizes Grant as follows: "'Familiar reverence' is about as far as Americans think it is proper to go in saluting a hero, while Grant's unheroic heroism was perfectly adjusted to the population he led to victory."

Keegan's fourth and final general was from mid-twentieth-century Europe: Adolf Hitler, whom Keegan aptly styles the False Hero. Today, most people think of Hitler as an evil and deeply flawed political leader, which he surely was. Yet his own self-image was that of a soldier, and he spoke often and with heartfelt emotion of his military experience in World War I. He was certainly viewed as a soldier by many around the world—and very much so by those in Germany. Often appearing in his own self-styled version of a German field uniform, he clearly was the commander of the Nazi war machine in very personal ways. He was, of course, a master manipulator. "The essence of Hitler's achievement of dominance over the German army may be briefly stated," Keegan says: "Finding it humbled and diminished, he gave it back its strength and pride, but he took from it in compensation, though in scarcely perceptible installments, its independence and autonomy and so eventually its dignity and conscience." It is hard indeed to think of Hitler as in any way a hero.

For Hitler's supreme command had been no more than a charade of false heroics. It had been based . . . ultimately on the ritual of suicide as the equivalent of death in the face of the enemy. Few suicides are heroic, and Hitler's was not one of them. Among all the epitaphs that have been written for him since April 30, 1945, "hero" is a word that finds no place among them. Nor is it probable that it ever shall. Heroes, in the last resort, die at the head of their soldiers and find an honoured grave. Hitler died in the presence of no man and his ashes are scattered in a place that today cannot even be found.

Keegan concludes by looking at "modern" leadership. He says, "Mankind, if it is to survive, must choose its leaders by the test of their intellectuality; and, contrarily, leadership must justify itself by its detachment, moderation and power of analysis. Hopes of transition to such a style of leadership need not be based on mere wish." The lesson for leaders in the twenty-first century is that the mask of command still pertains, although trying to put on the "hero's mantle" will fail. "Command, the cliché has it, is a lonely task. But so it must be. Orders derive much of their force from the aura of mystery, more or less strong, with which the successful commander, more or less deliberately, surrounds himself; the purpose of such mystification is to heighten the uncertainty which ought to attach to the consequences of disobeying him." Still so true (adding only "or her") in today's more complex and utterly transparent world!

Using these four models, Keegan leads the reader on a brilliant tour de force of modern military leadership. The lessons (and anti-lessons) are applicable to every walk of life. This is a true classic of leadership, and one that should be on the shelf of anyone engaged in leading others.

Leadership Lessons Summarized

The mask of command is a tool leaders must employ, but in a way that does not aggrandize the leader or place him or her on a pedestal above the followers. In today's transparent and complex world, the leader must still stand apart from the led—but in a way that recognizes the inherent role of leader as servant to the organization and above all to the followers.

— Adm. J. Stavridis

31 ⌇ *A Peace to End All Peace: The Fall of the Ottoman Empire and the Creation of the Modern Middle East*
by David Fromkin (Henry Holt, 1989)

Recommended by Adm. Michael G. Mullen, USN (Ret.), chairman of the Joint Chiefs of Staff 2007–11, Chief of Naval Operations 2006–7

A Peace to End All Peace is a book I often recommended to my team to better understand the complexities of the Middle East, which are in many ways rooted in the events of a century ago and the collapse of the Ottoman Empire. It is also a book full of lessons of leadership, both good and bad, with deep applicability to the ongoing challenges of the region and the world.

Quote from the book "Their [the European and American leaders who redrew the map of the Middle East after World War I] vision of the future of the Middle East was central to their idea of the sort of twentieth century they passionately believed would emerge as a phoenix from the ashes of the First World War" (David Fromkin).

About the Author
David Fromkin was born in the Midwest in 1932 and is a noted historian and author. He is also an accomplished lawyer. *A Peace to End All Peace* was originally published in 1989 and remains in print to this day. It is a superb account of the efforts of leading world powers—mostly European—to reshape the Middle East from 1914 to 1922 and was a finalist for both the Pulitzer Prize and the National Book Critics Circle Award. The "modern Middle East" thus created has been more or less a disaster. Fromkin has written many other books of history, including

well-regarded treatments of President Theodore Roosevelt and King Edward VII of Great Britain. A graduate of the University of Chicago, Fromkin taught for many years at Boston University. As a lawyer, he served in the U.S. Army Judge Advocate General Corps on active duty.

About the Book

This is a brilliant and foundational book for those who want to understand the enigma that is today's Middle East. If you are confused as to why Iraq is home to three competing ethnic groups—Kurds, Sunnis, and Shias—read this book. If you want to know why there is no Kurdistan despite a coherent religious and cultural grouping constituted by millions of Kurds—read this book. If the borders of Syria and Jordan look suspiciously simple and almost hand drawn—read this book. Fromkin's tour de force explicates the failure of leadership and cultural understanding that led to the poorly drawn and highly contentious borders of today's Middle East.

Beginning with the collapse of the Ottoman Empire—famously the "Sick Man of Europe"—to the postcolonial impulses of Great Britain and France, Fromkin tells this sweeping and largely tragic story with panache and style. Including the role of Russia and the Soviet Union in the region, he sketches the extraordinary characters who populate this narrative—from the youthful Lawrence of Arabia to General Herbert Kitchener (in his last command). Fromkin helps us understand the impact of Lloyd George's Zionism, the Balfour Declaration, and the infamous Sykes-Picot Agreement and how they created today's Middle East. In particular, we see the heavy thumb of Winston Churchill on the scales of the time alongside the nationalistic impulses of many of the regional actors.

The lessons of leadership (most often the failure of leadership) fall out clearly and collectively. First and foremost is the political "tone deafness" of the leaders of the world powers, who were utterly convinced that their vision of the world would triumph if only they sketched in the right lines on the map. The Arabists who actually knew the region and could have rendered more realistic advice were simply ignored in a triumph of idealism over realism. "Few Europeans of Churchill's generation knew or cared what went on in the languid empires of the Ottoman Sultan or the Persian Shah," Fromkin says. "Much of the Middle East still rested, as it had for centuries, under the drowsy and negligent sway of the Ottoman Empire, a relatively tranquil domain in which history, like everything else, moved slowly." This lack of cultural sensitivity sowed the seeds of the violence we reap today.

World War I in this out-of-the-way theater and its inherent leadership lessons receive excellent coverage, with the battles between Turks and the Allies highlighting the "great game" at play. Russian troops moved south wherever they could, the British and French had competing agendas, and the Arabs hoped for independence from the failed Turkish Empire. Prince Faisal, King Hussein, and other Arab leaders put their faith in T. E. Lawrence and other Europeans, but ended up largely betrayed. As the Ottoman Empire imploded and the "Young Turks" led by Kemal Ataturk rose to power, the European powers pushed hard to impose their own vision. This is the second great leadership lesson: outside solutions unanchored by an understanding of a given regional system are almost always doomed to fail. When the Americans, led by Woodrow Wilson, tried to intervene, the resulting confusion did little good for anyone's side of the argument. In the midst of all of this, of course, were the confusing and emotional questions surrounding the question of Palestine and the Jews' burning desire for a homeland. Summing up the disaster, Fromkin says, "The Middle East became what it is today both because European powers undertook to re-shape it AND because Britain and France failed to ensure that the dynasties, the states, and the political system that they established would permanently endure."

In the end, only questions and bad compromises remained. The world has reaped what was sown by the "peace to end all peace." Today Syria burns, Iraq is splitting apart, Jordan teeters, Yemen is racked by civil war, and the Gulf States are in domestic turmoil. The Shias and Sunnis are embroiled in the twenty-first-century version of the Wars of the Reformation. As Fromkin correctly concludes: "Decisions, by all accounts, including those of the participants, were made with little knowledge of, or concern for, the lands and peoples about which and whom the decisions were being made." It did not have to be this way.

Leadership Lessons Summarized

Begin by listening and truly understanding the culture, history, literature, and aspirations of any given group. Use the knowledge gleaned by listening and thinking before leaping into action. Recognize that solutions imposed from the outside will often meet vigorous resistance and are unlikely to succeed. Bottom-up solutions are the best.

— Adm. J. Stavridis

32   *A River Runs Through It*
by Norman Maclean (University of Chicago Press, 1976)

Recommended by Adm. Greg "Grog" Johnson, USN (Ret.), commander U.S. Naval Forces, Europe and commander NATO Allied Forces South 2001–4

I think the book is a very important leadership book in indirect and nuanced ways. It taught me about balance in life and to never delay doing something or saying something about relationships, especially family relationships or those with close friends. If we delay we may never get the chance. So as the father famously says in the eulogy to his son: "But we can still love them—we can love them completely without completely understanding." That can be a very difficult thing for those of us who set high standards and are competitive, self-demanding, type A personalities. We tend to be judgmental and find it difficult to be nonjudgmental and unconditional.

Finally, I think another important lesson comes from something Mr. Maclean recalled his dad saying: "My father was very sure about certain matters pertaining to the universe. To him all good things—trout as well as eternal salvation—come by grace and grace comes by art and art does not come easy." I am a big believer in God's grace, which in my mind is about the way people act toward one another—this matter of being unconditional, non-judgmental, a good listener, etc. Grace really is about art, and not everyone is accomplished at this art. All of us would be better and more effective if we were skilled in the art of grace.

Quote from the book "Eventually, all things merge into one, and a river runs through it. The river was cut by the world's great flood and runs over rocks from the basement of time. On some of the rocks are timeless raindrops. Under the rocks are the words, and some of the words are theirs. I am haunted by waters" (Norman Maclean).

About the Author

Norman Maclean (1902–90) was a writer and scholar who lived a long and productive life, raising two children and writing several highly regarded books. Too young for World War I, he spent much of his life teaching in a classroom, once proudly saying, "I would spend two weeks covering the first scene in *Hamlet*." Supreme Court justice John Paul Stevens said that Maclean's poetry class at the University of Chicago was the best he ever took and shaped him as a thinker and writer. Maclean's other most highly regarded book is *Young Men and Fire*, the story of the vicious 1949 Mann Gulch fire that took the lives of a group of young firemen. Of writing he said, "One of life's quiet excitements is to stand somewhat apart from yourself and watch yourself softly becoming the author of something beautiful, even if it is only a floating ash."

About the Book

A River Runs Through It is a largely autobiographical story (although nominally fictional) of the early life of author Norman Maclean. Set in Montana in the early years of the twentieth century, it is a book about brothers and fathers, about ranching and outdoor life, about courage and love, and above all about nature and its relationship to each of us. As Maclean says in a famous line from the book, "In our family there was no clear line between religion and fly-fishing."

This brilliant novella was not published until the late 1970s, decades after all the action in the book takes place. It has variously been printed as a stand-alone work and occasionally combined in volumes with several long short stories by the author. The short format is a difficult one in which to fit such a sweeping story, especially given the author's use of highly atmospheric prose. Until the 1992 film with Brad Pitt was released, the book's fame was somewhat limited to cognoscenti because there was never an attempt to advertise it widely. It is generally regarded today as a classic of American fiction, reminiscent of the best of Hemingway, Faulkner, or Steinbeck in portraying life in the United States in a specific region and time.

Set in and around Missoula, Montana, the novel/memoir tells the story of a stern Presbyterian minister and his two very different sons—one rebellious, the other reserved and studious—as they find their way through the plains and the mountains of Montana between World War I and the Great Depression. Much of the action is set during Prohibition (1919–33). Essentially a family story, *A River Runs Through It* tells the deceptively simple tale of a father and his sons. They live and love deeply, fight over women, make both good and bad choices, live and die. The leadership lessons are simple and profound: "[A]ll good things—trout as well as eternal salvation—come by grace and grace comes by art and art does not come easy." Despite this apparently simple philosophy, true life collides frequently, and a full understanding between the father and two sons of each other proves elusive. "It is those we live with and love and should know who elude us in the end."

The book is also profoundly respectful of nature. Good leaders have the ability to place themselves and their lives in the larger context of the world, indeed, of the universe. They appreciate how small we are—how trivial our day-to-day concerns are—in the face of the enormity of the natural world. Good leaders appreciate this balance between the size of the universe and our own small part in it and can still inspire their followers in the face of the small scale of our endeavors.

Leadership Lessons Summarized

There is a serenity that comes from engagement with nature that is deeply sustaining to a leader. Sometimes family leadership situations are the hardest to resolve, but the foundation of all our lives remains our families.

— Adm. J. Stavridis

33 *Balkan Ghosts: A Journey through History*
by Robert D. Kaplan (Vintage Books, 1993)

Recommended by Gen. William S. Wallace, USA, commanding general Training and Doctrine Command October 2005– December 2008

One can argue that there was no reason for the United States to get involved in the Balkans; there's no national security interests involved. I guess you can make the case that the Balkans glue the Middle East to the European continent, but I think that's "BS." You can make all kind of arguments, but the real issue became the pictures that we were seeing on TV of ethnic cleansing. You mention humanitarian suffering and our government because we have the capability and felt compelled to get involved, which of course we did in, I don't know, '97 I guess, '98, somewhere in there. We got involved in a conflict that we didn't understand, and that lack of understanding has a lot to do with our own culture and our own history. Our history is about three hundred years old; everybody else's is five to ten times that old. Other histories are infused with myth and innuendo that have been passed down from generation to generation, and not necessarily based on fact, and yet we were thrust in the middle of this conflict. So Robert Kaplan comes out with this book called *Balkan Ghosts.*

Bob Kaplan is a geographer—fundamentally a geographer—but he put the Balkan conflict in the context of first, geography; second, in the context of history; third, in the context of culture; fourth, in the context of ethnicities, none of which was high on the list of military folks paying attention to that sort of stuff. We worried about throw-weight of munitions; we worried about deployability; we worried about targeting. We didn't worry about cultures and history and ethnicity and all that sort of thing, and we found ourselves thrust into a kind of a policing role in a conflict that we frankly didn't understand. So *Balkan Ghosts* was kind of an eye-opener for anybody who was involved in those days, in the conflict, and to a larger extent, a broader audience, and the military who said, hey, there's something going on here that requires study and understanding, but it's not to be found in military history books. It's to be found elsewhere. In, you know, ancient history perhaps, or in a cultural anthology perhaps, or in some kind of geographical relationship to cultures and populations and migrations and all that sort of stuff.

He had insights that were much more fundamental to the conflict than just to factions arguing over political dominance of a region—much more fundamental than that, and going back hundreds and hundreds and hundreds of years. You know, it reminds me, a couple of years ago I saw a *Doonesbury* cartoon, which is unrelated to the Balkans but it's kind of illustrative. The first panel is a U.S. soldier and an Iraqi soldier riding along in a humvee. In the second panel the Iraqi soldier pulls out his weapon and starts shooting out the window of the humvee and the American says, "Hey, what are you doing? What's going on?" He said, "That guy killed my brother." And the American says, "Oh, really? When did that happen?" And the Iraqi says, "Twelve hundred years ago."

So, that's the kind of influence that book had, understanding that the roots of many of these conflicts both then and now are in deep, deep, long-standing historical arguments that have never been resolved and are unlikely to be resolved. And we as the military, we as the nation and our allies, if we're going to get involved, we at least need to understand that history, we need to understand the ethnical conflict, we need to understand that some of these opinions on one side or the other are irreconcilable.

I think our civilian leadership needs to understand it before we get involved, and at least have some kind of sense of what we're getting into. If the military wants to get involved, they have to understand the problem that they're dealing with and the fact that it may very well be more deeply rooted than just a military solution or a civil-military solution. So, anyway, that's my take on *Balkan Ghosts* and Kaplan.

Quote from the book "So what if the Balkans are a confused, often violent ethnic cauldron? Welcome to much of the world" (Robert D. Kaplan).

About the Author

A well-traveled foreign affairs expert and author, Robert D. Kaplan was born in New York City on June 23, 1952. The magazines and newspapers that he writes for, including the *New Yorker*, the *New York Times*, the *New Republic*, the *Washington Post*, and *The Atlantic*, give a clue to his left-of-center political persuasion. He writes frequently about the unsettled nature of the post–Cold War world, essentially traveling the globe and illuminating the challenges of history, geography, and culture as catalysts for conflict. In later years Kaplan has forged a reputation within the government for his insights and observations, and *Foreign Policy* magazine in 2011 named him "one of the world's top 100 global thinkers." Kaplan has lived in Israel—he joined the Israeli army while in residence there—as well as Athens, and makes his home today in Massachusetts.

About the Book

The Balkan countries are named for the mountain range that stretches from just east of Serbia to the Black Sea, covering about 4,500 square miles and stretching for 330 miles. The name derives from ancient Persian and means "Old Mountain" or "high, above." The Balkan region comprises more than 257,400 square miles of mostly mountainous territory that is home to nearly 60 million people. It begins in the west with Croatia, founded in the seventh century, and stretches eastward to Moldova and the Black Sea.

Humans have occupied this ancient land since the late Paleolithic period—the Stone Age. At about 8000 BC, the dawn of the Neolithic Age, there began a migration from Anatolia of people learned in agriculture and the manufacture of pottery. As time went on, the Balkan region became the portal for trade with the north, and people of many different backgrounds settled there.

Kaplan spent a great deal of time in the Balkans throughout the 1980s and writes about historical hotspots with a mixture of pathos and personal understanding. "The region was utterly fascinating," Kaplan eagerly shares, "the hotels inexpensive, and other journalists few and far between." We learn about Albania and its checkered past. It became independent in 1912 and existed as a kingdom until Italy invaded it in 1939. Then, in 1944, Enver Hoxha came to power and gradually sealed off the country's borders to the rest of the world as he governed—or perhaps ruled—with an iron fist throughout the Soviet era. For many years Americans were forbidden to travel there. Today, in the aftermath of the collapse of the Soviet Union, Albania has emerged as a parliamentary republic, a member of NATO, and a popular and inexpensive tourist destination. As recently as 2012, 4.2 million visitors contributed more than 10 percent of Albania's GDP. Islam is the dominant religion, with about 60 percent of the population, although 65 percent of that number claim to be "nondenominational."

On his web site Kaplan notes that "in July 1989, four months before the Berlin Wall fell and immediately before the East German refugee crisis that would precipitate that event, I warned in a 3,000-word article in *The Atlantic*: In the 1970s and 1980s the world witnessed the limits of superpower influence in places like Vietnam and Afghanistan. In the 1990s those limits may well become visible in a Third World region within Europe itself. The Balkans could shape the end of the century, just as they did the beginning."[14]

"*Balkan Ghosts* paints a grim picture of ethnic relations in south-eastern Europe," Kaplan continues,

> but it is only the grimmest human landscapes where military intervention has ever been required in the first place: for one need never idealize a human landscape in order to take action on its behalf. The prologue of *Balkan Ghosts* ends with the realization that the mundane, ethnic peace achieved in southern Austria as a result of economic development would soon be the fortune of the former Yugoslavia. Chapter One of *Balkan Ghosts*, about Croatia, is less about fate than about the moral choice that still awaited people there: whether to follow the path of ethnic division in the Balkans symbolized by Cardinal Alojzije Stepinac, or the path of ethnic reconciliation symbolized by Bishop Josip Strossmayer. Though my books and articles about the Balkans were read by the President and others, at no point did anyone in the Clinton Administration—whether the President himself or even an intern in the State Department—ever contact me in any way concerning my work, and how it might be applied to specific policy choices that arose long after the book was completed. The fact that *Balkan Ghosts* was reportedly used as an excuse for non-intervention in early 1993 will forever cause me great grief.

Balkan Ghosts found its way to the desktop of virtually every senior U.S. policy-maker involved in the series of decisions that governed the U.S. engagement in the Balkans throughout the 1990s. Both during the war in Bosnia in the early part of the decade and then later during the intervention on behalf of Kosovo against the Serbian regime, *Balkan*

Ghosts was required reading for anyone deploying to the region. It lays out the centuries of history, most of it bad and dangerous, in ways that helped us to eventually succeed in pacifying the region.

Leadership Lessons Summarized

Balkan Ghosts provides two striking lessons in leadership. The first is the need for leaders to read deeply about the history, culture, geography, and economics of a region before deciding on a coherent course of action. As an example of the type of book leaders need to read and study, it is difficult to top. The second lesson, drawn from the turbulence of the history Kaplan so vividly describes, is the need for leaders at some point to let go of the past and propel their people into the future. These two lessons, ironically, seem to contradict: one says to know the past deeply, the other to allow yourself to forget its impact. But taken together they represent a powerful recipe for leadership in geopolitics and, frankly, in our day-to-day lives. We should study and understand the past but not be imprisoned by it. Pretty hard to beat that as a prescription for leadership.

— R. Manning Ancell

34 *Gods and Generals: A Novel of the Civil War* (Civil War Trilogy)
by Jeff Shaara (Perfection Learning, 1998)

Recommended by Gen. William L. "Spider" Nyland, USMC, Assistant Commandant of the Marine Corps 2002–5

Fortunately, I became a voracious reader at a young age and that trait has continued to this day. I believe that professional reading is a key ingredient to sound leadership, as we can all learn new tools of the trade, reinforce our own leadership models, or review our models in light of the leadership traits and characteristics of others. My personal library is divided into sections for the Civil War,

World War II in the Pacific theater, the Vietnam War, and topical readings subsequent to 11 September 2001.

One of my favorites, *Gods and Generals*, is a very interesting development of in particular four Civil War generals—Jackson and Lee from the South, and Chamberlain and Hancock from the North. I personally think the Southern generals are better developed, in particular Jackson. Seeing the war through his eyes, his decision-making and war-fighting skill, makes it come alive and leaves one with a very special feeling for this incredible wartime commander. Had he not been mortally wounded, sadly by his own troops, who knows what he and Lee might have been capable of accomplishing. In sum, a great book with tremendous insights into one of our nation's most incredible periods and some of its leaders.

Quote from the book At the first meeting of Joshua Chamberlain and Sergeant Buster Kilrain, Chamberlain asks the burly Irishman if he is a veteran. Kilrain replies yes. "'Did the long walk with General Scott down south of the Rio Grande,' he said. Chamberlain nodded and said, 'Some of the men you fought with in Mexico are on the other side. Almost all their generals.' A strange look came across the sergeant's face. 'Oh, it gets worse than generals, Colonel. Some o' the lads that I left Ireland with are on the other side as well. Imagine that. Left together to escape a tyranny . . . and end up shootin' at one another in the Land of the Free.'"

About the Author

During the time Michael Shaara was trudging through the writing of his masterpiece, *The Killer Angels*, his son Jeff was drawn into the web of research, interviews, and the myriad other tasks that go into the making of a bestseller. Michael Shaara was teaching at Florida State University in Tallahassee at the time, and one day he packed up the family and drove to Gettysburg to see the famous battlefield up close.

The excursion drew Jeff further into the challenges of writing about a momentous battle that changed the direction of the Civil War, as well as the characters who were players on this giant chessboard in central Pennsylvania. Like his father, Jeff was particularly intrigued by the story of the 20th Maine and its miraculous stand at Little Round Top.

Gods and Generals was published with great success in 1996, followed by *The Last Full Measure*, the final book in the Civil War Trilogy, in 1998. Shaara subsequently wrote thirteen books—all but one historical fiction—about the Mexican-American War, the Revolutionary War, World War I and World War II, and additional books on the Civil War. He is at work on an exploration of leadership in the Korean War.

Jeff Shaara teamed up with producer and director Ron Maxwell in the years following his father's death and assisted in the production of the movie *Gettysburg* in 1993. It was a smash hit. In 2003 Shaara and Maxwell worked together again to bring *Gods and Generals* to the big screen. Word has it that they are looking for the right actors to play prominent roles in a movie version of *The Last Full Measure*.

About the Book

Shaara tells the reader up front that his book "is primarily the story of four men": Robert E. Lee and Stonewall Jackson of the Gray and Winfield S. Hancock and Joshua Chamberlain of the Blue. Woven into the three years leading up to the Civil War is the supporting cast that includes, among others, Jefferson Davis, "Lo" Armistead, Winfield Scott, "Old Pete" Longstreet, "Jeb" Stuart, John Bell "Sam" Hood, and George Pickett.

The more you know about the players in this melodrama of the prelude to the Civil War beforehand, the more you will savor the insights woven into the matrix—the commonality of backgrounds and relationships, the brotherhood of West Point, and the Mexican-American War that made a national hero of Winfield Scott and brought together scores of officers who would later wear the blue and the gray. We suggest you read *Reveille in Washington* by Margaret Leech, a superbly detailed recount of Washington, D.C., in the years 1860–65.

Only two of the characters in *Gods and Generals* were not graduates or former cadets at West Point: Winfield Scott and Joshua Chamberlain. Scott was born near Petersburg, Virginia, on June 13, 1786, and briefly attended the College of William and Mary before embarking on a career in the Army that spanned more than half a century. He was a towering figure in all respects, standing six feet five inches tall and earning accolades in the Mexican-American War as "Grand Old Man of the Army."

Joshua Chamberlain was a scholar rather than a soldier, but when the Civil War erupted he opted to sign up as colonel of the 20th Maine. He was a native of Maine, born near the small town of Brewer on September 8, 1828, the same year that Jefferson Davis graduated from West Point. Chamberlain attended Bowdoin College, having had to learn classical Greek and Latin in order to gain acceptance. The Chamberlain family had a long history of military service. Joshua's great-grandfather was a sergeant in the Revolutionary War, his grandfather was a colonel in the War of 1812, and his father was a volunteer in the obscure Arostook War in 1839 between the United States and Great Britain.

A moving review in the *Anniston Star* right after the book came out wraps up the heart and soul of *Gods and Generals*: "This heartbreaking story offers understanding of man's fascination with battle and made me marvel at how wave after wave of soldiers marched into sure death, driven there by generals who deeply believed in causes that to them were perhaps greater than any we hold today. The portraits of the battlefield are vividly horrid, of the men profoundly emotional, and of the war, intense. I wept as I turned the pages."[15]

Leadership Lessons Summarized

There are many lessons to be learned from Jeff Shaara's book, but one stands out in a brief conversation between Capt. James Power Smith and Gen. Stonewall Jackson. Smith asks Jackson, "How is it you remain so calm in the midst of battle?" Jackson's response should not be a surprise to those who have studied this man's leadership. "Mr. Smith, my religious faith teaches me that God has already fixed the time of my death; therefore, I think not of me. I am as calm in battle as I would be in my own parlor. God will come for me in his own time."

In the end, a leader's fundamental job is to bring order out of chaos, whether it occurs on a battlefield or in a boardroom. Leaders must stay calm, never lose their temper, and strive to bring that sense of order to the team.

— R. Manning Ancell

35 ⟿ *Grant Takes Command*
by Bruce Catton (Little, Brown, 1968)

Recommended by Gen. David Petraeus, USA (Ret.), commander U.S. Central Command, commander International Security Assistance Force Afghanistan, director of the Central Intelligence Agency

Grant Takes Command is full of leadership lessons that continue to resonate over the decades. I often recommend it to members of my team for the way it illuminates Grant's strategic vision, extraordinary determination, and unassuming sense of himself, qualities that are essential for any leader.

Quote from the book "The art of war is simple enough. Find out where your enemy is. Get at him as soon as you can. Strike him as hard as you can, and keep moving on" (Ulysses S. Grant).

About the Author
Bruce Catton was born in 1899 in upstate Michigan and in his youth heard the stories of the old veterans of the Civil War. He was a journalist for a time but quickly became enamored with the study and writing of history, with the vast majority of his work focused on the Civil War. He attended Oberlin College but never finished his degree (Oberlin awarded him an honorary one decades later) and also served briefly in the U.S. Navy in World War I.

A narrative historian of unusually easy grace and rhetorical brilliance, Catton's writing style has been compared with Winston Churchill's in both accessibility and the quality of the prose. Over the course of his long and prolific career he won both the Pulitzer Prize and the National Book Award. He became the founding editor of *American Heritage* magazine in 1954, saying at the time, "Our American heritage is greater than any one of us. It can express itself in very homely truths; in the end it can lift up our eyes beyond the glow in the sunset skies."[16] He was awarded the Presidential Medal of Freedom by President Gerald Ford in 1977, the year before he died.

Of particular note among his many books besides *Grant Takes Command* are a pair of trilogies about the Civil War. The first, Army of the Potomac, focuses entirely on the military aspects of the conflict and was issued from 1951 through 1954, concluding with *Stillness at Appomattox*, which won the Pulitzer Prize. He followed up with a second trilogy about the Civil War during the one-hundred-year anniversary of the conflict, the Centennial History of the Civil War, which is much broader in scope, including the social, economic, cultural, and geopolitical aspects of the war. These three volumes came out between 1961 and 1966 and were similarly well received. *Grant Takes Command* is the third book in yet another trilogy focused on the war, in this case a deep examination of Grant.

Catton also wrote many other books, some about various aspects of the Civil War and others about diverse topics including the death of President Kennedy, the early years of American history, and a history of Michigan. His memoir, *Waiting for the Morning Train*, published near the end of his life in 1972, captures a lost era in American history and culture from his boyhood in the rural Midwest at the turn of the last century. He died in his beloved upstate Michigan in 1978. Catton is today regarded as a preeminent narrative historian, and his work continues to attract readers and hold relevance for those studying leadership under the kind of extraordinary stress created by the terrible Civil War.

About the Book

The first two volumes of the trilogy—*Captain Sam Grant* (1950), written by Lloyd Lewis, and *Grant Moves South* (1960), by Catton—are also worth mentioning. The latter shows us the young military commander as he learns the craft of fighting major battles, including Shiloh, Vicksburg, Fort Henry, and Fort Donelson. Both are respected and readable, but neither contains the leadership lessons or the powerful narrative of *Grant Takes Command*.

Beginning with the difficult Chattanooga campaign of 1863 and ending with the final campaigns of the war against Gen. Robert E. Lee in Virginia, this book moves at a brisk but graceful pace through the pivotal battles of the war. One of the great strengths of the book is the level of character development, which allows the reader to effectively flow into the minds of Grant and his subordinates. What emerges is Grant's fundamental and defining trait as a leader: the ability to strategically focus on one key objective and hammer at it relentlessly. He quickly identified the Confederate forces under General Lee, the Army of Northern Virginia, as the center of gravity of the conflict. Once he ascended to supreme command after President Lincoln finally found "his general," he made finding and destroying the Army of Northern Virginia his principal—indeed only—objective. A leader's ability to succeed often depends on finding the single clear objective and narrowing focus to place it squarely at the center of the enterprise's effort.

Along the way Grant also demonstrated a textbook ability to work with both his seniors and his subordinates. He easily stepped into harness with President Lincoln, and they quickly—to the great joy of the president—found the appropriate division of responsibility between senior military commander and political master. Their relationship, while not always perfect, was vastly better than any Lincoln established with Grant's predecessors. Similarly, Grant was able to build a smoothly functioning team of subordinates who were devoted to him and understood his clearly defined priorities.

Grant also understood Lee's Achilles' heel: the need to protect Richmond. This limited Lee's maneuverability so long as the Army of the Potomac was within striking distance of the Confederate capital. Using this in careful balance, Grant was able to make a hammer and tongs and gradually grind down the undersupplied Confederate army week after week, culminating in Appomattox.

Throughout the book, a clear and appealing portrait emerges of Grant. He was an officer who experienced many ups and downs in his career, learned early the hardships of life, and eschewed any show of pomp and circumstance. Of his cultural knowledge he said once, "I only know two tunes—one of them is Yankee Doodle and the other isn't." In *Grant Takes Command* we see the humble leader who also emerges so clearly in Grant's own memoirs, written as he was dying of throat cancer. A plainspoken general of troops, he famously said, "I have never advocated war except as a means to peace."

Leadership Lessons Summarized

Leaders must be able to identify the center of gravity—the entity about which all else revolves—both for their own organization and for competitors. Once this center of gravity is identified, a good leader protects his or her center of gravity while focusing on overcoming the competitor's. A good leader also manages relationships in a 360-degree sense, up to seniors, out to peers, and down to subordinates. Last, an effective leader is most often humble in dress, projected status, and attitude.

— Adm. J. Stavridis

36 ⌒ Hope Is Not a Method: What Business Leaders Can Learn from America's Army

by Gen. Gordon R. Sullivan, USA (Ret.) and
Col. Michael V. Harper, USA (Ret.) (Crown Business, 1996)

Recommended by Gen. Ann Dunwoody, USA (Ret.), commanding general U.S. Army Materiel Command 2010–12

A high-performing organization is one that does routine things in an outstanding manner.

Quote from the book "The challenge for the leader is not to 'get it exactly right,' because there is no 'it.' The challenge is to become 'good enough': good enough to seize and exploit developing opportunities, good enough to deploy our forces more rapidly than competitors, good enough to get it 'about right' in execution."

About the Author

Gen. Gordon Sullivan was born in Boston in 1937 and was raised in Quincy, Massachusetts. Unlike many senior Army leaders, he was not a West Point graduate, instead attending Norwich University in Vermont. He had a long and distinguished career in the Army, culminating with four years as the chief of staff from 1991 to 1995. After his time as chief of staff he became the president of the Association of the United States Army, the professional organization of the Army. He passed the reins to Gen. Carter Ham in 2016.

Col. Michael V. Harper is a career Army officer who served as chief of staff to General Sullivan. He was the head of the U.S. Army Strategic Planning Group from 1991 to 1995 and helped create the plan used by the Army to create strategy for the twenty-first century. Colonel Harper holds an MA from the Naval War College and an MBA from the University of North Carolina. He continues to consult on long-range strategy for organizations.

About the Book

Bringing to bear a long career of leadership and management experiences, former Army chief of staff Gordon Sullivan and his chief of staff, Col. Mike Harper, have produced a powerful book that is in effect a series of case studies. Using the restructuring of the U.S. Army after the end of the Cold War as a template, they offer a series of powerful "lessons learned" gleaned from the dramatic downsizing—some would say the precipitous and dangerous drop—in the size of the Army as the nation chased the chimera of a post–Cold War "peace dividend."

Of note, the authors were dealing with a 40 percent reduction in staff and funding as well as what was perceived at the time as an utterly new set of missions. It is hard to imagine a large organization facing more wrenching change than was the massive U.S. Army, which at the time had around 1.5 million people and a budget in excess of $70 million. The authors address the challenges of significant change by focusing on ten key areas of endeavor. They discuss change itself, leadership, vision, human activities, thinking and doing (essentially execution), team building, creating (innovating), campaigning, transforming organizations, success, learning, training, and the future.

General Sullivan and Colonel Harper begin by making the case that leadership techniques and tools are quite transferrable from the military to the business world because many of the imperatives and challenges are identical: a rapidly changing competitive environment, swiftly emerging technology, the need for technical skills on the part of the workforce, the emergence of unexpected new tasks, and financial pressures to downsize/right-size large enterprises.

Clearly articulating the links between ends, ways, and means that constitute the building blocks of strategy, they also use the Army's six imperatives: Quality People, Leader Development, Modern Equipment, Doctrine, Force Mix, and Training. When these six imperatives are in balance, a trained and ready force emerges—whether you are running an Army with 600,000 soldiers or a Starbucks coffee shop with 10 employees.

They also outline what leaders need to do at the beginning of their engagement in an organization—starting with the "Leader's Reconnaissance," which consists of three key questions: What is happening? What is *not* happening? What can I do to influence the action? While this seems deceptively simple, so often leaders do not take the time at the very beginning to understand the basics outlined here. The authors draw these questions from the combat experiences of the famous battalion commander (and later three-star general) Hal Moore and the battle of the Ia Drang Valley in 1965 in Vietnam. His unit was almost destroyed but managed to outfight a vastly stronger North Vietnamese force. The questions are what Moore kept asking himself throughout the running battle, and they are quite applicable to any leader today.

The book also offers some valuable rules:

Rule 1. Change Is Hard Work. It creates two jobs at once: keeping the organization flowing but also implementing change. It doubles the workload.

Rule 2. Leadership Begins with Values. They become the anchor that keeps the organization from drifting in the uncertain seas that everyone faces.

Rule 3. Intellectual Leads Physical. Essentially, we must envision what we want before we actually do it.

Rule 4. Real Change Takes Real Change! So many of us have the tendency to nibble around the edges. It takes courage to drive change.

Rule 5. Leadership Is a Team Sport. Collaborate to graduate, as they used to say at the U.S. Naval Academy. Building alliances, coalitions, and teams is vital work for a leader.

Rule 6. Expect to Be Surprised. This is especially true in today's complex world, with change accelerating constantly.

Rule 7. Today Competes with Tomorrow. The job of the leader is to find the time and resources to ensure that we prepare for what must come, balancing between the present and the future.

Rule 8. Better Is Better. All organizations must seek to improve and find an edge. Better, in effect, is how we win.

Rule 9. Focus on the Future. This is the heart of a leader's job.

Rule 10. Learn from Doing. Leaders need to be practical and hands on, and that ethos will gradually fill an organization.

Rule 11. Grow People. The greatest leverage leaders own is the ability to train and educate their subordinates. This is the lifeblood pumping through any organization.

This is an exceptionally simple and readable leadership book. While building *The Leader's Bookshelf*, we were surprised how few "leadership books" our interviewees cited—but this one was the exception. It provides a highly readable, example-filled, and coherent roadmap to improving leadership. Indeed, the book is full of very practical examples drawn from the Army's domestic and global experiences. The Civil War, Panama, the Persian Gulf, Somalia, Task Force 51, the post–Cold War downsizing, and many other scenarios are used throughout the book to very good effect.

Leadership Lessons Summarized

It is hard to imagine a simpler set of leadership tenets than the eleven listed above. The book also emphasizes the need for the leader to reflect on what is happening and constantly ask himself or herself: What is happening? What is *not* happening? and What can I do about it?

—Adm. J. Stavridis

37   LeMay: The Life and Wars of General Curtis LeMay
by Warren Kozak (Regnery, 2009)

Recommended by Gen. Carroll "Howie" Chandler, USAF, commander in chief Pacific Air Forces 2007–9, vice chief of staff U.S. Air Force 2009–11

I always enjoyed biographies and autobiographies, and I have read a lot of them frankly since I've been a general officer, to be honest about it. I like the personal sides of some of the stories in this book as well as his tireless efforts on strategic bombing during the war and in the years he headed SAC. I read *The Life and Wars of General Curtis LeMay* when I was on the Air Staff. There are some interesting parallels here, plus the personalities. Strangely enough, we lived in the same house at Bolling Air Force Base, where he had lived at the time he was vice chief. They had one daughter who went to the National Cathedral School where our daughter went. I have a lot of respect for Curt LeMay, even though he unfortunately got himself kind of tangled up with George Wallace there toward the end. Certainly he was a great airman.

Quote from the book "I don't differentiate between unlucky and inept" (Curtis E. LeMay).

About the Author

A native of Milwaukee, Warren Kozak was born in 1951 and graduated from the University of Wisconsin–Madison. He is the author of three books and a regular contributor to the *Wall Street Journal*'s op-ed pages. "I have the opportunity to meet fascinating people who have lived great lives," he says on his web site.[17]

About the Book

Curt LeMay had a lifelong love affair with airplanes that began in earnest when he was a student at Ohio State University. Like many Americans he was mesmerized by the memorable journey of Charles Lindbergh in May 1927 and the daring flights of Amelia Earhart. Kozak goes into great detail about LeMay's involvement in the growth of military aviation, his meteoric rise to prominence and high rank as a proponent of strategic bombing, and, most important, his role in the birth of the Strategic Air Command and its incredible influence not only on the Air Force specifically but on the American people as a whole during the long Cold War that saw the spread of knowledge of—and fear of—"the bomb."

General LeMay evinced a determined demeanor throughout his life, and as he rose to prominence in the postwar Air Force his stony character became the thing of legends. The late Gen. David C. Jones, who was an aide to LeMay as a lieutenant colonel, told me LeMay was a good judge of character. "He didn't have much contact with a lot of the very junior people [but] he knew a lot of colonels. I think he was a good judge of which ones were the most capable. He very carefully watched these people, particularly wing commanders. Every time there was an aircraft accident that wing commander, within twenty-four hours, would have to stand in front of LeMay and explain the accident. And LeMay didn't want to give them a week to prepare; he wanted to see what they knew about the wing at the time of the accident rather than a week later. And the worst thing a wing commander could do was use the word 'luck.' LeMay had a favorite saying. 'I don't differentiate between unlucky and inept.'"

By early 1942, before he was thirty-six years old, LeMay was himself a bird colonel and commander of the 305th Bombardment Group, which was sent to the small village of Chelveston, England, in Northamptonshire. His pilots prepared for the long journey across the Atlantic from their temporary base in New England, knowing the flight would be perilous and challenging. Daylight hours were spent in fundamental duties and training, evening hours were given to personal matters. "LeMay continued to keep an emotional distance from his men," writes Kozak. "But the group had now been together for months and they began to solidify. In spite of himself, there were some men he could not help feeling closer to."

Throughout his life LeMay was stoic, unemotional, and taciturn in interactions with others. One night shortly before the 305th left the States he walked into the room occupied by Bill Sault, one of his pilots. "Get dressed, Sault, we're going downtown." Sault knew from the expression on LeMay's face that there was no room for discussion, and during the drive into the heart of the city conversation was typically clipped. "They stopped in front of a downtown hotel where they got out," Kozak continues. "LeMay took him inside, went to a room and there, to Sault's surprise, were their wives." Colonel LeMay had made arrangements for the farewell get-together without giving any hint of his actions. "He was abrupt, caustic, seldom complimentary," recalled Sault many years later. "I never saw him smile. But there wasn't anything he wouldn't do for us and he never forgot us." Kozak presents the case for commanders at all levels to know their subordinates and give them direction when necessary, find opportunities and occasions to reward great performance, and have the fortitude to reassign those who fail.

Under LeMay's leadership the 305th Bombardment Group pioneered daylight bombing over Nazi-controlled Europe in 1942–43. Those techniques were passed along to the brave bomber pilots in the Pacific theater in the waning moments of the war. "LeMay knew that what he had to do—what the entire Army Air Force had to do—was destroy Germany's ability to wage war," Kozak writes. "But he also understood that victory in war is inevitably purchased with the lives of young men. If a country was hesitant to spend this capital, LeMay believed, there was no sense in fighting a war in the first place, a belief shared by William T. Sherman, Ulysses S. Grant, and even Abraham Lincoln." We are unlikely to see anyone like Curt LeMay emerge on the scene ever again, certainly not a four-star general at the age of forty-four who served fourteen years wearing those four stars.

Leadership Lessons Summarized

One powerful leadership lesson we can take from the life of Curtis LeMay is what might be called the "LeMay Doctrine," formulated and practiced in World War II. It says that once a nation has made the decision to go to war, "that nation should be willing to hit the enemy with every conceivable weapon at its disposal to end the conflict as quickly as possible." This kind of devotion to mission is something good leaders are willing to demonstrate. Additionally, despite his introverted personality, LeMay also personified the kind of leader who quietly supports his subordinates and earns their admiration and trust. While not an open and transparent twenty-first-century leader, LeMay personified the strong, silent leadership of many World War II leaders.

— *R. Manning Ancell*

38 *Buffalo Soldiers: A Narrative of the Black Cavalry in the West*

by William H. Leckie (University of Oklahoma Press, 1967; updated with Shirley Leckie, 2003)

Recommended by Adm. Michelle Howard, USN, Vice Chief of Naval Operations 2014–16

The Buffalo Soldiers: I was fascinated by that group of soldiers, and what they had to go through in post–Civil War society to gain acceptance.[18] Don't let the nay-sayers stop you. You have to believe in yourself and a lot of times it's your family and friends who help you get to "yes." So don't give up on your dreams, ever.[19]

Quote from the book We Can: We Will (motto of the 9th Cavalry Regiment). Ready and Forward (motto of the 10th Cavalry Regiment).

About the Author

William Leckie was born in 1889 in Runge, Texas. After volunteering for the Army Air Corps in World War II he commanded a battalion of African American soldiers in the Pacific. He was deeply offended by the prejudice and racism of the time and throughout the remainder of his life did all that he could to fight against injustice, from racism to McCarthyism. He earned a PhD in history from the University of Oklahoma and focused much of his research and publications on the American West. During his academic career he served variously as a professor, a dean, and an administrator at Texas A&M University, the University of Toledo, and other institutions. In addition to *Buffalo Soldiers* he wrote several books about the frontier. He and his wife, Shirley, also a historian, updated *Buffalo Soldiers* extensively in 2003. Leckie died in 2012.

About the Book

Until the late 1960s almost nothing was known about the hard and heroic work of African American soldiers in the West after the Civil War. This brilliant and highly readable short book by William Leckie changed all that with its publication in 1967. Widely regarded as a true classic of American history, *Buffalo Soldiers* describes the life and challenging times of these pioneering military figures in vivid, approachable prose. It was updated in 2003 to include more information about the lives of buffalo soldiers in the 10th and 9th Cavalry Regiments.

Life in the West was hard for everyone, but it was particularly grinding for the buffalo soldiers and their families. They faced all of the typical prejudices of the time—beginning with the pejorative description of their dense, curly hair that reminded some racists of buffalo hair. Given the attitudes of the times, African American units were invariably led by white officers. The units on which this work focuses operated in some of the harshest regions of the West, notably in pre-statehood Arizona, literally "the Wild West." Formed almost immediately after the Civil War, the buffalo soldier units operated from 1866 to 1891 and were active participants in numerous skirmishes, battles, and campaigns against the Native American tribes fighting throughout the region. Despite all of the prejudice and racially inspired hatred directed against them, the buffalo soldiers developed a reputation for superb fortitude and bravery.

Organized into nine tightly written chapters, and replete with period photographs and maps, the book moves through the history of the soldiers at a gallop. It begins with the early years, quickly retelling the long history of "Negro Troops" going back to the Revolutionary War, the War of 1812, and of course the Civil War. When the 10th Regiment was posted in the West, the white officers assigned to command knew their men must outride, outshoot, and outsoldier other troops—and in large measure they did. While the 10th Regiment fought in the central plains the 9th Cavalry was equally occupied in West Texas in the post–Civil War years. By the 1880s the 10th Regiment was relocated to Texas as well, patrolling a massive area with distinction, even as the 9th Cavalry moved to what is today New Mexico and Arizona to deal with the Apaches. Both units continued to serve in very challenging circumstances throughout their two decades of operations, including much combat in the Red River War and the Victorio War.

As a sort of epilogue (not covered in the book, but still relevant as we consider these brave but highly underrated soldiers), it is worth knowing that far from the deserts of the American Southwest, the buffalo soldiers were also deployed to Cuba for the Spanish-American War in 1898. After the sinking of the USS *Maine* (later determined probably to have been the result of an internal explosion, not the work of

Spanish "commandos" as the Hearst newspaper chain and others in the "yellow press" shrilly claimed), the United States declared war on Spain and invaded the Spanish colony of Cuba. The exploits of the Rough Riders and Col. Teddy Roosevelt have been well known for more than a century, but the good work of the buffalo soldiers was not illuminated until far later. The buffalo soldiers in Cuba helped rescue the Rough Riders, volunteered for service in yellow fever camps, and fought bravely throughout the campaign.

By the early 1890s the long history of the two cavalry regiments on the frontier was coming to a close as the region gradually took on the appearance of civilization. As Professor Leckie summarizes toward the end of this work, "The experiment with Negro Troops launched in 1866 proved a success by any standard other than that of racial prejudice. By 1891, the combat record spoke for itself. They had fought on the plains of Kansas and in Indian Territory, in the vast expanse of West Texas and along hundreds of miles of the Rio Grande and in Mexico, in the deserts and mountain of New Mexico and Arizona, in Colorado, and finally in the rugged grandeur of the Dakotas." While there were failures and setbacks, and the troopers were not "all Angels," their combat effectiveness is unquestionable in the clear light of history.

Leckie concludes, "The Ninth and Tenth Cavalry were first-rate regiments and major forces in promoting peace and advancing civilization along America's last continental frontier. The thriving cities and towns, the fertile fields, and the natural beauty of that once wild land are monuments enough for any buffalo soldier." This books stands as well as a testament to all they accomplished.

Leadership Lessons Summarized

Leaders must sometimes overcome deeply rooted prejudice in order to create winning outcomes. This requires perseverance, courage, endurance, and patience—along with superb performance. A climate of racism is among the most challenging circumstances a leader must deal with and will not be solved overnight, but winning the battle of perceptions can and must be done.

—Adm. J. Stavridis

39 — *The Foundation Trilogy*
by Isaac Asimov (Doubleday, 1983)

Recommended by Gen. John P. Abizaid, USA, commander U.S. Central Command 2003–7

Whenever I go somewhere I always have to come back and read some history. I read some history before I go and I read some history after I go to try to put it into context. I should mention that when I was a young reader, before I was in the Academy, Isaac Asimov really got my attention with his Foundation Trilogy. The way he talked about how the future could be really fascinated me. I read a lot—I love history in particular—but I like to pepper in some science fiction and I like to look at authors like Asimov and Stephen King. There's not a day that goes by that I don't read two or three different things. That gets me interested in other things that are happening around the world. Of course, I read a lot about the Middle East, as you can imagine.

Quote from the book "It has been my philosophy of life that difficulties vanish when faced boldly" (Isaac Asimov).

About the Author

One of the best known and certainly one of the most prolific writers of science fiction, Isaac Asimov was born in Russia in 1920 and immigrated to America as a youth. He earned a PhD from Columbia in 1948 and taught biochemistry at Boston University for the rest of his life. In 1988 Asimov sat down for an interview with young Slawek Wojtowicz, a native of Poland, who asked Asimov about his introduction to science fiction. "I started reading science fiction when I was nine years old," Asimov said. "I sold my first story when I was eighteen and my first book when I was thirty. Since then I have published 394 books. I have twenty-five other books in press. Some of these are mysteries, some are children's books, others are on straight science, literary subjects, humor, mythology—on everything I can think of." He explained that his day was well planned. "This morning I did my weekly science column for the *Los Angeles Times* Syndicate. I'm working on a novel—it is little over half finished in first draft. Pretty soon it will be time to write my monthly essay for *Fantasy and Science Fiction.* I'm writing a big *History of Science* and I've got up to 1945, so it is only little over forty years left, but they were very hard forty years, so I've got lots of work." He paused and smiled. "All I do is write. I do practically nothing else, except eat, sleep and talk to my wife."[20]

Between 1948 and his death from heart and kidney failure on April 6, 1992, Asimov published more than five hundred books. Ten years after his death it was discovered that he died of complications from HIV as the result of a blood transfusion during his final hospital stay.

About the Book

Foundation, first published in 1951, was Asimov's fourth book. He later expanded it into a series of three books: *Foundation, Foundation and Empire,* and *Second Foundation.* For thirty years it was known as a trilogy. In 1981 Asimov added two sequels: *Foundation's Edge* and *Foundation and Earth,* and then two prequels: *Prelude to Foundation* and *Forward the Foundation.*

It's important to understand Asimov's vision of humankind's future to understand and appreciate what he writes about that future. His views of the future are a mixed bag. He told Wojtowicz:

> I have several—some bad, some good, depending on what we do. I can see a computerized world, with robots doing most of the dull work, or a space-centered world with people moving out into orbit about the Earth and reaching the asteroids. But I can also see a polluted world in which the quality of life stinks and one in which there is a nuclear war and we destroy ourselves. There is nothing that MUST be, everything depends entirely on what we decide to do. Naturally I would like to see civilization to continue and improve. I think everyone would. But still, people tend to do things that harm humanity.[21]

The Foundation series takes place well into the future at a time when humankind has expanded deep into the Milky Way. Mathematician Hari Seldon has created a branch of mathematics known as psychohistory that enables him to predict future events provided they are on a grand scale. By this time in its history humankind inhabits planets all across the galaxy, all under the rule of a single emperor. Seldon sees this human empire disintegrating and requiring 30,000 years to rebuild. But he also discovers an alternative future in which the decline could well be only a mere one thousand years, so he gathers a "foundation of talented artisans and engineers" and places them at the extreme end of the galaxy where they are protected from the cataclysm.

Leadership Lessons Summarized

Perhaps the most important leadership lesson in these three fascinating books is that leaders must constantly consider the future of their enterprise, using all the tools at their disposal, but the big decisions are theirs to make. The leaders have new tools available to predict events—in a sense, the use of metadata. Yet in the end, it is the leader's ability to use the data with real judgment and passion—as well as intuition—that will determine whether or not a particular course of action will be successful. In other words, use all the tools at your disposal, but recognize that decisions will have to come from the heart and the mind of the leader, not from data or a formula.

— R. Manning Ancell

40 *Ender's Game*
by Orson Scott Card (Tor Books, 1985)

Recommended by Gen. James "Hoss" Cartwright, USMC (Ret.), commander U.S. Strategic Command and vice chairman of the Joint Chiefs of Staff

Ender's Game is a creative and brilliant exploration of leadership set against the backdrop of a digital future. The main character is confronted with leadership challenges in a world driven by game theory and swarm warfare. The reader is exposed to a world immersed in automation and robotics. Above all, this book is about leadership in a world where human and machine will be partners. The process of creating leaders is complex and challenging, but reading *Ender's Game* will help a leader develop his or her own skills and build a team that can succeed under the harshest conditions.

Quote from the book "I don't care if I pass your test, I don't care if I follow your rules. If you can cheat, so can I. I won't let you beat me unfairly—I'll beat you unfairly first" (Ender Wiggins).

About the Author

Orson Scott Card, born in 1951, provides a vision of the world many centuries in the future in a steady stream of extremely well regarded science fiction. His breakthrough novel, *Ender's Game*, rises above the futurist genre and displays Card's wide-ranging views on leadership, government, warfare, and destiny. The book and its nearly equally good sequel, *Speaker for the Dead*, won the Hugo and Nebula Awards in 1985 and 1986. This achievement puts Card at the top of science fiction writers in terms of formal recognition.

Distantly related to Brigham Young, the founder of the Church of Jesus Christ of Latter-day Saints (Mormon church), Card lives in Greensboro, North Carolina, and has written books about creative writing and numerous columns on religion, today's society, and politics in the United States. He performed his Mormon mission in Brazil and began his publishing career as a poet. *Ender's Game* began as a short story that eventually grew into a novel and then an entire series of works. Card is the father of five children, each named after an author he and his wife admire—Geoffrey Chaucer, Charles Dickens, Emily Dickinson, Margaret Mitchell, and Louisa May Alcott.

Describing himself as a social liberal and a moral conservative, Orson Scott Card has a wide-ranging intellect that he applies to thinking about the future in the context of war, politics, and power. *Ender's Game* has been translated into dozens of foreign languages and was produced as a major motion picture in 2013.

About the Book

Ender's Game is a science fiction classic set in the distant future. Earth is under attack by an alien species of insect-like creatures who have a high degree of intelligence and much advanced technology. Earth has thus far survived two major attacks and is preparing for the anticipated third attack, trying to identify the most capable of its youth in order to train them to defend civilization. The central protagonist is a young boy, Ender Wiggins, who is selected after a rigorous process and begins training at the Battle School, a high-level center orbiting the earth in zero gravity. The three central ruling cliques of Earth have come together to face this global threat, and an international fleet is constructed to face the insects. The training program is ultimately looking for strategists, but also for individuals with extreme mental toughness in the face of adversity.

As a trainee, Ender has many difficult moments, including challenges involving his highly intelligent but essentially psychopathic brother, Peter. He battles fellow students—mortally wounding one—and gains the attention of the school's leadership. Ender is isolated from the other cadets at the Battle School. Warfare simulations follow—essentially cyber conflicts directed by the young trainees—and Ender proves a tactical genius, sort of a nascent Napoleon of the cyber world. When he is ten years old, Ender meets a hero of the previous wars, Mazer Rackham, who puts even more pressure on the young warrior. In a climactic battle that Ender is led to believe is a training simulation, his brilliant tactics destroy the insects' planet. More adventures will follow for Ender, who is shaped in the crucible of combat despite thinking it is all a game. As the novel repeatedly points out in one way or another, in Ender's world, "sometimes lies were more dependable than the truth."

At its heart the book is about the intersection of combat training, deception in pursuit of national goals, and the brutality of war. This is not an antiwar book, but rather a clear-eyed look at what is necessary to overcome an implacable foe. It also manages to convey a sense of the absurdity of war when opponents stumble into conflict without really understanding each other's culture, history, aims, and political objectives. Ender says at one point, "In the moment when I truly understand my enemy, understand him well enough to defeat him, then in that very moment I also love him. I think it's impossible to really understand somebody, what they want, what they believe, and not love them the way they love themselves. And then, in that very moment when I love them . . . I destroy them." There are frequent echoes of Sun Tzu in *Ender's Game*, and in some sense the entire book reflects Sun Tzu's dictums of how the underdog can triumph through cunning, treachery, endless preparation, and determination.

Another important contemporary theme in the novel is the power of youth. Much of Ender's clique is composed of very young warriors. The idea that the future rests with the young is not of itself profound or interesting; but in the context of this novel it reflects the shift in societies toward the computer literate—the "digital natives" who have full facility with the complex tools of technology. Indeed, the idea of building a "cyber force" that is beginning to gain traction in many nations (including the United States) will often require using very young "warriors" who have the ability to conduct significant cyber operations. That branch of the services will be young, dynamic, flexible, inventive, and highly technically capable—much like Ender in this novel. Leading such a group will be challenging for more mature leaders and will require flexibility on the part of the chain of command.

Another theme in *Ender's Game* that has high relevance today is the emergence of deeper interstate conflict in the cyber realm. Much of the battle Ender fights is played out from a computer terminal and resembles a video game. In today's highly fraught cyber sphere, where nations such as China, the United States, and Russia are in constant "combat," it is becoming increasingly clear that nations will need a dedicated cyber

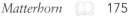

force much like our U.S. Air Force, which emerged only when armies began to operate continuously in the air. The debate today about the role of cyber in combat is front and center, and the leadership challenges of inspiring in a highly technical environment are part of this superb novel.

At its very heart, this is a coming-of-age story of a young, impressionable, and supremely talented young man. Compelling and thoughtful on every page, *Ender's Game* is rightly regarded as a classic of science fiction and of combat in the cyber age. As Ender comes to know, for a young man learning his place in a brutally challenging world, "perhaps it's impossible to wear an identity without becoming what you pretend to be."

Leadership Lessons Summarized

Ender's Game focuses on the importance of tactical training and the balance between harsh methods and true mentoring. The idea that "the more you bleed in training, the less you die in war" is central. The book also uses innovation and creativity in strategic and operational ways to triumph over a foe with greater firepower. Finally, it is a book about the need to overcome adversity to be an effective leader, whatever your age, and also a cautionary tale about the need to lead the very young differently and more creatively.

— Adm. J. Stavridis

41 *Matterhorn: A Novel of the Vietnam War*
by Karl Marlantes (Grove/Atlantic, 2010)

Recommended by Gen. Charles C. Krulak, USMC (Ret.), 31st Commandant of the Marine Corps, 1995–99

The son of Lt. Gen. Victor H. "Brute" Krulak, Chuck Krulak served two tours in Vietnam after graduating from the Naval Academy in 1964. "I literally 'lived' the first battle in that book. Small unit fighting at its best . . . and worst."

Quote from the book   "China threw his hands open in disgust.
'OK. You be the preacher man. You tell me. Who Mose Wright?'
'You ever hear of Emmett Till?'
'Wha'chew think?'
'Yeah. I be seven and I see that puffy face with the eye hanging out
in *Ebony* magazine and I never, *never,* forget that face. But *I* don't
live in Mississippi. *You don't live in Mississippi.* Mose Wright, he
Emmett Till's uncle, and *he live* in Mississippi where they hang you
from a tree with you nuts cut off and throw you in the river with
iron fan blades wrap 'round you black dead-ass neck. You speak
up against that shit in Mississippi, you as good as dead."

About the Author

You don't receive the Navy Cross (second only to the Medal of Honor),
the Bronze Star, and two Purple Hearts for leading from behind. Karl
Marlantes served as a company commander during the toughest and
most challenging years of America's presence in Vietnam: 1968–70. Born
in Astoria, Oregon, the day before Christmas 1944 and raised in nearby
Seaside, where his father was principal of the high school, young Marlantes attended Yale on a National Merit Scholarship and studied at
Oxford University on a Rhodes Scholarship, but dropped out after one
semester to join the Marine Corps. After his duty with the Marine Corps
he returned to Oxford to complete a master's degree, then embarked on
a career as a business consultant in Europe. All the while he had a book
about Vietnam and a young Marine lieutenant on his mind.

In an interview with Lt. Col. Ralph Peters on cable television's *After
Words,* he responded to a question about *Matterhorn*'s main character,
Waino Mellas, who transitions from boy officer to a leader of men in the
jungles of Vietnam not far from the Laotian border. "It's a novel about a
young man learning compassion in the middle of a war," he said, which
is "something all young men have to learn."[22] Marlantes claims that
Mellas is not himself and that the fictional lieutenant is an amalgam
of a lot of people he served with or observed during the Vietnam War.

About the Book

During the Civil War Robert E. Lee observed, "What a cruel thing is war; to separate and destroy families and friends, and mar the purest joys and happiness God has granted us in this world; to fill our hearts with hatred instead of love for our neighbors, and to devastate the fair face of this beautiful world."[23] Lee knew only too well the futility and finality of a war's many battles and skirmishes and lamented the necessity for leaders to send their troops to certain death. Little had changed when the mid-twentieth century brought the world into two great wars, a conflict in Korea that nobody won, and a drawn-out and increasingly unpopular war in the jungles of Southeast Asia. By the summer of 1968 a majority of Americans had lined up in opposition to the Vietnam War. A year later, from May 10 to May 20, 1969, a battle for Hill 937, otherwise known as Hamburger Hill—a heavily defended but "strategically insignificant" target—that led to more than four hundred American casualties drew the disgust and outrage of the American people when the troops that took the infamous hill were ordered to abandon it. "Either win the damn thing or get the hell out" was the growing sentiment in the United States, "and when the Johnson administration seemed unable to do either, the American people's patience ran out."[24]

There are similarities between Hamburger Hill and Marlantes' *Matterhorn* to be sure. Marlantes offers up glimpses of Bravo Company, its commanding officer, and his men before and after engagements with the enemy, suffering the heat and incessant rain, wild animals, leeches, swarms of insects, and a constant clash of race, education, and disparities in rank and age among the troops. He skillfully lets us sit by the campfire and soak up the conversation much like the proverbial fly on the wall.

Mark Bowden, author of the bestseller *Black Hawk Down*, has the highest praise for Marlantes' book:

> *Matterhorn* is a great novel. There have been some very good novels about the Vietnam War, but this is the first great one, and I doubt it will ever be surpassed. Karl Marlantes overlooks

no part of the experience, large or small, from a terrified soldier pondering the nature of good and evil, to the feel and smell of wet earth against scorched skin as a man tries to press himself into the ground to escape withering fire. Here is story-telling so authentic, so moving and so intense, so relentlessly dramatic, that there were times I wasn't sure I could stand to turn the page. As with the best fiction, I was sad to reach the end.[25]

In complex, detailed, and lengthy novels such as *Matterhorn*, in which the development of characters and attention to detail are crucial, the author writes what he believes his characters would say and think and believe, whereas in nonfiction the characters are flesh and blood and the author is required to write accurately and honestly all the elements that enable the subjects to jump off the page. Back on April 30, 2010, Evan James from *Mother Jones* asked Marlantes if he had spoken with Vietnam veterans about *Matterhorn*.

A guy came up to me at a reading in Seattle and he had five books with him. I said, "Wow, how come you're buying five books?" He said, "I'm married, four kids, and I served as a Marine in the area the novel covers. And every time I try to tell them about the war, I'd start shaking or start to get nervous and clam up and I couldn't go through with it. I've been trying for four years and I'm gonna buy the book, because this book will tell it exactly the way it was." And that made me just almost cry.[26]

Leadership Lessons Summarized

The leadership lesson in this epic book is as basic as battle itself. The key to winning a war lies in cohesion of small units around a knowledgeable, well-trained officer or NCO who doesn't hesitate to show initiative at the right moment. The enlisted troops want someone to whom they look for decisions that lead to success without squandering lives needlessly.

— R. Manning Ancell

42 ⚔ *Patton: Ordeal and Triumph*
by Ladislas Farago (Ivan Obolensky, 1963)

Recommended by Gen. John H. Tilelli Jr., vice chief of staff U.S. Army 1994–95, commanding general U.S. Forces Command 1995–96, and commander in chief UN Forces Korea 1996–99

My first battalion commander, Col. Jesse Wheeler, a VMI graduate, mentored young lieutenants and captains on the profession of arms. He did discuss professional development and the necessity to read. Reading was a part of self-development as well as unit development. You not only had to read, but you also had to understand. And you had the challenge of other people reading the same books and not only quizzing you but in some cases countering what you had to say.

As an armor leader I read books about Patton, of course—you would expect that. Farago wrote a book about Patton that I thought was a great, great biography. It showed he was a risk taker and somewhat of an audacious, ostentatious leader, and it talked about his World War II experiences and his growing experiences from the time in West Point onward. I've kept that book on my shelf.

Quote from the book "I can't decide logically if I am a man of destiny or a lucky fool, but I think I am destined. Five more days will show. This may sound like junk, or prophesy, within a week" (Gen. George Patton).

About the Author
The author of fourteen books, Ladislas Farago was born in Hungary in 1906. His first book, *Abyssinia on the Eve*, appeared in 1935. He had a lifelong penchant for military history and the spy business, but his most

commercially successful book, *Patton: Ordeal and Triumph*, which was made into an immensely popular movie starring George C. Scott and Karl Malden that won seven Academy Awards, bolstered his reputation and popularity. His final book, *The Last Days of Patton*, was released the year after his death in New York City in 1980.

About the Book

Well into the book, as Patton's Third Army is storming into the heart of Germany, Hauptmann Oskar Steiger, a member of Generaloberst Alfred Jodl's staff, is incinerating materials that the Germans don't want to fall into the hands of the Allies. He comes to an intelligence photo of Patton and pauses before throwing it into the trashcan of burning materials, muttering, "Der reine Krieger. Ein grossartiger Anachronismus" (The pure warrior. A great anachronism).

Truer words were never spoken. Patton was a man for the ages. Roger Nye, author of *The Patton Mind*, writes about a letter George wrote to Beatrice, his future wife, from the Eagle Hotel in Gettysburg on May 11, 1909, shortly before his graduation from West Point. This letter goes to the very roots of Patton's character as he embarked on his incredible Army career:

> This evening after supper I walked down alone to the scene of the last and fiercest struggle on Cemetery hill. To get in a proper frame of mind I wandered through the cemetery and let the spirits of the dead thousands laid there in ordered rows sink deep into me. Then just as the sun sank behind South Mountain I walked down to the scene of Pickett's great charge and seated on a rock just where Olmstead and two of my great uncles died, I watched the wonder of the day go out.
>
> The sunset painted a dull red the fields over which the terrible advance was made and I could almost see them coming, growing fewer and fewer while around and beyond me stood calmly the very cannon that had so punished them. There were some quail calling in the trees nearby and it seemed strange that they could do it where man had known his greatest and last

emotions. It was very wonderful and no one came to bother me, I drank it in until I was quite happy. A strange pleasure but yet a very real one. I think it takes an evening like that to make one understand what men will do in battle.[27]

George Patton firmly believed that he had been born time after time through history, and these beliefs framed and gave focus to his successes—and losses, though few and far between—in World War II. You need not share his beliefs, but accepting that he was sincere will make Farago's book more revealing. General Marshall understood and supported him in times when Patton stepped across the line, as in the famous incident of Patton slapping an enlisted soldier who was suffering from what we would today term post-traumatic stress disorder. General Eisenhower stood by Patton when he could well have sent him back to the United States to a do-nothing and probably humiliating job. And Gen. Omar Bradley could have left Patton on the wayside when he was promoted above him, but he was a bigger person than that and retained his respect for Patton. Likewise, it is much to Patton's credit that he accepted his former junior as his immediate boss.

A final thought about Patton's belief about past lives. Early in the war he visited an ancient battlefield and felt right at home. Farago writes that Patton remembered "the Carthaginians defending the city were attacked by three Roman legions. The Carthaginians were proud and brave but they couldn't hold. They were massacred. Arab women stripped them of their tunics and their swords and lances. The soldiers lay naked in the sun. Two thousand years ago. I was there."

Leadership Lessons Summarized

Patton was the ultimate warrior, and his ethos was one of direct action. While there are times a leader needs more subtle approaches, when you are faced with a truly dire situation, turn to Patton. Despite the power in clever and subtle approaches, there are times when only one tool is in the kit, and that is fury. Perhaps a good way to emphasize this is to bring out Patton's thoughts on leadership in his own words:

On the fury of war:

- "In case of doubt, attack."
- "War is simple, direct, and ruthless."
- "Attack rapidly, ruthlessly, viciously, without rest, however tired and hungry you may be. The enemy will be more tired, and more hungry. Keep punching."
- "In war the only sure defense is offense, and the efficiency of the offense depends on the warlike souls of those conducting it."

On the role of fate in our lives:

- "A man must know his destiny. If he does not recognize it, then he is lost. By this I mean once, twice, or at the very most, three times, fate will reach out and tap a man on his shoulder. If he has the imagination, he will turn around and fate will point out to him what fork in the road he should take. If he has the guts he will take it."

On decisions and planning:

- "Many, who should know better, think that wars can be decided by soulless machines rather than by the blood and anguish of brave men."
- "No good decision was ever made in a swivel chair."
- "A good plan, violently executed now, is better than a perfect plan next week."

— R. Manning Ancell

43   *Goodbye, Darkness: A Memoir of the Pacific War*
by William R. Manchester (Little, Brown, 1979)

Recommended by Adm. Michael G. Mullen, USN, Vice Chief of Naval Operations 2003–4, commander in chief U.S. Naval Forces Europe, commander Allied Joint Force Command 2004–5, 28th Chief of Naval Operations 2005–7, and chairman of the Joint Chiefs of Staff 2007–11

Ten years ago, while serving as CNO, Admiral Mullen declared that "reading fosters critical thinking and critical thinking makes us better leaders and better warfighters."[28] When asked to provide us with a list of the books that most affected his life and career, he gave us a short and intriguingly eclectic group of books that includes current events, military history, and historical fiction.

Quote from the book "One difficulty in re-creating the past is that the reader knows how it will turn out, so that events have an air of inevitability" (William Manchester).

About the Author

Born and raised in Massachusetts to a father who served in the Marine Corps in World War I, it came as no surprise to Manchester's family when he enlisted in the Corps shortly after the attack on Pearl Harbor. Expecting to get immediate duty in Europe, Manchester instead was ordered back to college to await call-up, which didn't come until 1944 when he was sent to Guadalcanal as a corporal. For reasons he was reluctant to share he had chosen to drop out of Officer Candidate School before receiving a commission; he ended the war as a sergeant.

After the war Manchester joined the reporter staff at the *Baltimore Sun*, where he met H. L. Mencken and published his first book, *Disturber of the Peace: The Life of H. L. Mencken*, in 1951. Manchester was a master at crafting remembrances that drew in not only people who vividly affected his life, such as Mencken and later John F. Kennedy, but those on the periphery who had an influence—some large, many rather small—on his life and career. His follow-up book to *Portrait of a President*, published in 1964, was the immensely popular bestseller *The Death of a President* in 1967.

Goodbye Darkness came in 1980, followed by a series of books on a wide array of subjects rooted in Manchester's life and experiences, ranging from a biography of Gen. Douglas MacArthur to *The Arms of Krupp* about the German armament industry. His biggest work was a three-volume treatment of the life of Winston Churchill, which was widely applauded. Sadly, he was unable to finish the third volume of his trilogy on Churchill, *The Last Lion*. He turned over the incomplete manuscript to a friend and colleague and disappeared from the American landscape after eighteen well-received books, passing away at the age of eighty-two on June 1, 2004.

About the Book

Back in 2006 C. Peter Chen wrote a review that encapsulates the thoughts of the many people who made this a bestseller:

> What makes this book truly stand out to me is that while most memoirs are only a list of events, occasionally diving into emotions, *Goodbye, Darkness* goes much deeper philosophically. For instance, it touches upon the concept of survivor's guilt. On a patrol on Guadalcanal, the entire group Manchester fought with was struck by Japanese mortar, with Manchester being the only survivor. "It isn't fair, it isn't fair, they're dead, why can't I be dead," Manchester told himself as he shook in fear and in shock on the battlefield that day, "it isn't fair." What is survivor's guilt? Does it originate from the brotherhood shared between Marines on the front lines? Or is it simply a hallucination experienced by the lone soldier trapped in a foreign environment?[29]

Reading this book is like putting on a pack, picking up a rifle, and heading into perhaps the most horrific conditions of chaos the American military faced in the Pacific island-hopping campaign of World War II. What it emphasizes for leaders today is the level of utter fear and uncertainty a team can face, and its effects on the men and women who find themselves where darkness is literally quite visible. Set up as a series of dreams that recall to Manchester his own passage through combat, the book provides extraordinary views of the battles of Guadalcanal, Tarawa, Pelieu, Iwo Jima, Okinawa, and others. It is perhaps the best depiction of combat from that period and stands as a companion piece to E. B. Sledge's *With the Old Breed*.

This is a travelogue to the past, a return to the places where men fought and died, and some, like Manchester, made it through and lived. The early chapters were difficult to write, he says in his author's note. "My feelings about the Marine Corps are still highly ambivalent, tinged with sadness and bitterness, yet with the first enchantment lingering. But by mining that tough old ore, and altering the order of those personal events, I have, I believe, been able to present a sequential account of war which still confuses most Americans. This, then, was the life I knew, where death sought me, during which I was transformed from a cheeky youth to a troubled man who, for over thirty years, repressed what he could not bear to remember."

The book is also an excellent source of first-person observations on the tactics of small-unit combat, many of which were reflected in U.S. military activity in Vietnam. Manchester was a historian, not a warrior, but his acute ability to translate the past into vivid prose echoes in American literature today.

Leadership Lessons Summarized

For leaders, this book is most strongly a cautionary tale about the potential effects on teammates resulting from chaotic conditions and extreme pressure. It is also a vivid glimpse into the human costs of participating in high-end hand-to-hand combat that resonates today as our nation treats hundreds of thousands of veterans from Iraq and Afghanistan. Leaders need above all to understand what their followers endure, and this book helps any leader to understand the human pain that can flow from hard decisions.

— R. Manning Ancell

44 To Kill a Mockingbird
by Harper Lee (Grand Central Publishing,
Hachette Book Group USA, 1960)

Recommended by Gen. Dan K. McNeill, USA, commander Coalition Forces in Afghanistan 2002–3, commanding general U.S. Forces Command 2004–7, and commander International Security Assistance Forces in Afghanistan 2007–8

Books certainly had prominent roles in my life. Just for example, the Bible, Rommel's *Infantry Attacks*, and *Once an Eagle*. Those were fairly routine. I'm gonna give you one that had profound effects on me that might not pop up as often. This one is *To Kill a Mockingbird*, by Harper Lee, which I read when I'm not even sure I was in high school yet. I could've been. If I was, I was no more than a freshman. It has many lessons about where I came from, because she wrote about a small Alabama town. Well, it could've been where I lived. And taking a stand, and the issues of right and wrong, were woven in very skillfully, and very prominently. It was also a good movie.

Quote from the book "Atticus said to Jem one day, 'I'd rather you shot at tin cans in the backyard, but I know you'll go after birds. Shoot all the blue jays you want, if you can hit 'em, but remember it's a sin to kill a mockingbird.' That was the only time I ever heard Atticus say it was a sin to do something, and I asked Miss Maudie about it. 'Your father's right,' she said. 'Mockingbirds don't do one thing except make music for us to enjoy. They don't eat up people's gardens, don't nest in corn cribs, they don't do one thing but sing their hearts out for us. That's why it's a sin to kill a mockingbird'" (Jean Louise [Scout] Finch).

About the Author

Nelle Harper Lee passed away on February 19, 2016, a little more than two months from her ninetieth birthday. She was born in Monroeville, Alabama, in 1926, and she died in that small town. Perhaps her roots were planted far too deep there for her to contemplate meeting her maker anywhere else. Nelle—her longtime friends and family didn't call her Harper—would have been a card-carrying member of the Association of American Recluses if such an organization had existed, joining fellow novelist J. D. Salinger, aviator Charles Lindbergh, and actress Greta Garbo, among many others.

Beginning in 1949, Harper Lee lived for a time in New York City, far removed from the tiny town of about six thousand souls where she grew up. It was in Manhattan that British journalist Michael Freedland of *The Guardian* was able to arrange an interview in 1978, which he boldly titled, "I'm the only journalist alive to have interviewed Harper Lee—and it's all thanks to Gregory Peck." Alan Pakula had picked the noted Hollywood star to play Atticus Finch in the movie version of *To Kill a Mockingbird*, a role for which he won an Oscar for Best Actor. During the filming of the movie Lee and Peck became very close. "It was while I was writing my authorized Peck biography that the relationship between author and star of the film adaptation was revealed," Freedland writes. "Plainly, it seemed they loved each other— but like a daughter loves a parent. They were only 10 years apart in age, and yet it seemed to me that he was sort of a surrogate father, even when her own father, on whom Peck's role as Atticus Finch was based, was still alive."[30]

About the Book

The Guardian published a glowing report of this bestselling American classic: "If you are a human being with emotions, this book will impact you, regardless of age, gender or background. This book makes you FEEL: that's the best way to describe it. Ultimately, there's a reason why people still read this book. It's a reason you won't understand until you pick up the book and feel the words."[31]

The book takes place in a fairly typical small town in the Deep South named Maycomb, Alabama—a fictitious hamlet patterned after Monroeville, Alabama—in the 1930s. The book is a snapshot of a three-year period and a courtroom drama that captivates the town. At center stage is a highly principled white attorney and single father named Atticus Finch, with two children. Scout is a resolute tomboy, unafraid to use her fists to settle a discussion. Her brother, Jem, doesn't understand why his sister acts more like a boy than a girl, and their relationship is at times contentious. Weave in Arthur "Boo" Radley, a neighbor who "never comes outside"; another neighbor's cousin, Dill, who comes to visit Maycomb in the summertime; and Tom Robinson, a black man accused of raping and beating a white woman. Atticus takes on the defense of Robinson, and the community begins to fall apart. The rest is left to you to enjoy in book or movie form.

If you have an interest in visiting Monroeville—aka Maycomb— the town puts on performances of *To Kill a Mockingbird* every year from mid-April to mid-May. While there you can visit the clock tower and tour the Old Courthouse Museum, both of which feature prominently in Harper Lee's jewel of a book.

Leadership Lessons Summarized

Atticus Finch displays a human quality that is all too often elusive in difficult situations: courage of conviction—doing the right thing no matter the cost to you or the loved ones who share your life. In Finch's case the price is shared by his children, who bear the brunt of the townspeople's anger for his decision to represent a young black man charged with the rape of a white woman. Harper Lee's sensitive portrayal of Atticus Finch on a tightrope will live on through the ages and resonate in the minds of leaders—who know that the "hard right cause" is vastly better than the "easy wrong one."

—R. Manning Ancell

45 ⁓ The Soldier and the State: The Theory and Politics of Civil-Military Relations
by Samuel P. Huntington (Belknap Press, 1981)

Recommended by Gen. Martin E. Dempsey, USA, commanding general of Training and Doctrine Command 2008–11, chief of staff U.S. Army 2011, and chairman of the Joint Chiefs of Staff 2011–15

I started reading, I suppose, when I was very young. If you talk about reading in the context of the profession, I had no interest at all in military history or the military profession until I went to West Point. I was determined to go to Manhattan College in New York City, and probably as a prelaw student, so I was always kind of inclined toward the humanities. Then I went into the engineering school. I started reading voraciously, really, at West Point. I've always believed that reading is an important part of who I am. Not that I read a book hoping to gain some discrete insight out of it, but rather to find something that I can tie to something else. I read Shakespeare, for example, avidly.

I went back to West Point as an instructor in the English Department, and one day the department head held up two books in front of the new instructors, and he said, "This is the dictionary. This'll give you the definition of words, the words of the English language." He was holding in the other hand the complete works of Shakespeare. "This is where you'll go to find out what they mean." I was kind of captured by that idea, that there's the definition of words and then there's their application. In the '70s I was reading about the aftermath about Vietnam. I don't remember any of the works in particular, to my discredit. I was reading a lot of the things coming out of TRADOC [the U.S. Army Training and Doctrine Command], interestingly, about how we change our Army paradigm from one that was focused exclusively on counterinsurgency in Vietnam into something that became Army doctrine. But I was reading avidly.

When I went to grad school and then back to West Point on the faculty, I became interested in the profession. If you remember, that period of time in the late '70s was a transitional and transformational time from the conscript Army to the volunteer Army. We were examining our profession, and I think Samuel Huntington's *The Soldier and the State: The Theory and Politics of Civil-Military Relations* probably, at that time, was the seminal work on what it means to be a member of the military profession.

Quote from the book "The only theory of civil-military relations which has had any widespread acceptance in the United States is a confused and unsystematic set of assumptions and beliefs derived from the underlying premises of American liberalism. This collection of ideas is inadequate in that it fails to comprehend many important facts, and it is obsolete in that it is rooted in a hierarchy of values which is of dubious validity in the contemporary world" (Samuel P. Huntington).

About the Author

A conservative political scientist but a lifelong social democrat, Samuel P. Huntington was born on April 18, 1927, in New York City. He was gifted with a superior intellect, graduating at age eighteen from Yale and earning a master's degree from the university while serving in the U.S. Army. By the time he was twenty-three he had earned a PhD from Harvard and was teaching there. All told, he taught at Harvard more than fifty years.

The Soldier and the State was his first book, and it earned him wide acclaim. A follow-up book, *The Clash of Civilizations*, cemented his reputation. In that book Professor Huntington was prescient to a broad degree about future events. He believed that future wars would be fought not between countries but between cultures, and that Islamic extremism would become the biggest threat to Western world domination. Huntington died on Martha's Vineyard on December 24, 2008. At that time it was obvious that his look into the future was proving to be highly accurate.

About the Book

Huntington spends some time discussing what Professor T. Harry Williams, a distinguished historian at Louisiana State University, identified as two military traditions in the United States: the Ikes and the Macs. "One is represented by the friendly, folksy, easygoing soldier who reflects the ideals of a democratic and industrial civilization and who cooperates easily with his civilian superiors. This 'Ike' tradition is exemplified by Zachary Taylor, U.S. Grant and Dwight D. Eisenhower. Opposing this is the 'Mac' tradition, embodied in Winfield Scott, George B. McClellan and Douglas MacArthur—brilliant, imperious, cold, dramatic officers deriving their values and behavior from an older, aristocratic heritage and finding it difficult to subordinate themselves to civilian authorities."

Huntington's book is a hefty read at 534 pages, but it is arranged so that you can stop and start reading with ease. It should be required reading for anyone serving in the Pentagon or other agencies and entities that employ military personnel.

Leadership Lessons Summarized

The essence of Huntington's book is the absolute necessity for leadership to rest at the core of the military profession. This has much wider applicability, of course, than simply the military profession. In all of the professional walks of life—medicine, the law, politics, the arts, and so on—the ability to rationally describe and ultimately perform the function of leadership is essential. The heart of truly professional activity is a sense of community, an accepted set of norms, traditional processes of advancement, and an orderly application of effort in pursuit of important goals. None of that can occur without leadership, and this incisive book shows us why.

— R. Manning Ancell

46 ⟶ *Master and Commander* and the Other Sea Novels of Patrick O'Brian

Recommended by Adm. Kurt Tidd, former assistant to the chairman of the Joint Chiefs of Staff and currently commander U.S. Southern Command

I began reading this series of novels when I was in command of USS *Arthur W. Radford* (DD 968) and read all of the books straight through over the course of my command. I did not stop until finishing the final book at the time of the author's untimely death. Spent many a delightful hour in the captain's bridge chair enjoying a volume. There are a million leadership lessons throughout, something for everyone and just about every possible situation encountered in command and after.

Quote from the book Captain Jack Aubrey is preparing to board his first command, HMS *Sophie*. "Walking down to the waterside . . . he felt a curious shortness of his breath; and as he sat in the waterman's boat he said nothing but the word, *Sophie*, for his heart was beating high and he had a curious difficulty in swallowing. 'Am I afraid?' he wondered." Later, "as he rowed back to the shore, pulled by his own boat's crew in white duck and straw hats with *Sophie* embroidered on the ribbon, a solemn midshipman silent beside him in the stern sheets, he realized the nature of this feeling. He was no longer one of 'us': he was 'they.' Indeed, he was the immediately present incarnation of 'them.' Thus appears the loneliness of leadership."

About the Author

Born Richard Patrick Russ to English-Irish parents in 1912, Patrick O'Brian changed his name in 1945 at the end of World War II. He washed out of the Royal Air Force and was medically rejected by the

Royal Navy but served in intelligence and drove ambulances during World War II (although there is some controversy and murkiness about the former). He left his first family after the war and settled into a long and happy marriage with his second wife, Mary, in the south of France, where he wrote most of his novels. He was by all accounts a shy, scholarly man with a voracious ability to read and synthesize the world. O'Brian's obsessive focus on detail about eighteenth- and nineteenth-century sailing warships is legendary, and the novels reflect a real feel for life at sea, command of warships, interactions between officers and enlisted men, and an understanding of the geopolitics of the Napoleonic era in which the saga is set. He died in Collioure, France, in 2000.

About the Books

The opening scene of this series of twenty sea novels is set in a Mediterranean port at a concert in a very upper-class house. We meet a young naval officer, Jack Aubrey, who has a spat with a rather seedy medical doctor, Stephen Maturin; after that initial disagreement the two become friends. When Jack is given command of a small British warship he asks Stephen to join him as the ship's surgeon. Thus begins a long friendship that spans the Napoleonic Wars and follows the ups and downs of Jack's career as a fine seagoing captain and Stephen's increasingly complex assignments as an undercover naval intelligence officer.

Captain Aubrey, whose character and adventures are loosely based on a nineteenth-century British naval hero, Lord Cochrane, is a superb war fighter who has plenty of success in command, winning prizes and promotions—he is a heroic commander and leader at sea. Ashore, however, he is a bit of a boob who has many problems with the leadership of the Royal Navy, his own pursuit of a wife, and especially management of his money. Dr. Maturin, on the other hand, is all thumbs at sea and constantly has to be rescued from his own incompetence and clumsiness; but ashore, his skill with a blade and a pistol and his virtuosity with languages make him a formidable intelligence professional. He is a brilliant and innovative surgeon as well as an enthusiastic naturalist. Together Aubrey and Maturin fight at sea and pursue love ashore across a couple of decades, ending finally with Aubrey attaining flag rank after many, many detours and diversions along the way, including a disgraceful turn in the stocks for bankruptcy. The series takes place all around the world, including voyages in the south Atlantic, the central and western Pacific, the waters of Australia and the Indian Ocean, and of course the Mediterranean and northern Europe. While their principal foe is Napoleon's France, they also constantly battle tumultuous storms, encounter vile characters at sea and ashore, and fight with creditors and Jack's superiors at the Admiralty.

Master and Commander, the first book in the series, is a good place to begin, especially with an eye toward leadership lessons. As Jack takes over his first command, the "sweet sailing brig HMS *Sophie*," in Port Mahon, he is frozen with trepidation, even though he has spent his life at sea preparing for this moment. He and his crew of "Surprises" sail into the Mediterranean and conduct a series of battles against determined opponents and commercial vessels alike, quickly earning a reputation for taking prizes and audacious action in combat. Stephen Maturin uses his skills as a linguist (he is fluent in English, French, Spanish, and Catalan) to help the cause of both England (about which as an Irishman he is somewhat ambivalent) and his friend Aubrey. The final set piece in the novel is a pitched battle against a comparatively huge Spanish frigate that significantly outguns and outmans *Sophie*. The book is a stirring beginning to the entire series of novels, which I read one at a time sitting in my bridge wing chair on USS *Barry* from 1993 to 1996. I dip back into them from time to time, and returning to any of the novels is like catching up with two good friends. They still ring with action, humor, human nature, and above all the lessons of leadership.

Leadership Lessons Summarized

While it is difficult to summarize all that can be learned from Jack Aubry and Stephen Maturin over the course of this twenty-volume voyage, a few fundamental leadership lessons jump out. First and foremost is the importance of both compassion and high standards on the part of leaders. Throughout the novels we see instances of military martinets, on the one hand, and slovenly slugs who care nothing for the mission, on the other—Jack finds his way to the balance of leadership that creates a taut but happy ship. Balanced and calm in the stormiest moments (despite his hot temper), Jack Aubrey is human in scale but memorable in his accomplishments as a fair-minded leader. Second is the vital importance for leaders to have good friends and confidants. In today's world, the role of Stephen Maturin afloat would best be filled on a ship by either the executive officer or the senior enlisted man or woman, called the master chief petty officer of the command. But the key principle is simply that a leader in any well-run enterprise needs a near-peer who can honestly provide a different point of view. Peers are important sources of "true north" for any leader. Third, a consistent message in the novels is the need for leaders to be innovators. Both Jack and Stephen are able to try new methods, especially when in dire need, to succeed. It is a quality that saves both them and their ships many times over. Fourth and finally is the role inspiration plays: having a leader like Jack Aubrey, for all his flaws, is a huge force multiplier for his team. Why? Because, like Napoleon, his archfoe, Aubrey is almost always a "dealer in hope," the kind of captain we all would want. And that need applies across the spectrum of human organizations, from the smallest family to the U.S. Department of Defense and the largest commercial companies in the world, and pretty much everything in between.

—Adm. J. Stavridis

47 — *The General*
by C. S. Forester (Michael Joseph, 1936)

Recommended by Gen. John F. Kelly, USMC, commander in chief U.S. Southern Command 2012–16

I grew up in a working-class, Roman Catholic, Irish family in Boston. My father worked two jobs, so it didn't leave him much time for reading because he would leave the house at 5 a.m. and wouldn't come back to the house until midnight. But certainly the nuns and the Christian brothers in my high school had me reading a great deal. I've loved history from the very beginning. When I graduated from high school I went on to just a year of college—I wasn't very interested in it, frankly—and then went into the Merchant Marines for a little over a year. Then I went into the Marine Corps for two years, followed by college at the University of Massachusetts. When I came back in the Marine Corps as an officer—close to my first days as a second lieutenant—I ran into a fellow named Capt. Ed Wells, a Harvard-educated, upper-crust guy. That first day I knew him he started talking to me about professional reading and how the real professionals read and study their professions. A doctor who doesn't read peer articles and stay attuned to the developments in his field is not the kind of doctor you would want to go to, and the same is true for officers in the Marine Corps. He got me going on reading, specifically focused on military things, and I just never stopped. When I read a new book I wrote a notation in the front of the book what billet I was in, the date I finished reading it, and where in the world I was.

I first read *The General* by C. S. Forester when I was a very, very young officer. In a way it changed my life. It's a post–World War I novel about a man, Curzon, who started out in one of the elite British regiments. In this period in the British Army if you read books you were some kind of a geek. People avoided going to staff colleges or any professional military education; it was all spit and polish. Curzon goes through his career, kind of the perfect British officer, and World War I starts. He is a brave guy, a dedicated guy, a noble guy, but a guy who in the end has become a corps commander—a three-star general—and when presented with an overwhelming German attack couldn't figure out how to deal with it because he'd never developed himself intellectually. He didn't know the great lessons of the great master, if you will, and then he just decided one day to go down to his horse, grab his sword, and attack—with the intent of dying.

I've read this book every time I got promoted just to remind myself of the effect. I've noted where I was when I finished reading it the last time, then when I read it again I will try to remember what it meant to me as a major and, depending on as you get older and higher in rank, it's a different book every time you read it. When a lieutenant reads that book it's different from when a lieutenant general reads it. And I think the same is true for every book. So it's just kind of a fun thing I've done over the years and with this book in particular just to remind me of the critical importance of thinking.

Quote from the book "There were twelve years of peace between the two wars. It was those twelve years which saw Herbert Curzon undergo transformation from a young man into a middle-aged soldier, from a subaltern into a senior major of cavalry. A complete record in detail of those twelve years would need twelve years in the telling to do it justice, so as to make it perfectly plain that nothing whatever happened during those twelve years; the professional life of an officer in a regiment of cavalry of the line is likely to be uneventful and Curzon was of the type which has no other to record. They were twelve years of mess and orderly room; twelve years of inspection of horses' feet and of inquiry why Trooper Jones had been three days absent without leave. Perhaps the clue to Curzon's development during this time is given by his desire to conform to type, and that desire is perhaps rooted too deep for examination. . . . Frequently it is assumed that it is inherent in the English character to wish not to appear different from one's fellows but that is a bold assumption to make regarding a nation which has produced more original personalities than any other in modern times. It is safer to assume that the boldness and insensitiveness which are found sporadically among the English have developed despite all the influences which are brought to bear to nip them in the bud, and are, therefore, should they survive to bear fruit, plants of sturdy growth."

About the Author

A popular and prolific English novelist, C. S. Forester was born Cecil Louis Troughton Smith on August 27, 1899, in Cairo, Egypt. When the marriage of his father and mother dissolved, he accompanied his mother back to London, where he attended Alleyn's School and Dulwich College and studied medicine briefly at Guy's Hospital. Unable to enlist in the British Army in World War I because of his eyesight, he instead turned to writing and began a very successful literary career.

In addition to *The General* Forester penned the twelve-volume Horatio Hornblower series, which follows the career of a dashing officer of the Royal Navy during the Napoleonic Wars, beginning as a midshipman and ending as an admiral. Besides scores of books with nautical themes, Forester wrote two very popular books that became extremely successful movies. *The African Queen*, which came out one year ahead of *The General*, was a monster hit in Hollywood in 1951, directed by John Huston and starring Humphrey Bogart and Katherine Hepburn, who won Oscars for Best Actor and Best Actress. Another book, *Hunting the* Bismarck, became the 1960 film *Sink the* Bismarck.

Forester served with the British Information Service in World War II and was sent to the United States to write publicity encouraging Americans to support Britain in the rapidly expanding war. He ultimately settled in Berkeley, California. He died in Fullerton, California, on April 2, 1966.

About the Book

Forester attempts to understand how "simple determination to do his duty" could translate to Curzon and men like him "order[ing] the cream of their country's manhood to sacrifice themselves in senseless battles." This is a book about a culture imbedded in the British military centuries ago and how it festered in times of war.

The book must be read with an understanding of World War I as a backdrop. When the "lights went out in Europe" and much of the advanced world was plunged into war, much of the old military doctrine was unready to meet the new advanced technologies. As the tank, the airplane, the zeppelin, radio, and other "advancements" emerged, military thinking was still stuck on the fields of Waterloo—cavalry charges to break the will of the infantry, long-range bombardments, and determined assaults against heavily fortified positions. This mismatch of killing technology and incapable leadership led to millions of deaths on the battlefields of central Europe.

General Curzon is an example of the military mind that refuses to prepare for a new world. In that sense he stands as an exemplar of all leaders who do not innovate and are somehow afraid of changes—especially fundamental ones in the profession—and therefore fail those they seek to lead. The novel follows his career from the Boer War through his initial command in the Great War, then the series of accidents, coincidences, and an advantageous marriage that advance his career. Curzon is not a vile or cowardly man; indeed, he is brave and virtuous. But his skill sets are utterly inadequate to the task set before him, and many, many soldiers die as a result. By the end of the novel he has lost a leg and sinks into retirement, never quite understanding what has happened to his nation or why so many had to die.

Leadership Lessons Summarized

There is a good reason Gen. John Kelly read and reread *The General* throughout his career. Great leaders will tell you that there is as much to be learned from leaders who fail as there is from superior leaders who succeed. The difference, of course, is to observe what not to do while filing away in your memory bank positive characteristics to emulate. In the case of *The General*, the lessons are crystal clear: leaders must keep up with the times, educate themselves, be ready to innovate, and care for their subordinates enough to think through how to succeed when old methods are clearly failing. General Sir Herbert Curzon will live on in the memory of leaders as an object lesson in what not to do. Such cautionary tales have tremendous value.

— R. Manning Ancell

48 *Captains Courageous*

by Rudyard Kipling (first edition published in 1896,
followed by serialization in *McClure's Magazine* 1896–97)

Recommended by Adm. Timothy J. Keating, USN, commander
U.S. Northern Command 2004–7, commander in chief U.S. Pacific
Command 2007–9

I grew up in South Dayton. I began reading earlier than later
because, as a typical middle-class family, we had no television and
I spent many nights under the covers with books. I remember when
the Kettering-Moraine branch library was built in a field not one
thousand yards from our house. How fortunate we were! My dad
recommended books for me to read—mostly fiction—and *Captains Courageous* was the very first book I ever read.

I don't remember a required reading list as such at the Naval
Academy, but many different kinds of books were suggested by
others, all by word of mouth. Frankly, I have never been a fan of
the *New York Times* and its list of bestselling books. During the
time I was aide to Adm. Bill Crowe he knew I read a lot. He couldn't
understand why I and my fellow aviators didn't pursue further education instead of only reading and flying!

Quote from the book "She was a black, buxom eight-hundred-ton craft. Her mainsail was looped up, and her topsail flapped
undecidedly in what little wind was moving. Now a bark is feminine beyond all other daughters of the sea, and this tall, hesitating
creature, with her white and gilt figurehead, looked just like a
bewildered woman half lifting her skirts to cross a muddy street
under the jeers of bad little boys. That was very much her situation.
She knew she was somewhere in the neighborhood of the Virgin,
had caught the road of it, and was, therefore, asking her way."

About the Author

Rudyard Kipling was born one day from year's end in 1865 in Bombay (now Mumbai), India. At the age of six he was taken to England by his father, John Lockwood Kipling, a scholar of the arts whose works and influence played a great role in young Kipling's literary successes. Kipling's childhood was largely unhappy; he attended United Services College in North Devon, a new, inexpensive, and inferior boarding school. Immediately upon returning to India in 1882 Kipling embraced all the sumptuousness and subtleties of India that he remembered from his childhood and wove his experiences and observations into the seven years he spent as a journalist there writing short stories, poetry, and other recollections of life in India.

In 1889, now twenty-four, Kipling returned to England as a well-established author known for his "brilliant prose."[32] In the 1890s and into the following century Kipling enjoyed immense popularity despite his "imperialist attitudes" about the people who lived beyond the boundaries of the United Kingdom.

In 1892 Kipling married Caroline Balestire, the sister of his collaborator. The young couple moved to the United States and settled in a home on Kipling's mother's property in Vermont, but Kipling would not—or could not—shake off his deeply imbedded conviction that people who didn't have British roots and reside within the confines of the empire were inferior. So he and Caroline moved back to England in 1902 and purchased a house in Burwash, Sussex, about fifteen miles inland of the port of Hastings, where they remained until his death on January 18, 1936.

The Nobel Committee selected Kipling for the Nobel Prize in Literature in 1907, the first British subject to be so honored. Diamond magnate Cecil Rhodes presented Kipling with a house in South Africa in recognition of Kipling's longtime relationship with the country and especially with Rhodes, who shared Kipling's proclivity for British imperialism.

The year after his death, three decades after Kipling had received the Nobel Prize, *Captains Courageous* was filmed in Hollywood. Directed by Victor Fleming, who would later direct *The Wizard of Oz*, *Gone with the Wind*, and other hits, *Captains Courageous* starred teenage actor Freddie Bartholomew, Melvyn Douglas, Lionel Barrymore, Mickey Rooney, and Spencer Tracy, who won the Oscar for Best Actor for his portrayal of Manuel Fidello.

About the Book

This is a classic coming-of-age story centered on the imperious twelve-year-old son of millionaire Harvey Cheyne. He and his father are on the ocean liner *Queen Anne* headed to Europe when, after consuming six ice cream sodas and vomiting over the side, Harvey is swept overboard. Nobody notices he is missing. Luckily a fishing dory is nearby, and a curly-haired Portuguese American doryman with a thick accent hauls the water-soaked boy on board. This is Harvey's first introduction to Manuel Fidello, who declares, "Fifteen years I've been fisherman—first time I ever catch a fish like you."

Manuel brings Harvey to the dory's mother ship, the schooner *We're Here* home-based in Gloucester, Massachusetts. Dried off and cleaned up, Harvey is introduced to Captain Disko Troop—who is not impressed with the rude, obnoxious youngster. He is taken around the ship and meets the other crew members hailing from varied and picturesque backgrounds, typical of a Kipling novel. During the course of the novel Harvey matures and develops a more agreeable personality as he works hard on the ship and learns to fish from the motley crew of blue-collar sailors. He becomes particularly close to Manuel, eventually becoming a sort of surrogate son to him, and also develops a warm relationship with young Dan, who is close to him in age. Many adventures unfold as the ship works the cod fishery. Kipling keeps the reader interested and involved by describing the maturation of a young man who has found his way in the heart of the sea. The eventual reunion of Harvey and his father is logically portrayed from a plot perspective and quite emotional.

Leadership Lessons Summarized

Leaders are often confronted with wrenching changes in their lives. In the case of young Harvey, the sudden jump from a life of privilege to one of hard work provides him the opportunity to develop in a direction utterly different than he might have expected before he took the metaphorical plunge into the ocean and emerged, baptized, as a different person. The lessons Harvey learns are those all leaders must learn about relationships: trust, honesty, teamwork, and kindness. Kipling lays out the buffet table of human engagement and teaches all who would lead some fundamental and valuable lessons in the process.

— R. Manning Ancell

49 *Commander in Chief: Franklin Delano Roosevelt, His Lieutenants, and Their War*
by Eric Larrabee (Harper & Row, 1987)

Recommended by Gen. Peter Chiarelli, USA, vice chief of staff U.S. Army 2008–12

I was extremely fortunate to have served as senior military assistant for Secretary of Defense Robert Gates for seventeen months before receiving my fourth star and spending the last four years of my forty-year career as vice chief of staff of the Army. . . . One day early in his tenure as secretary of defense when we were traveling overseas, just after we took off, he came to the area on his plane where [his ten or so advisors] congregated and gave us each a copy of Eric Larrabee's *Commander in Chief: Franklin Delano Roosevelt, His Lieutenants, and Their War.* As he passed the books he told us that if not his favorite, Larrabee's work was one of the best books he had ever read and he wanted to share it with us. Gates is a voracious reader and, taking note and impressed with his endorsement—to a person—we all began to devour the more than 650 pages. It was a multistop visit to Europe with an unannounced stop in Iraq, and by the time we touched back down at Andrews Air Force Base outside Washington, D.C., we had all finished Larrabee's magnificent work.

For me, the experience was an epiphany. Prior to reading *Roosevelt's Lieutenants* Anton Myrer's *Once an Eagle* had been the book with which I compared all others. Larrabee's account of the men who executed the war effort was riveting. Giants for sure, but many with issues or transgressions that today would make the front page of the *Washington Post*—above the fold—and would quickly end their career regardless of their operational or strategic brilliance and value to the war effort. It put into perspective how much war had changed in the sixty years from the beginning of World War II to the events of 9/11. It was amazing to relearn that firebombing in Japan, which killed more civilians than the atomic bombs that were dropped on Hiroshima and Nagasaki, was an accepted strategy in World War II, while it seemed that we were being brought to task every time a targeting error accidentally killed or injured a civilian in Iraq or Afghanistan.

I wish that I had read Larrabee's book when it was first published in 1987, when the majority of my career was in front of me. Nevertheless, reading it when I did gave me a new perspective before I reached the pinnacle of my career and allowed me to recommend it to all I touched in my almost four years as VCSA. If you plan to dedicate your life to public service, or have dedicated your life to public service, this is a must read. If you could pick only one book to keep with you while stranded on a desert island, I strongly recommend that the book be Eric Larrabee's *Commander in Chief: Franklin Delano Roosevelt, His Lieutenants, and Their War*.

Quote from the book Larrabee sums up Adm. Ernest King's early involvement and influence among the Joint Chiefs who orchestrated the war from the War Room at the White House: "He took charge of the Navy at the depths of its despair and lifted it to the heights of triumph. He was a hard man in a hard time, well suited to lead a fighting fleet, but he was also a thoughtful man of a breadth and incisiveness that gave him an early and enduring grip on Allied strategy."

About the Author

Eric Larrabee was born in Melrose, Massachusetts, on March 6, 1922. His father was a professor of philosophy at Union College in Schenectady, New York. After graduating from Harvard cum laude in 1943 Larrabee earned a commission as a military intelligence officer, served in Europe, and was awarded the Bronze Star. From 1946 to 1963 he was an editor at *Harper's* magazine, *American Heritage*, and *Horizon* before switching to academia. His monumental treatise on military and naval leadership in the Roosevelt years came about from a suggestion made by Arthur M. Schlesinger Jr. that he write a book similar to Douglas Southall Freeman's classic *Lee's Lieutenants* but about the generals and admirals of World War II. "I read for thirty years and wrote for three and a half," he quipped, the final result being the lengthy book that British historian Sir John Keegan called "the most comprehensive collective portrait of the American war leadership to date."[33]

Larrabee never repeated the splash he made with *Commander in Chief*, but he left behind a choir of voices who admired and appreciated his love of the arts and genuinely missed him when he died at his home in Manhattan at age sixty-eight.

About the Book

Larrabee opens his book with chapters about FDR and Gen. George Marshall, the most dominant figures of the war early on, who in turn influenced the appointment of the field and fleet commanders who aggressively took the war to the enemy and brought home victory to the Allies. It is important to understand FDR's unusual but integral role in the war. Larrabee explains that the wartime Roosevelt is a stilted and less substantial figure than the man who shaped domestic issues beginning with his first term. Yet this would not have been his perception of himself. Roosevelt took his position as head of the Armed Services more seriously than any other President but Lincoln, and in practice he intervened more often and to better effect in military affairs than did even his battle-worn contemporaries like Churchill or Stalin. Every President has possessed the Constitutional authority which that title indicates, but few Presidents have shared Mr. Roosevelt's readiness to exercise it in fact and in detail and with such determination.

On the face of it, any effort to have a closer look at him in his war-making capacities would seem to be hampered by the fact that he left no memoirs and was accustomed to keep his own counsel. Sometimes, for his own reasons, he would give the impression that he thought military matters belonged in military hands.

From the very beginning, Roosevelt "defined American involvement in World War II as an all-out endeavor in pursuit of high principle. 'We are all in it together, all the way. Every single man, woman and child is a partner in the most tremendous undertaking of our American history.'"

It is easy to understand why Larrabee places Marshall at the top of the list of Roosevelt's lieutenants. He was by most accounts the greatest man ever to wear the uniform of an American soldier, and there is much a reader can learn about leadership from him. Take, for example, a comment he made in a letter on September 23, 1941, to Charles Graham, president of the Pittsburgh and West Virginia Railway, declining an invitation to attend an event that would give him an opportunity to meet Wendell Willkie. "Am sure that I would enjoy meeting Wendell Willkie, particularly under such informed and agreeable circumstances, and as to my political faith—I have never voted, my father was a democrat, my mother a republican, and I am an Episcopalian."

This book provides an extraordinary and intimate portrait of all the senior leaders who served under Roosevelt and guided the nation through its most dangerous war since our own Civil War. Every page brings an interesting revelation about someone whose public persona can be revisited through the depth of Larrabee's research. As a portrait of the "back office" of World War II as well as a guide to the front-channel history, this book is brilliant.

Leadership Lessons Summarized

Three principal leadership lessons emerge again and again in this riveting book. The first is the need to delegate. Successful leaders (such as General Marshall) are masters of managing talent, picking the right people for the job, and delegating to them. A second key lesson is the need to keep events in perspective. As General Chiarelli points out above, many of the transgressions and individual idiosyncrasies on the part of the various leaders would cause major stumbles today. Good leaders can separate the wheat from the chaff in this regard, and subordinates with baggage, such as Admiral King, can be retained nevertheless. Third is the vital importance of peer relationships for leaders. While there will always be rivalries and disagreements, the ability to direct a high-powered group of subordinates working together as a team is perhaps the most important skill a leader can display—and of course Roosevelt was a master of that art. As we saw in *Team of Rivals* and again in *Lee's Lieutenants*, *Commander in Chief* gives us a portrait of a leader who managed peers with real skills.

— R. Manning Ancell

50 — *How: Why HOW We Do Anything Means Everything*
by Dov Seidman (John Wiley & Sons, 2011)

Recommended by Adm. James Stavridis, commander U.S. Southern Command 2006–9, supreme allied commander NATO 2009–13

This is a book that reaches into the soul of what leaders must do: create a climate of doing the right thing—not because of onerous rules and regulations, but because the leader convinces everyone that morality and ethics are at the heart of what makes organizations succeed. *How* is the bedrock upon which leaders can build world-class organizations from the ground up.

Quote from the book "Behavior is something you can control. If you reach out and inspire more people throughout your global network, you win. If you collaborate more intensely with your co-workers, you win. If you keep promises 99 percent of the time and your competitor keeps promises only 8 out of 10 times, you deliver a better customer experience, and you win. When it comes to human conduct there is tremendous variation, and where a broad spectrum of variation exists, opportunity exists. The tapestry of human behavior is so varied, so rich, and so global that it presents a rare opportunity, the opportunity to out-behave the competition" (Dov Seidman).

About the Author

Dov Seidman is widely regarded as one of the top philosophers to study both behavior and leadership. He routinely advises top executives from all walks of life—particularly in business—about his ideas on the importance of *how* we do things, and has built a fundamental philosophy around these ideas. Educated at UCLA and Harvard Law School, he lived much of his early life in Israel. Today he leads a company that constantly seeks the positive connections between life, success, leadership, and our ethical compass. In person he is passionate, energizing, and deeply committed to the idea that we can succeed while still doing the right thing. He has worked with hundreds of companies around the world employing more than twenty million employees, and President Bill Clinton penned the foreword to this book following the work Dov did with the Clinton Global Institute. Married and the father of young children, he lives and works in Manhattan.

About the Book

At its heart, *How* is about the increasing importance of the way an enterprise does its business, which is very often more important than what is actually done. Success is more about the "how," and less about the "what." Seidman focuses throughout the book on how we do four things, the pillars of his philosophical approach: the ways we think, lead, behave, and govern. Using a rich mix of case studies, primary-source research, interviews, and personal experience, the author gradually builds a powerful and compelling case that doing the right thing is not only the right moral choice but will also lead inexorably to the most successful outcomes for any enterprise. He offers a convincing counterargument to the seductive qualities of crisis management. It is easy to lead through a combination of cutting corners, pressuring our people in inappropriate and immoral ways, enforcing an artificially successful culture of endless rules and regulations, and failing to provide fundamental guidance to our teams about how to take the moral and ethical path. In the business world a competitor can reverse-engineer a product or provide a parallel service; but only through focusing on the *how* of customer relationships can long-lasting connections be built and maintained. Over time, that approach will succeed far more often than any other.

In addition to powerful approaches to thinking, behaving, and governing, Seidman provides fascinating views on leading. In particular, he points out that over the long throw, neither compelling performance with endless rules and ruthless oversight nor paying for it with huge bonuses and other incentives is a winning strategy. Rather, we need to inspire people to succeed, ensuring that we do not fall into the trap of coercion or simple motivation. Neither sticks nor carrots are quite right, but rather a workforce that can relate to colleagues around the world through respect for their culture and the study of their languages. Our team members must create unique and genuine experiences and honorably represent the company not only while they are at work but wherever they are. This is critically important in a world with Facebook, Twitter, LinkedIn, and other social networks driving transparency. How many enterprises these days suffer serious blows because of inappropriate e-mails? Drunken posts on blogs? Foolish tweets? A team at any level is only as good, moral, and ethical as its weakest link.

The essence of this easy-to-read book that will resonate with any leader for a long time is simple: *what* you do—commodities, structures, services—can be duplicated easily; it is *how* you do things that will be memorable, build a reputation, and succeed in the long term. This is especially true in a world categorized by rapid acceleration of information and transparency, where long-term survival is increasingly rare. Dov Seidman tells us that it is the realm of *how* we do things that is the "new frontier of conduct."

Leadership Lessons Summarized

Leadership cannot be sustained through simply using a whip in one hand and a sugar cube in the other, as though our teammates were horses. We have to inspire good and honorable behavior because the world is transparent, flat, instantaneous, and judgmental. We have to do the right thing, not the expedient or profitable thing. An easy wrong never trumps the hard right choice. Reputation is the sum of all our *hows* and is the ultimate long-term game. It is also extremely fragile. You can build a thousand bridges perfectly, but if you cheat but once you will always be regarded as a cheater. *How* true that is in today's world.

—Adm. J. Stavridis

READING LISTS

R. Manning Ancell

Of all the inanimate objects, of all of man's creations, books are the nearest to us, for they contain our very thought, our ambitions, our indignations, our illusions, our fidelity to truth, and our persistent leaning towards error. But most of all they resemble us in their precarious hold on life.

—Joseph Conrad

Why worry about reading lists? There are several reasons a young professional in any walk of life might want to have access to reading lists.

The first is simply to obtain good ideas about what to read to improve performance and understanding of the profession. Whether the military, medicine, the law, accounting, technology, or any other reasonably defined area of professional endeavor, there are countless books to help you improve performance. Where do you start? A list of books compiled from a respected source is an excellent place to begin.

A second reason is that many book lists are arranged by level or zone in ways that can help you organize a self-reading program. Within the U.S. military, for example, the various geographic combatant commanders have reading lists that are focused on the region for which they hold responsibility: Africa, South America and the Caribbean, Europe, or Korea. Some are prioritized from most important to less important works. The thicket of potential choices is pruned into a more cultivated garden.

Third, working through a reading list can give a younger professional a sense of belonging in the community, a basis for conversation with peers, subordinates, and more senior people. Some organizations—accounting firms, banks, and credit unions—will have required reading, with testing; not always fun, but certainly a motivator.

Fourth, a reading list is in many ways a conversation about what is good to read. Many lists provide a means for leaving feedback directly on the web site, or at least describe a formal or informal mechanism to provide reactions, comments, and ideas for additions or deletions.

Within today's military the service chiefs, the chairman of the Joint Chiefs of Staff, many four-star admirals and generals who head major commands such as the U.S. Southern Command and Training and Doctrine Command, and some top civilians such as the secretary of defense and the various service secretaries often provide their subordinates with lists of suggested books. In addition, major institutions of higher learning such as the Command and General Staff College at Fort Leavenworth, the Army War College, the Naval War College, and other organizations seek to encourage reading books as an integral part of self-development. We use the words "suggest" and "encourage" because it is similar to the old epithet "you can lead a horse to water but you can't make it drink." Many in the military like to read books and find the time to read despite a busy schedule. Many more don't. Capsulizing "great reads" into easy-to-manage lists is a natural step forward for those who require a bit of structure in their reading in order to make it a part of their routine, a part of their lives.

Gen. John Kelly, USMC, a former commander of U.S. Southern Command, was a young major when the Marine Corps' visionary Commandant Gen. Al Gray made the important decision to put a backbone to informal reading lists by having them originate in the Commandant's Office. That was 1988, and Kelly was tapped to work with officers handpicked by General Gray to make the Commandant's Reading List happen, including Paul K. Van Riper, a brigadier general at the time, and Col. Patrick G. Collins.

Gen. John Allen, USMC, another participant in the process, told us that to his credit, Gray knew this was a revolutionary new concept and it couldn't be pushed or forced into being overnight. His approach was simple and unhurried: "'I don't need a perfect solution this year,' he said. 'I just want these schools right now to be sources of education and training. We'll go for perfection over three or four years with the next Commandant.' Well, it revolutionized the Marine Corps."

Much of the first Commandant's Reading List originated in Kelly's personal library, which then numbered about three hundred titles. This was an unwieldy number for a reading list, of course, but "we pared it down and we put it into blocks," Kelly explained. "Then we made it a requirement to read. You could look and see, if you were a sergeant, there might have been twenty books in the sergeant group that you could pick from. The expectation from General Gray and others was that the senior officers would have the book discussions. I mean, back in those days the first question you'd almost always ask someone is, 'What are you reading?' I still ask people that all the time, and people who know me, especially people who are junior to me but know me, say 'Sir, what are you reading?' I'll have people contact me a lot to say, 'You know, sir, I was just thinking, can you give me an idea of a book to read on military intelligence or something like that?' I would say, sure; these are four or five really good books on that."

Kelly admits that the challenge continues to be the viability and variety of the list. There is a lot of territory in terms of life experience and educational level between a seventeen- or eighteen-year-old recruit and a fifty-something general officer. "I think the popularity of the books are they're usually an easy read," Kelly continued, "but if you get into military history books and biographies, it's a hard read, it's a real intellectual read, so I think that's why. You know, the Pressfield books on the Spartans and all of that. People love to read, but I guess in our everyday kind of modern-day, materialistic lives, you don't have a lot of those noble events in your life, you know what I mean?"

Particularly for the younger enlisted people, early on it was difficult to motivate these junior Marines to sit down and read a book. There were myriad other things on their minds, and most of them were far from sitting in the barracks and reading a complex book. It seemed illogical to assign them to read Sun Tzu. Kelly agreed. "But you might assign them a novel that teaches Sun Tzu. You might not give them a history book about Gettysburg, but you give them *The Killer Angels*. That's good education in those books, and the beauty is the young people don't know they're getting educated as they read it, you know? They'll do what they're told, but it's how you design the reading list. Again, you wouldn't require a nineteen-year-old to read the classic *On War* or something like it, but there's a lot of good books out there to get the same kind of lessons out."

The Marine Corps soon realized that the various groups of Marines—enlisted, NCO, junior officer, senior officer, and general officer—have different needs and tastes in the books they read. In many ways it's an evolution; learning at an early age, reinforcing mid-career, situational reading later in positions of responsibility, whether a gunnery sergeant or a lieutenant colonel. If you're on the docket for an assignment to East Africa, read what others have experienced there. Put yourself in their shoes. Get to know the territory, the people, the customs, and the challenges you will likely face as a "stranger in a strange land." Benefit from the experiences of those who have been there, done that. The lessons are there. It's all in the history. "There's people who wrote books during the Iraq War when we were going into insurgency ops, a lot of people who went out and wrote good books, and they're good books about insurgency and cultural sensitivities and that," Kelly said. "But at the end of the day they already exist. I mean, the French in Indochina and the French in Algeria. There are books about the dos and don'ts of warfare in their country. There were units in the French army that did super well in Algeria, and there were units that were just kinetic, and we had the same thing in Iraq and Afghanistan."

John Kelly was a popular and frequent speaker at a variety of Marine Corps functions while on active duty, and he always emphasized the honing of war-fighting skills and the importance of reading. "When I speak to graduations, like OCS classes, or commissionings, when I'm commissioning them, I always put in there that it is a moral and ethical responsibility to read. If there's not a war going on, the only way to learn about war is to read about it, and to read about how other people did war, if you will. Otherwise, if you're preparing for war—which is what you should be doing all the time because it is the moral and ethical responsibility of any officer, for sure, and any NCO—and so if you're preparing for it, which you should be, you should be reading about it. It's the only way to get the experience.

"When I came back from Iraq in 2003, the first time I saw Al Gray, General Gray, he just came up to me and said, 'The 1st Marine Division, led by Jim Mattis, did a hell of a job in Iraq. We did a hell of a job; 650 miles in 28 days.' It was the longest attack of any force since World War II. Just think. I don't know how far it is from Normandy to Berlin, but I bet it's not much further than 650 miles. [It is 1,200 kilometers, roughly 750 miles.] But we went from Kuwait all the way to the heart of Iraq and a little bit beyond. I was one of his students, if you will, and I just looked at him and said, 'You know, sir, it worked.' When I said that I meant the study of the art and science of war. It worked. We all knew what we were doing. We weren't surprised by anything. I looked at General Mattis and said to him when he came up to see us, 'Were you surprised by anything?' He said, 'No. And you?' I said, 'Sir, it was like watching a video. I mean, it just felt like I had been there before.' And of course, I don't mean to get too metaphysical here, but you know, I'm not suggesting I lived another life, but it was because of how much I talked about it, studied about it, I knew what I was doing, and I didn't have to think too much. You know, I didn't think back and say, ah, this is like when Stonewall Jackson was in the First Battle of Bull Run. It wasn't that at all, it was just that I had a sense for what we were doing. Then when we switched into the phase four [the war-fighting phase of a campaign], so to speak, and we started the insurgency ops, we had no problem switching to that. It had a lot to do with how much people were educated in the art and science of war. It's all out there in the history, in cyberspace. People will never stop writing books about, say, T. E. Lawrence, because he's such a remarkable character. At the end of the day, if you read *Seven Pillars of Wisdom*, you got it."

It's important to note that Gen. Jim Mattis, a well-known general within the Corps and one of the greatest proponents of reading, who had a personal library of nearly seven thousand books before he retired, deferred to John Kelly as "the only man I have ever known who reads more than I do."

For the reader seeking to start learning about leadership we have provided the fifty books on this list. They can help the professional in any occupation find his or her way to better leadership. The lists in chapters 6 and 7 offer additional suggestions that may help make your own reading program vibrant and organized.

CHAPTER
FIVE

WRITING AND PUBLISHING
The Blueprint for Success
Adm. James Stavridis

There are books which take rank in our life with parents and lovers and passionate experiences, so medicinal, so stringent, so revolutionary, so authoritative.

—Ralph Waldo Emerson

One of the best parts of doing a lot of reading to improve your skills as a leader is that it will also make you a better writer. The more you read, the easier writing becomes. This is true for several reasons: First, the kind of reading recommended here in *The Leader's Bookshelf* is uniformly good, well structured, clean, direct, and in virtually every case quite compelling—that is, of course, why so many senior leaders chose these particular books. The human brain is quite capable of retaining almost everything it observes, hears, and reads. There is an intuitively sensible linkage between reading good prose and improved writing. Sir Winston Churchill, one of the truly great writers ever to put pen to paper in the English language, often said that when he was stuck on a passage that just would not come out well in a draft, he would put aside the writing and pick up the King James Bible, letting its beautiful phrases and cadences wash over his mind. He would then return to drafting whatever he was working on and invariably found the correct "turn of phrase." This same process works well over the long term for any of us.

A second reason that reading helps with writing, quite obviously, is that it exposes us to new and challenging ideas—as well as providing new facts that can be incorporated into our own writing. The opportunity to learn new things, encounter the very best thinkers on a given topic, and dispel previously held beliefs through reading new information is invaluable in any profession.

Finally, reading widely allows us to discover new sources of published works. Learning about the vast array of publishing houses, self-publishing routes, blogs, web sites, and social media networks permits us to find outlets for our own thinking. While doing a lot of reading is helpful, the next logical step is writing. After we have written good blog posts, short articles for online journals, op-eds for newspapers, columns for magazines, and ultimately chapters for books, the really important step is to then take "the leap of faith" and publish a book.

Using the Navy as an example profession—it is one both of us know well—let's talk a bit about why a good leader not only *reads*, but also presses on to write, and then to publish.

Benjamin Franklin once said, "Either write something worth reading or do something worth writing." The really good advice, we would say, is "do both!" Live well, write about it, and write it well. Life in today's military certainly takes care of the "worth writing" part of Franklin's advice by providing a broad, rich array of *worthy* experiences and ideas, worthy of living, but also worthy of reading, documenting, discussing, and—above all—publishing. And the good news is that in virtually *any* profession in today's exciting and dynamic world there will be experiences worth writing about.

Much as the sea has been the inspiration for many writers—poets, novelists, journalists, even scientists—the military profession itself is a sea of inspiration. It is ever changing, nearly boundless, and often Hollywood-style exciting; and it begs to be interpreted, presented, and debated. Indeed, we already have a well-established literary heritage ranging from purist strategy and tactics to fiction and even science fiction, but each of us has a role to play in continuing and improving on this heritage. And it has never been easier to get started. All you need are some ideas you care about and pen and paper—or more likely, a computer keyboard.

All of us who have served have observed or lived something worth writing *and* something that would be good for others to read. Naval officers, for example, often express these ideas and observations in wardroom discussions, which are critical elements of personal and unit development. But these discussions usually make a local impact only and stay within the ship or unit. Publishing your thoughts for others to see, however, extends the reach of your ideas and sparks a larger discussion, a larger professional conversation. In the case of widely read journals— whether service specific like *Proceedings* and the *Marine Corps Gazette*, or broader-reaching joint or international publications like *Foreign Affairs* and the *Harvard Business Review*—your ideas can influence a great many and inspire conversations in numerous wardrooms or even academic centers, boardrooms, and cafés.

But here is the catch: your ideas will not go anywhere unless you have the courage to "hang them out there" for others to see. Publishing can be a daunting task. In our professional lives we can rationalize and mitigate the risks of holding station alongside an oiler in heavy seas or landing an aircraft on a pitching carrier deck; but for many, the thought of having our ideas read by others pegs the risk meter as unacceptable. Once our thoughts are out there, we feel we have lost control.

Let's face it, sometimes mentors even advise people *against* publishing because it is perceived as a "career risk." Don't be afraid. Have the moral courage to vet your ideas responsibly and sensibly. In virtually every case of which I am aware, even the most controversial articles (and I've written my share) are accepted as attempts to contribute and are respected as such.

The key to publishing and mitigating any risk is twofold: finding the appropriate venue and writing the best you can with complete honesty for that audience. And it all begins with reading, which is the gateway activity for energizing the mind and providing the grist for the mill of writing and publication.

Let's take each of those in turn.

Obviously, this entire book is about the value of *reading*, which is where any writer must begin. With the advent of instantaneous search via the Internet, the vast body of knowledge in online services such as Wikipedia, and the easy access to a "common conversation" via endless web sites, chat rooms, and blogs, primary-level research is incredibly easy. The caveat, of course, is to ensure that you do not take everything you read on the Internet as gospel—it most assuredly is not. This is where the value of books comes in: because they are vetted, are edited, and often have a publisher's credibility standing behind them, books more typically have enduring value. But both the "quick hits" on the Internet and the long-term reading of classics—like the books herein— have value at the start of a writing project.

Next is thinking about where to publish.

Finding a venue is getting easier all the time. There are many print journals, for example, eager to publish the ideas, stories, and articles of young professionals, especially professional military journals. In the context of the U.S. Navy, for example, you don't have to be the Chief of Naval Operations or a combatant commander like the supreme allied commander of NATO to get them published, although one day you might find yourself in those shoes. After all, just look at three young officers who have published in *Proceedings* over the years, names any Navy officer will recognize: Lt. Ernest J. King, Lt. Chester Nimitz, and Lt. William F. Halsey. Whatever happened to those guys? Each became a five-star admiral, and collectively they led the U.S. Navy and the U.S. military throughout World War II in the Pacific.

In fact, *Proceedings*, or any professional journal, would become irrelevant without the youth of the force publishing ideas and taking interest in the greater professional conversation. If you look at the more exciting, thought-provoking, and innovative articles printed today, you more than likely will find young minds behind them—lieutenants, lieutenant commanders, and commanders. And the best ideas often come from unlikely sources and certainly are not the sole dominion of the "brain" or "genius" of the unit.

Options for publishing and testing ideas are also ever expanding. The Internet and electronic publications afford ample opportunity to match our ideas against those of others. Blogs and Internet forums are great arenas for testing the waters, sharpening arguments, and crystallizing thoughts. Perhaps these forums even reduce the perceived risk level of publishing, lowering the "whole Navy will read this" anxiety factor. To a certain extent this is true, and electronic forums serve a great messaging purpose. But military professionals should be cautioned always to keep the conversation aboveboard and to avoid anonymous posting while keeping classification and good judgment in the forefront of our minds. I'm sure we've all learned the lesson of the e-mail we wish we hadn't sent—the one that got forwarded well beyond our small organization and returned to haunt us. So use all the media available, but do so within the bounds of common sense, command policy, regulation, and especially classification. This is good advice for *any* leader, of course, whatever your profession.

Even though publishing opportunities are growing, that does not mean writing well is getting any easier. As Nathaniel Hawthorne once observed, "Easy reading is damn hard writing." Writing is a skill that needs continuous honing through practice, study, and formal mentorship if possible. Just as physical fitness and technical proficiency require dedicated time and effort, so too does writing. In fact, writing is a key skill for all leaders, regardless of rank, and must be exercised, evaluated, and rewarded when done well.

Of course, we have to keep in mind that not all of our writing will be worth reading. All of us will create some losers—we both have in the course of our voyages as writers. Indeed, even the best writers have had their flops. The key is to keep writing and publishing anyway. Much as a baseball player who bats .333 (only one in three successes) is having a great season, a writer can also have hits and misses and still be successful. Of course, through bouncing your ideas off your peers and through honest editing you should be able to turn your thoughts into a well-written argument and better position it for success. Always show a draft article to a few trusted advisors for comments and criticisms before turning it loose like a fawn in the forest for the real world to see.

Perhaps the most important aspect of this is quite simple: dare to speak out and challenge assumptions and accepted wisdom. Do not be timid. But be sensible and balanced.

Finding the balance between "bomb throwing" and providing responsible, interesting, controversial, and challenging commentary can be tricky, of course. Think of the terrific opening scenes of the film *Jerry Maguire*. The title character, a sports agent played by Tom Cruise, pulls an all-nighter to write a scathing indictment of his own profession. He prints up a couple of hundred copies and distributes them in everyone's inbox. While most of his colleagues are applauding his verve publicly, one of them whispers, "He'll be out of here in three weeks." And so he is. Criticism needs to be constructive, based on sensible interpretation of the facts, and not personal.

When writing a professional article, I think of Mark Twain—who has the best advice: "The time to begin writing an article is when you have finished it to your satisfaction. By that time, you begin to clearly and logically perceive what it is you really want to say." Rewriting is essential. But, on the other hand, do not let the perfect article be the enemy of the very good one. The perfect article does not exist! Trying to make it so will only guarantee you never publish it. By all means rewrite, edit, deliberate, think; but ultimately, launch your ideas and see what comes.

Be prepared to face criticism. Despite your best efforts to formulate an idea and write it well, there will be critics. But you should look at criticism as a strength of the system. It means people are reading your work, that they are thinking, and that the environment is set for overall professional development. Besides, your argument, if written well, might persuade, inform, or influence the audience just as you intended.

Taking a good idea beyond the article phase can also be rewarding and make a lasting contribution to our literary legacy. An article or series of articles can germinate and grow into a full-length book. And probably the best way to master your subject of interest is to research and write a book about it. This is true for any profession, but in the naval service especially we have many published authors whose works still influence new generations of mariners. The same is true of doctors, lawyers, businesspeople, academics, and many others.

Capt. Alfred Thayer Mahan is legendary for his classics on naval strategy, but after he wrote his defining opus, *The Influence of Sea Power upon History, 1660–1783*, Mahan was sharply admonished by a superior officer. In a famously quoted fitness report (the Navy's annual evaluation form), the reporting senior said, "It is not the business of a Naval officer to write books." Hmmm. Mahan went on to become a rear admiral and stood by his right—indeed, his responsibility—to write and publish.

Plenty of mentors today, in any profession, will tell you not to write and publish. I disagree. Don't feel you have to write a book, but on the other hand, don't rule out the possibility that eventually you may want to do so. And don't forget that Mahan ended up retiring as an admiral. No one remembers the officer who wrote the fitness report; but everyone in the Navy knows Admiral Mahan, and the *Arleigh Burke* destroyer named for him proudly sails the seas today.

A few final thoughts to consider in this turbulent world:

In this rapidly globalizing twenty-first century, our nation and our military are competing in a marketplace of ideas. Indeed, so are all the elements of our society, from media to business to medicine to tech and everything else. We live in a 24/7 news cycle with near instant reporting and widespread dissemination of stories. It is a teeming, tumultuous, and exhausting marketplace. There has been a tremendous push for professionals to understand, quantify, and assess their ability to compete in this arena. On all fronts, we must excel at strategic communication—the ability to get our message out to the right audience, at the right time, with the proper effect, and in all media.

Each of us has a clear obligation to contribute to this effort, to be a part of the conversation, to help our ideas compete—whatever our particular niche or level in any profession. This is what leaders do.

Our nation was founded on two ideas that could not be repressed: freedom and liberty. In 1776 our ancestors launched these ideas into a world ruled by a different system. Our ideas faced stiff competition, and throughout the years we have even suffered wars to defend them—wars like today's struggle against extremists who use terrorism as a weapon, often to suppress freedom of expression. Our second president, John Adams, a founding father and one of the iconic American leaders, once wrote that the best way to defend our ideas was through using our minds: "Let us tenderly and kindly cherish, therefore, the means of knowledge. Let us dare to read, think, speak, and write."

So, wherever you are on the road to becoming a leader, dare to begin to read and develop your understanding. Carve out the time to think and form new ideas. Dare to speak out and challenge assumptions and accepted wisdom if your view differs from them. Have the courage to write, publish, and be heard. Launch your ideas and be an integral part of the conversation.

Why? Because it makes our nation and your profession—whatever it is—vastly stronger. In the end, no one of us is as smart as all of us thinking together. Leaders are deeply influenced by all that they read; but reading is only the first step on the path to thinking, writing, and publishing. The best leaders are constantly willing to share their ideas and wisdom with the widest of audiences. Be that kind of leader.

CHAPTER SIX

WHAT ARE YOUNG LEADERS READING?

Adm. James Stavridis

The writings of the wise are the only riches our posterity cannot squander.

—Walter Savage Landor

People often ask me what I am reading, and I love conversations that begin that way because they offer me the chance not only to enthusiastically expound on good books—something central to my life—and also, and perhaps more important, to learn about new books I can look forward to reading when I turn the question around. No one can get through every good book ever written, obviously. As I mentioned in chapter 1, the French intellectual and Enlightenment scholar Voltaire said that a man could begin to read in the first room of the French National Library and die before he ever finished the first alcove. So true; and all the more reason to hear from lots of different voices about what is worth reading.

In chapter 3 we shared with you fifty books recommended by senior four-star officers. The list is based on interviews with nearly two hundred very senior leaders who have spent their lives serving their country and focusing on how to lead effectively. It is a good and powerful list for anyone at any age in any profession.

But listening only to the voices of the most senior officers does not give a full picture of what books shape leaders. Every day, young women and men in their very early twenties embark on leadership roles throughout the armed forces. Newly commissioned ensigns and second lieutenants take charge early, standing in front of their division or platoon or on the deck of a small craft, and actively exercise leadership at the deck-plate level. Many of them are surprisingly voluminous readers, honing their skills not only through the deck-plate advice of their chain of command and by experiencing the challenges firsthand, but also through reading and learning about leadership situations. What books are they reading? And how do they choose them? When do they find time to read? There are profoundly important recommendations and ideas in the voices of these junior officers.

To gain their input we turned to a handful of senior mentors who are in touch with large numbers of junior officers through their work and personal lives. These include Capt. Fred Kacher, who leads a U.S. Naval Institute "young leaders" group, many of whom routinely exchange their ideas about reading and leading. Another is Ryan Evans, who runs a popular site focused on security, *War on the Rocks*, and is a champion of young voices in publishing and dialogue generally. A third is Fred Rainbow, a longtime journalist and editor at *Proceedings*. And I myself am in frequent touch with many junior officers I have mentored over the years.

In putting this list together we polled officers from a wide variety of backgrounds—all of the five services are represented, as are the service academies and other commissioning sources. Jet and helicopter pilots, ship and submarine drivers, and infantry officers and other ground combat arms are all represented. Lots of combat experience is represented, too, of course, given the experiences of the past ten years for the U.S. armed forces. The ages of those surveyed run from early twenties to early thirties, and they include very career-oriented leaders and some who cannot wait to complete their commitments and head off to the civilian world.

What they all have in common is a desire to read and to be good leaders. And generally they recognize that leadership is not something one can learn exclusively from reading books, but that reading can energize and act as a sort of "force multiplier" alongside the experiences, lessons and advice from mentors, classes, and other sources of inspiration. This particular group has strong opinions, and you can hear them on a wide variety of web sites that are tuned to this group, as well as finding their occasional articles in the various journals of the profession of arms, including the U.S. Naval Institute *Proceedings*.

We asked them collectively to name the books they regard as "classics," books they had read at some point in their lives (even as youths) that were seminal in shaping their worldview and especially their sense of how to lead. We also asked them what books they had read in the past year that particularly impressed them and enhanced their understanding of the wider world and how leaders shape it. Their response was very strong and included a wide selection of viewpoints. In the material below we try to capture the spirit of a significant batch of responses, giving emphasis to books that were repeatedly named as well as identifying some outlier choices.

None of this represents a comprehensive or scientific survey. It is not driven by a detailed or even a uniform format of questions, but rather by an open-ended set of queries to a broad group of interested and engaged junior officers. While their time in leadership roles does not compare with the admirals and generals whose views and recommendations form the basis of *The Leader's Bookshelf*, they add a powerful set of opinions to the mix.

It is fascinating and well worth noting how few book recommendations overlap between the most senior officers and the most junior (we have placed an asterisk next to the books that appear on both lists). Of all the metrics we could use to determine whether we were offering up the right set of books, this is the one that gives us confidence that our effort is a worthy one, producing as it has a full shelf of not only the fifty books the most senior and accomplished leaders recommend but also a nice group that comes from very junior officers at the very heart of the leadership challenges in today's turbulent world. The scope and span of the two lists together are heartening. We hope the senior folks will find some of these ideas intriguing, and vice versa. Let the book talks begin!

Combat Leadership

At the top of the queue from many junior officers are timeless classics reflecting the dynamic challenge of leadership under stress and crisis. This type of reading and leading is fundamental not only to the military but to the worlds of business, finance, law, international relations and diplomacy, negotiation, and any other high-stress/fast-paced endeavor as well. So it is not surprising to see the following books on the junior officers' list, all of which, interestingly, are novels.

The Centurions, by Jean Larteguy, is a searing novel that poses the deepest moral questions about how to fight and lead in the postheroic age. Set in the colonial battlefields of post–World War II France, Vietnam, and Algeria, it guides young leaders to think about the moral and ethical questions at the heart of combat.

Gates of Fire*, by Steven Pressfield, tells the story of the three hundred Spartan warriors who held out for crucial days against the vastly larger Persian forces and helped save Greek civilization. It is full of the lessons of personal leadership in combat, personified by King Leonidas of Sparta, who inspires, goads, pushes, and loves his men throughout their epic and ultimately tragic battle.

The Killer Angels*, by Michael Shaara, won the Pulitzer Prize for Fiction in 1975 and brilliantly tells the story of the Battle of Gettysburg through the eyes of the commanders from the North and the South. By contrasting the styles of leadership on the battlefield that day, readers can consider the variety of styles and personalities that can make for successful leadership.

Master and Commander*, by Patrick O'Brian, is the first of a twenty-volume series of sea novels about Royal Navy captain Jack Aubrey that take place in the late eighteenth and early nineteenth centuries. In the course of following Aubrey's career through the Napoleonic Wars, O'Brian gives us timeless lessons in how a leader inspires loyalty and performance through equal measures of discipline and respect.

Once an Eagle*, by Anton Myrer, is a classic Army story of the rise of two very different officers—one a polished, ambitious staff superstar and the other a mud-on-his boots true warrior. This is a book read by virtually every officer in the U.S. Army, and its portraits of the two leading characters have had a profound cultural effect on Army leadership styles for decades.

Memoir

The memoir is another popular category among junior officers. Here, as you would expect, there is less of a tendency to reach back into the more distant past, but rather a desire to read inside accounts of recent events. A group of books mentioned by several of the junior officers included the following.

Duty, by former secretary of defense Robert Gates, is a hard book to read in that it is a harshly realistic view of the twisted environment of Washington, D.C., during the height of the wars in Iraq and Afghanistan. The consummate professional, Secretary Gates stayed at his post across Republican and Democratic administrations and always believed in his troops.

The Accidental Admiral was often cited for honesty and sweep of topic— obviously a gratifying reaction for me personally, since I wrote it. There are chapters on leadership, strategic communications, smart power, threat convergence, and strategic planning as well as the story of NATO operations in Afghanistan, Libya, the Balkans, Syria, Iraq, and at sea on counterpiracy missions.

Four Weeks in May, by Captain David Hart Dyke, is a very personal memoir from the captain of HMS *Coventry*, which was sunk during the Falklands War in the spring of 1982. His leadership in the most trying conditions a sea captain can face—the sinking of a ship and the deaths of many in the crew—is invaluable and resonates with junior officers.

It Worked For Me, by former secretary of state Gen. Colin Powell, is a collection of stories, tricks of the trade, and leadership tips by the most accomplished military officer of his generation. General Powell served as the chairman of the Joint Chiefs of Staff as well as national security advisor and ultimately as secretary of state, and his story-telling is superb.

Thoughts of a Philosophical Fighter Pilot, by James Stockdale, relates the story of the more than seven brutal years Vice Admiral (then Captain) Stockdale spent as a prisoner of war in the infamous Hanoi Hilton during the war in Vietnam. Of special note is the way he weaves his study of the ancient Greek and Roman philosophers (especially the Stoics like Epictetus) into his leadership approach. Because he was one of the most senior officers in captivity, his memoir is also a case study in leadership in a crisis situation.

History

In terms of history, the junior officers tended to read books about the history, context, and background needed to understand war, especially the wars they have themselves fought, or perhaps those they expect to fight in the future.

Invisible Armies, by Max Boot, recounts the long history of special operations and sheds considerable light on how these shadow warriors have evolved from a culture that is more than two thousand years in the making—much of it driven by personal leadership.

The Twilight War, by David Crist, is the story of the thirty-year undeclared war between the United States and Iran. Using a wide variety of previously unavailable sources, Crist reveals a story that might be crucial for junior officers to understand if our differences do flare up into war, even given the possibilities for peace opened (just a crack) by the nuclear agreement.

Rules of the Game, by Andrew Gordon, tells the inside story of the Battle of Jutland in World War I. The failures of command and control as well as the insidious results of decades of peacetime operations by the Royal Navy came home to roost in a failure of leadership at the highest levels. The book is a fascinating choice by junior officers, and one that has enormous resonance today.

Six Frigates, by Ian Toll, is a long love sonnet to the six original frigates of the U.S. Navy, only one of which survives to this day as the oldest commissioned warship in the world actually afloat: USS *Constitution*. The story of their design, funding, construction, and seagoing operations is a powerful set of lessons for any leader.

Practical Tools

The current generation of junior officers is pragmatic and focused on practical tools they can use. Theory seems of less interest to them, reflecting their backgrounds as primarily Millennials. Thus the "leadership" books they reach for are full of concrete suggestions for improving themselves as leaders and as people.

What Got You Here Won't Get You There, by Marshall Goldsmith, provides tips and advice from a famous executive coach on how to lead your way to the very top.

The New Digital Age, by Eric Schmidt and Jared Cohen (chairman of the board and head of Google Ideas at Google respectively), is about the rapid and accelerating change brought about by the fusion of information technology, quantum computing, artificial intelligence, and the Internet—and how leaders can best adapt its power to motivate and inspire.

Going Big by Getting Small, by Col. Brian Petit, explains how special operations teams can lead in the operational space between strategy and tactics in places such as Colombia, Yemen, and Indonesia, creating real effect through dynamic, on-the-ground leadership with small teams.

Thinking, Fast and Slow, by Nobel Prize–winning economist Daniel Kahneman, helps leaders tap into their intuitive, quick-thinking brain as well as the slower, more contemplative processes. Essentially a book about how we think and what we can do to optimize our thought process, this is a focused tool for developing leadership skills.

Team of Teams, by Gen. Stanley McChrystal, draws upon his deep experience with special operations teams in changing outcomes in large, complex organizations and systems. Most important, he shows how such an approach can succeed in any setting.

The Road to Character, by David Brooks, contrasts the balance between our "eulogy values" of goodness, honesty, character, and selflessness and our "résumé values" of accomplishment, rank, reputation, and achievement. Good leaders know they need both, and the ability to balance these qualities in a world that seems to overvalue the "résumé values" is a true challenge.

Classics

Despite all of the focus on relatively recent books, modern wars, and well-known current figures, the junior officers cited three truly classic works.

Meditations, by Marcus Aurelius, outlines how we should all live our lives through harnessing stoicism, honesty, and the best we can offer.

The History of the Peloponnesian Wars, by ancient historian Thucydides, tells the story of the great war between two rival systems of city-states in Greece, Athens and Sparta. It is one of the earliest and best descriptions of political power and geostrategic thinking, and a book often taught in the nation's war colleges.

The Art of War[*], by Sun Tzu, is a staple of every war college curriculum. What is interesting is that very young leaders are immersed in this thirteenth-century work, which is divided into thirteen chapters and runs the gamut of tactics, operational art, strategy, and grand strategy in clear and lucid prose.

International Relations

Books that explain the world are popular among junior officers, who must adapt their leadership style to the world they expect to encounter. It's no surprise that this trio of geopolitical experts appears on several of the junior officer lists: Kaplan, Kissinger, and Friedman.

Asia's Cauldron, by Robert Kaplan, describes the history and current tensions that surround the South China Sea.

World Order, by former secretary of state Henry Kissinger, draws on well over half a century of personal experience at the highest levels of academe, government, and business to describe the shape of today's world.

On China, also by Henry Kissinger, is a sweeping story of more than two millennia of Chinese history that helps junior officers understand the impact of culture, literature, and history on how a leader governs an enormous and complex society.

The Next Hundred Years, by George Friedman, reads like a gripping novel but is in fact a very realistic set of predictions about the century ahead—some of which are already coming to pass.

Wars to Come

Over time, the tools of war will evolve and new ways to both attack and defend will emerge. It is only natural that junior officers will look ahead to those challenges, and two books that were often cited in that regard are a bit of a matched pair.

Ghost Fleet, by Peter Singer and August Cole, is a novel about a war between the United States on one side and an alliance of China and Russia on the other. It begins with a surprise attack on Pearl Harbor using a great deal of emerging technology for warfare, all of it set a decade from now in 2025.

Cyberwar and Cyber Security: *What Everyone Needs to Know*, by Peter Singer, is a matched piece with *Ghost Fleet*, except it is nonfiction. Taken together, the two books provide a chilling outline of where conflict is headed and have great appeal to junior officers.

Quirky Outliers

Several books mentioned by one or more of the junior officers do not fit logically in any of the categories above but are fascinating choices. All are works of fiction, and each is quirky in some fundamental way. We offer them as examples of books that are distinctly outside the norm of reading for many, and that therefore may be all the more valuable to those in uniform today who seek a fresh insight or viewpoint.

Infinite Jest, by David Foster Wallace, set in an addict's halfway house and a tennis academy, is a long and highly entertaining meditation on the importance of entertainment in our lives. It is an utterly fresh portrait of today's America written by a gifted author who committed suicide at the peak of his career.

Atlas Shrugged, by Ayn Rand, is a classic American novel about individualism, the power of society, and the determination of self-selected leaders. Complex and difficult in places, it is in many ways the first postmodern novel.

Starship Troopers, by Robert Heinlein, is set in the future, with Earth under attack from a species of large insects with advanced technology. Heinlein gives us a vivid portrait of battlefield leadership and military preparation in a vivid, dramatic storytelling format that has high appeal to many junior officers.

The Secret Agent, by Joseph Conrad, is a tale of anarchism, terrorism, and espionage set largely in the United Kingdom in the late nineteenth century. Written by the brilliant seafaring author Joseph Conrad, it is an example of his later writing, which branched into the political. Superbly plotted, it provides ample lessons in leading through complex missions even at a very junior level.

Overall, it is interesting to note that there is only a 10 percent overlap—quite small—between the reflections of the very senior leaders in chapter 3 and the very young leaders represented here. This makes general sense, given age and demographics; but it also reflects the time senior leaders have spent honing the craft of leadership in real-world situations. As a result, they are more likely to pick books of history, memoir, and politics; and the touchstones to which they look tend to be older figures in history. So *vive la différence*! The common threads in the commentary from both groups are quite striking: a sense that history matters most, however it is received (fiction, memoir, classic historical study, etc.); that novels can provide excellent insights, especially into character; that memoirs provide invaluable "inner dialogues" from leaders under stress and strain; and that some of the classics have a place on a leader's bookshelf.

Clearly, the overall lesson for any student of leadership seeking to build the right kind of bookshelf is to listen to some of these younger voices as well as the older ones.

CHAPTER
SEVEN

BUILDING A PERSONAL LIBRARY

R. Manning Ancell

It is a man's duty to have books. A library is not a luxury, but one of the necessities of life.

—Henry Ward Beecher

Over time, any professional will gradually assemble a library of books that have particular meaning for him or her. This is true of any profession, from accounting to wine making, and often begins with the books that formed the basis for study in college, university, or graduate school. Such books tend to be touchstones to which professionals return from time to time, and they are often heavily annotated, tabbed, or marked in some way. They are the cornerstone of your library, and even when they become outdated in some way (think of the book of computer programming from the 1980s full of how to code in COBOL), they still have value if only in your heart.

As you move forward in your profession you will add updated volumes on the profession itself. In the Navy, for example, new books emerge every few years on ship handling, engineering, watch standing, and career advising, and those purely professional books should stand alongside the cornerstone volumes from education.

A serious reader's tastes will broaden over time, and new volumes reflecting new interests and ideas will be added to the library. These can and should include fiction, perhaps works that deal in some way with the profession. Historical fiction that helps a professional understand how the profession evolved can be particularly helpful and useful. Additionally, you will want to explore other aspects that may be tangential but important to your profession—a chef, for example, may become interested in wine making or architecture or interior design. More books are added to the library.

The use of reading lists can be particularly valuable when adding to a personal library. And, of course, individual recommendations from mentors and peers can be valuable sources of additions to a library as well.

A threshold question today is whether to use traditional paper books or an electronic format. There are good reasons on both sides of the equation. Paper books can be marked and tabbed at will, leaving personal footprints and path markers when a reader returns to them. This also has a certain emotional and psychological appeal for many readers, essentially being markers that they have conquered a particular work. Additionally, paper books—if purchased carefully in first editions and hardback—can become valuable over time (although not if heavily marked in ink, so if you are buying with collectability in mind, use only paper slips inserted in various sections with notes on them). And last, paper books make a visual statement in a home or office that many esteem.

On the other hand, there is much to recommend electronic libraries. First and most obviously, there are no cartons of weighty books to be lugged around at every move. When Admiral Stavridis returned from serving as supreme allied commander of NATO in Europe, he moved four thousand professional books, all of which he unpacked in his new home, the seventeenth relocation of his thirty-five-year career. His wife was (as always) resigned to the paper library. How many of those books could have been eliminated if they were stored electronically? A second advantage of electronic books is the increasing level of tools available to search, scan, and mark them. All of that can be stored perpetually in the Cloud. Third, electronic books are somewhat cheaper, and many of them—most notably classics—are available for free. They can also be accessed on a temporary basis through most libraries over the Internet and downloaded.

So the decision—paper or electronic—is up to you. A hybrid or blend between the two is an increasingly popular option, with readers opting to buy a limited number of paper books (generally nice volumes in first editions) for their permanent "bricks and mortar" library. The majority of "quick reads" are often purchased electronically and stored in the Cloud. Admiral Stavridis is following this approach today because his wife finally cut him off at around five thousand books on the shelves in their home.

One way to explore the books you might want to read and add to your personal library is to look inside the notable libraries accumulated by two successful four-stars of different time periods in American history, remembering that you must carefully cull the subject matter and the authors to uncover the base upon which you will chart a course to literary literacy in matters of military history, leadership, and allied subjects.

Library of Gen. George S. Patton Jr., USA

Throughout the final two years of World War II, when he commanded the Third Army, Lt. Gen. George Patton (he wouldn't be promoted to full general until April 14, 1945, just before his death) transported a small library of books he liked to read "for relaxation." His widow, Beatrice Patton, recalled after the war that the books were "a Bible, prayer book, Caesar's *Commentaries* and a complete set of Kipling."[1] Quite an undertaking with Kipling's books given that he published scores of collections of his short stories, poetry, travel and military writings, and individual books—both novels and nonfiction. Huge collected sets like the Edition de Luxe published in thirty-eight volumes in

London, and the Burwash Edition in New York in 1941, consisting of twenty-eight volumes, were popular after Kipling's death in 1936.

Beatrice was amused by the story of a clergyman who interviewed Patton during the harsh winter of 1944. The minister spotted a Bible on Patton's bedside table and "thought it had been put there to impress the clergy, but had to admit later that the general was better acquainted with what lay between the covers than the minister himself."

The Patton family was a tiny throng of inveterate readers who read not only individually but also out loud to one another. Most important, they took on roles of characters in books. "It began with the classics," Beatrice remembered, "for the Pattons felt that life was too short to get one's education unless one started early, and the family loved to read aloud. By the time the future general had reached age eight he had heard and acted out *The Iliad*, *The Odyssey*, some of Shakespeare's historical plays, and such books of adventure as *Scottish Chiefs*, Conan Doyle's *Sir Nigel*, *The White Company*, *The Memoirs and Adventures of Brigadier Gerard*, *The Boys' King Arthur*, and the complete works of G. A. Henty" (another prolific author who wrote from the mid-nineteenth century literally up to his death in 1902). We would not be surprised if you are scratching your head over most of these titles. They are certainly not on bookshelves in a majority of homes, nor do they often (if ever) show up in the curriculum of America's schools.

Patton spent one year at Virginia Military Institute, transferred to the U.S. Military Academy, and graduated number 46 out of a class of 103 in 1909. While at West Point he embraced the study of classics and began to make extensive notes in the books or on three-by-five cards and undertook to catalog the growing number of books in his personal library. He was one of only a few Americans who owned translations of *Mein Kampf* and works of Lenin and Marx, "believing," Beatrice explained, "that one can only understand Man through his own works and not from what others think he thinks." Patton was particularly drawn to biographies of Civil War leaders. "He was an intensive student of the Civil War," Beatrice continued, "and one of his regrets was that his favorite military biography of that period was by a foreigner—Henderson's *Stonewall Jackson*. Imagine his delight when Freeman's *Lee* began to appear. He bought and read them one volume at a time, and when I showed it to the author—crammed with my husband's notes and comments—he smiled: 'He REALLY read it, bless his heart.' "

Transferred to duty in Hawaii in 1925, Patton was greatly distressed to learn that his entire library and his household goods had been ravaged by a fire in the hold of the SS *Grant* en route to Hawaii. One entire box of books was completely destroyed, and 75 percent of the others lost their covers. "Patton undertook a massive rebinding process in Hawaii," notes Roger H. Nye in *The Patton Mind*. "Today those books are identified by straw-colored buckram covers, hand-printed titles and names of authors and the occasional 'R' indicating Patton had read them. For example, Patton's copy of William Ganoe's *History of the United States Army* was bought in 1924, damaged in the 1925 fire, and rebound in 1926."[2]

Duty in Hawaii in 1925–28 was a turning point for George Patton as he intensified his reading of strategy and the big picture of warfare. He annotated the books he read and typed his reactions to those books on note cards. An examination of his books and cards reveals whether Patton agreed or disagreed with the author on a particular point or premise. Judging by the sheer volume of comments and annotations, Patton was most impressed with Colonel Ardant du Picq's *Battle Studies*, which was published after du Picq's death from wounds suffered at the Battle of Mars-la-Tour near Metz. This important engagement took place on August 16, 1870, during the Franco-Prussian War and was one of the very last occasions that a cavalry charge was employed in modern warfare (modern in terms of the timeframe in which it took place).

Du Picq wrote about the "moral and psychological aspects of battle," noting that "the soldier is unknown often to his closest companions. He loses them in the disorienting smoke and confusion of a battle which he is fighting, so to speak, on his own. Cohesion is no longer ensured by mutual observation."[3] The philosophy of *offensive à out-rance* (excessive offensive) that du Picq proposed and the opposing forces in the opening battles of World War I accepted was synthesized to "he will win who has the resolution to advance" without consideration of how, under what circumstances, and over what terrain. Patton subscribed to this theory in World War II when he declared, "I don't pay twice for the same real estate," or words to that effect.

Patton produced 138 notes on 26 cards from his reading of du Picq. The example below we offer to illustrate that Patton was honing his own leadership skills through his reading:

50. ANCIENT BATTLE RESEMBLED A DRILL. There is no such resemblance in modern battle. This leads to confusion (since drill is regulated and battle is not drill is detriment as now taught, WE SHOULD HAVE ONLY DRILLS FOR FIGHTING).

51. Man can stand only so much terror. Now he gets it sooner (the approach) and in more appauling [*sic*] forms. Also fire makes dispersion necessary discipline and dispersion are opposed. Hence we need it more and have more trouble in getting it. It must spring from long accuaintance [*sic*] with comrades, trust in officers who must be present and from (FEAR OF PUNISHMENT AND HABIT).

52. In former times man fought against man now he fights FATE in the form of blind bullets. He seems to be alone it is easy to skulk. (Squads should have rollcalls at objectives and the skulkers should be dealt with by the men. (HOW CAN NATIONS IN ARMS U.S. MODEL DO THESE THINGS?)

During his adult life George Patton had a love affair with books, and they became in some ways members of the family. The best-loved books received his annotations, and some even got note cards as well, as with du Picq's book. Patton enjoyed sharing books with friends and close associates and took pleasure in urging them to read particular books. On July 9, 1926, he wrote to Dwight Eisenhower, who was class of 1915 and therefore six years junior to him: "First read *Battle Studies* by Du Picq (you can get a copy at Leavenworth) then put your mind to a solution."

Patton's reading was limited to ancient warfare down through the ages to World War I, with limited availability for English-language editions. Thus in the 1930s he scoured bookshops for books in English about Prussian leaders, strategy, and tactics, and to some degree geography. Books about the Japanese and the Russians generally made the "b list" rather than the "a list."

Patton's nephew Frederick Ayer Jr. published a thought-provoking book in 1964 entitled *Before the Colors Fade* that sheds some interesting light on his late Uncle George. While Patton was stationed in Hawaii he sent his nephew a photograph with a note attached: "This is my war face which I have been practicing before a mirror all my life. I am going to use it again to scare hell out of the Germans."[4] Ayer wrote that Uncle George was convinced the Treaty of Versailles "left things unbalanced" and "disarmament was dangerous and that certainly there would be another war. Sometimes he said it would be against the Japanese, sometimes against the Russians, but he was always sure it would come."

Ayer related a second incident during the war that spelled out the sum of all George Patton's reading and study over the years. This was how Ayer remembered a short speech to staff members at Third Army. "I have studied the German all my life," Patton said. "I have read the memoirs of his generals and political leaders. I have even read his philosophers and listened to his music. I have studied in detail the accounts of every damned one of his battles. I know exactly how he will react under any given set of circumstances. He hasn't the slightest idea what I'm going to do. Therefore, when the day comes, I'm going to whip hell out of him."

At the time of his untimely death in 1945 Patton had accumulated an impressive library, including many books that were filled with his annotations. When Patton's widow was asked to prepare a list of her late husband's all-time favorite books, she came up with the following:

Biographies and Memoirs

R. E. Lee: A Biography, by Douglas Southall Freeman

Charles XII of Sweden, by Carl Gustafson Klingspor

Genghis Khan, Alexander, and other biographies by Harold Lamb

Maxims of Napoleon, and all the authoritative military biographies of Napoleon, such as those by Bourienne and Sloane

Memoirs of Baron de Marbot of de Fezansec, a colonel under Napoleon. Mrs. Patton noted, "We were translating the latter when he went to war in 1942."

Memoirs of Ludendorff, von Hindenburg, and Foch

Memoirs of U. S. Grant and those of George McClellan

Stonewall Jackson, by G. F. R. Henderson

Current Events

The Crowd: Study of the Popular Mind, by Gustave Le Bon

Leadership

Alexander, by Arthur Weigall

Anything by J. F. C. Fuller, especially *Generals, Their Diseases and Cures*. "He was so delighted with this that he sent a copy to his superior, a major general," recalled Mrs. Patton. "It was never acknowledged. Later he gave 12 copies to friends, colonels only, remarking that prevention is better than cure."

Lee's Lieutenants: A Study in Command, by Douglas Southall Freeman

Military History

Anything by Basil H. Liddell-Hart, "with whom he often loved to differ."

Art of War in the Middle Ages, by Charles Oman, and other books by him

Fifteen Decisive Battles of the World, by Sir Edward S. Creasy

Military History of Greece, by Thucydides

The Influence of Sea Power upon History, by Alfred Thayer Mahan, and other books by him (the trilogy)

Novels
Rudyard Kipling, complete works

Other History
Anything by Winston S. Churchill
Decline and Fall of the Roman Empire, by Edward Gibbon
Gallipoli, by Sir Ian Hamilton
The Prince, by Niccolò Machiavelli
Years of Victory and Years of Endurance, by Arthur Bryant

Other Categories
Commentaries, by Julius Caesar
Maxims of Frederick the Great Strategicon, by Marcus Vitruvius Pollio
    and Oliver L. Spaulding
The Home Book of Verse, American and English 1580–1912, by Burton
    Egbert Stevenson
Treatises by von Treitschke, von Clausewitz, von Schlieffen, von Seeckt,
    and other Napoleonic writers[5]

Patton's boss during World War II, Gen. George C. Marshall, believed that history provides insights necessary in modern decision making. He told an audience at Princeton University after the war that he doubted "whether a man can think with full wisdom and with deep convictions regarding certain of the basic issues today who has not at least reviewed in his mind the period of the Peloponnesian War and the fall of Athens." Marshall read books on history and biography but did not accumulate a library approaching the size of Patton's. Marshall read for relaxation, too, and among the books in his Leesburg, Virginia, library were biographies of Queen Victoria, Ben Franklin, Will Rogers, and Clara Barton, as well as such classics as *Sherlock Holmes* and *Treasure Island*.

Library of Gen. James K. Mattis, USMC
(from an Interview with R. Manning Ancell)

General, you are a legend in the Marine Corps, and probably the armed forces as a whole, as a tough-as-nails commander with a soft heart. *Stars and Stripes* reporter Jeff Schogal wrote in a blog back in February 2011 that if you were parachuted unarmed "onto an island inhabited by psychotic ninja robots" you would "get more kills than famed Scottish warrior William Wallace." He went on to relate an occasion during Gen. Chuck Krulak's time as Commandant when he made the rounds of Marine Corps commands in and around the nation's capital on Christmas delivering cookies and discovered that you—a brigadier general at the time—had sent the designated officer of the day home to be with his family and took over his duties as OOD; most unusual for a senior officer, much less a general officer, to do this. In between these two extremes lies a Marine who has accumulated perhaps one of the largest personal libraries of an active-duty military officer ever known in the modern world. What was behind this?

I'd like to tell you mine was designed with purpose in mind. In fact, it was to read everything interesting in the world and ignore the boring, which was about the only challenge. I learned a lot from it, obviously. I was never perplexed for more than a moment when the enemy did something strategically or operationally or tactically, and I learned a lot about human nature from Sherman's book and Marcus Aurelius and Mandela's memoirs and everyone else's. I don't have a good storyline for what I did. Part of it, of course, was the Marine Corps had a reading list, and every boss I worked for seemed to have one, and they had rather a lack of sense of humor if I decided I didn't need to read what they thought was important. They were not there to help me through my midlife crisis or find my inner child, so it was rather a blunt organization in terms of taking responsibility for your own development. History was just natural as well as biography, and for me, even fiction must be a part of it.

Well, I read an article that said you've kept track of everything that you've read. When your library started to grow, what were the major titles that you had decided on that would be the foundation of your library? I mean, looking at reading in its basics as one of the three legs of the stool of personal development.

Well, personal development is a broader issue when you deal with violence. If you don't have an understanding of a letter from a Birmingham jail, and how Sherman put the enemy on the horns of the dilemma, and how Scipio Africanus was able to triumph, if you can't take those lessons of life and tie them together as a military commander, you're going to have a hell of a difficult time, especially in a democracy where if you rise to high rank, you're selected for tactical reasons, and operational, but then you have to deal with strategic reasons, and often you're bringing war's grim realities and trying to reconcile those with the political leaders you eventually deal with, their human aspirations, which are for a much better world than the primitive, atavistic one of the battlefield. So you develop by broadening your understanding of human nature, of the ascent of man and everything else so that you can reconcile war's realities, grim as they are, atavistic and primitive, with human aspirations, without becoming a narrow-minded person who at that point, you ought to give good military advice, but you can't do so without trying to achieve a better peace, and so you need to have that broader reading as you grow and personally develop so you can actually do the job as a military officer, if you're so fortunate that they keep you around long enough that you get promoted for a while.

I guess on a tactical level there was a novel by M. M. Kaye called *The Far Pavilions*, and, of course, Guy Sajer's *The Forgotten*

Soldier. Nate Fick had *One Bullet Away*, and there's some others on the tactical level. I think probably Alistair Horne and his *Savage War of Peace*—that was certainly one. Let me think. E. B. Sledge *With the Old Breed* was a really good one.

When you go up to the operational level of war, where you look at operational and strategic, you can't go wrong when you read Grant's *Memoirs* or Viscount Slim's *Defeat into Victory*. Oh, gosh, Liddell Hart and his book on Sherman and also his book on Scipio Africanus. I think Colin Gray's *Fighting Talk* and *The Future of Strategy* are just two tremendous ones. Williamson Murray's *Military Innovation in the Interwar Period*, up on the strategic level, plus Tony Zinni's *Before the First Shots Are Fired* and H. R. McMaster's *Dereliction of Duty* are really first-rate.

But you have to understand how they walk those paths, too, so you've got to read Colin Powell's *My American Journey*, and you have to keep your peace up there, so you'd better read Marcus Aurelius' *Meditations*.

And when you read books like Guy Sajer's *The Forgotten Soldier*, it just reminds you of the penalties that are paid by the private soldiers who have to carry out your orders. Then you read things like Nelson Mandela's *Long Walk to Freedom* or Steven Pressfield's *Gates of Fire*, and you realize we're not asked to do anything that's all that much greater than what others have done before.

If you look at Bob Gates' book—I was the executive secretary for two secretaries at Defense, I worked closely with three others— and when you read Gates' book *Duty*, you get a real sense of the breadth and the gravity of what faces people at that level. And in some way you look back on Will and Ariel Durant's *The Lessons of History* or Ron Chernow's book on Alexander Hamilton, and you realize, man, you can get an awful lot out of people who have been through this sort of thing and studied the ones who did it before. Then you realize how few things are really new under the sun if you do good reading. Any Marine who has not read Lucas Phillips' book *The Greatest Raid of All* should. This is about the raid that shattered the dry dock at Saint-Nazaire, France, so that *Bismarck* would never have a place to be repaired if they went out to sea. You see how you can apply strategy to operations to the tactical costs and all.

You look at our reliance on communications today, on cyber and all this stuff, and then you read Andrew Gordon's book on the rules of the game about what went wrong for the Royal Navy between Nelson's navy at Trafalgar and Admiral Jellicoe's navy one hundred years later at Jutland, and you get a real reminder of how you can take fundamental errors that just screw you up royally. Certainly you get that too if you look at our nation, where we're at right now, if you read Barbara Tuchman's *March of Folly* or *The Guns of August*, or you read Paul Kennedy's *Rise and Fall of the Great Powers* or Henry Kissinger's *Diplomacy* and *World Order*, you can see what's happening to a nation in a broader context, which I think is critical.

At the same time, you've got to study ethics and not confront your ethical dilemmas for the first time on the battlefield, so you read Michael Walzer's *Just and Unjust Wars* or Malham Wakin's *War, Morality, and the Military Profession*. Sometimes you can actually write books about the specific job you're in. For example, there's a lady named Gail Shisler, who is related to General O. P. Smith. She wrote a book called *For Country and Corps: The Life of General Oliver P. Smith*. He was the general who brought the 1st Marine Division on its way out of North Korea when it was surrounded there in that first bad winter in 1950 at the Chosin reservoir.

So again, you don't end up flatfooted—if you know what I mean—but there's a host of these things that help guide you. They don't tell you what the answers are, of course, they help guide. I hope that's some help to you, Bob. That sort of approach to how I looked at strategy versus operations, tactics versus ethics, and the spiritual sense shows up repeatedly in many of these.

When I started getting rid of books it was heartbreaking because I had to get rid of thousands because I was tired of hauling them all around. I knew I wouldn't read them again. I kept my geology books, some of my military books, a lot of my history, especially of the West, the American West.

So as you think through how to put together a personal library, remember that it is an intensely personal adventure. You may be entranced with the ability to hold a book in your hands, scribble in the margins, show the volume to friends who are visiting. Or you may want an entirely electronic library that resides remotely in the Cloud, available in a moment over your smart phone, tablet, or home computer. Your personal library may be seven books you deeply value or seven thousand, and it may be beautifully organized and alphabetized or simply arranged by the color of the book's cover. What matters is that it is *your* library, invested with your intellectual capital, and serves as a garden of the mind to which you can return again and again.

READING AND LEADING
The Big Lessons
Adm. James Stavridis

> When others fail him, the wise man looks to the sure companionship of books.
>
> —Andrew Lang

As we look back on the "Top 50" books of leadership lessons, each of them recommended by a senior military leader of the United States, it is possible to synthesize some of the concepts of leadership that collectively emerge. Perhaps these could be thought of as the "tricks of the trade" of being a good leader. Let's explore a few of them.

Key Lessons for Senior Leaders

Carve out time to read. You know this will be at the top of the list in a book about reading and leading! Without finding the time to build real intellectual capital you will soon burn through what you have. A good leader is constantly recharging the knowledge bank, and reading is the best and most efficient way to do that. Each leader needs to take a balanced approach to his or her reading. As the "Top 50" list shows, your "reading diet" needs a mix of novels, plays, poetry, biography, autobiography, history, memoir, and on and on. You have to balance fiction and nonfiction based on the current needs of your present assignment and keep up with the professional journals as well.

Find the time to think after *you read*. So often leaders are nearly over-whelmed by incoming information. A key attribute of a good leader is being able to prioritize what comes in and find the time to create "white space" that can be used to create intellectual capital. This, of course, is where reading comes into the picture. It is not enough to simply read, however; a strong leader reads but also processes what he or she is reading to create real thoughts. These should be more than just musings that pass along like shadows over a field; they must be considered and recorded. Good leaders write down their thoughts. Finally, it is necessary but insufficient to read, consider, and record your thoughts—they must be sent into the world to survive contact with friends, allies, critics, and enemies alike. Share the product of this critical time in the form of thoughts with others whose opinions you respect or who challenge you critically.

Speak and write with simplicity and precision. Communication is the ultimate skill of a leader. If there is anything that emerges from the study of these marvelous books, it is the power of communication. Good leaders not only take the time to read, they then organize their thoughts into written products that can be used effectively to move their organizations with power and speed.

Be humble and use humor often. Through each of the books presented here we find a continuing thread of humility and lack of preten-tiousness on the part of effective leaders. We often see leaders using humor and not taking themselves too seriously. The mission, of course, is taken seriously; but the ability to see the humor in even the darkest moments is powerful. Doing so can relieve tension in every setting from the largest meetings to the most intimate one-on-one conversations.

Focus and prioritize, then prepare deeply for the key events. Making sure you understand which events truly matter is a key skill for a leader. We are too often distracted by the mundane and day-to-day pressures of our e-mail and our inbox and forget to step back and put things in a prioritized queue. The best leaders know what *truly* deserves their attention and refuse to be dragged into the less important.

Stay physically fit. This is not always clear, and we can certainly find examples of leaders who drive themselves into the ground. An exhausted, and therefore less than optimally performing, leader is not useful. Regard sleep as a weapon that leaders must deploy to keep themselves sharp. Related to this, and a frequent failing for the classic type A leader, is ignoring medical issues—that nagging cough, the swollen joints, the sleepless nights. Pursue medical issues aggressively: it is part of being a good leader.

Be your own spokesperson. Leaders need to be out front on issues. So often it is a subordinate who is sent out to explain a disaster of some kind—perhaps a public affairs "expert" or a deputy or some head of a subordinate organization. This is the wrong approach, and many of the books on this list show that the very best leaders are willing to stand up in the strong winds that blow after a setback. There are certainly times to delegate, but in the face of real challenges, be the leader. Sun Tzu said, "When on death ground, fight." True words.

Spend the most time on personnel matters. Spend at least one-fourth of all your disposable time on personnel, and probably more. The most important decisions that a leader makes are about the people who will work for and with him or her. This applies to new hires as well as the team you currently have. Ensure that your team moves on to the very best jobs. A leader's reputation is often made by the jobs that his or her subordinates attain later in *their* careers. And it is often said, "Be kind to those you meet on the way up the ladder, because you will see them again on the way down." The fate of a leader is intrinsically tied up in the people around him or her—make sure you are spending a significant amount of your time on them.

Have a relaxing weekend routine. Virtually every good leader manages stress and is capable of taking real breaks. This means putting down the smartphone, ignoring the computer, not returning phone calls, and turning off the television every weekend for at least a day. Two days are better. Naturally, there will be times when a leader's job is in fact 24/7, but not all the time. As a general proposition, good leaders have built organizations capable of running without direct, constant engagement. This lifts a leader up and over the organization and provides the opportunity to recharge out of the immediate venue—and that is priceless.

Don't lunge at the ball. The temptation for every leader is to make quick, decisive decisions. This is built into our notion of a stereotypical leader. Indeed, many decisions as a result are made in haste, under pressure, as an emotional reaction, or with incomplete facts. Take the time to gather the information you need. Don't be driven by anyone else's timeline unless absolutely required (i.e., by direct policy guidance, your boss's dictates, or the law).

Details matter, but think big thoughts. Balance the time spent on both—absorbing and understanding details *and* sitting back from the thicket of the day-to-day and trying to think through new ideas, concepts, and necessities for the nation or organization. One of the toughest things for any leader to do is find the balance between focusing on details ("you get what you inspect, not what you expect" as our friends in the nuclear Navy say) and thinking strategically about your organization. Naturally enough, where you set the rheostat between detail and strategy sometimes reflects where you sit in an organization; a line division officer with a dozen men and women reporting to him or her must be more of a detail person than a senior leader with nearly a million people in the report chain. But sometimes it is the youngest members of the team who have the most startling insights about the big-picture items because their vision is fresh and untainted by tradition. Other times it is a senior leader who swoops into a workshop and uncovers the most fine-grained point. Finding the right balance—depending on where you sit in the chain—is a crucial skill for a leader.

Understand the process. Everyone loves to criticize "the process." We so often hear the tired phrase "the [fill in the blank] process is broken." It might be the accounting process, the procurement process, the interagency process, the leadership process—we are too quick to judge failure as being the result of some mysterious process. Good leaders know that the process is only a tool for the leader to use in achieving results. Learn the process, know the nuances of it, and you will find in most cases you can make the process work for you by bringing others into it early on, not springing surprises on people, and considering the "right limit, left limit" of any given way of doing business. Indeed, often the outcome is paradoxically less important than getting the process right in the eyes of all the participants, and thereby creating real confidence in the outcome. Another way to simply say this is "in on the takeoff, in on the landing."

Look at the law or the regulation for yourself. This is a corollary of the idea that good leaders dip into the details from time to time. So often your team—at whatever level you are leading—will say, "Hey boss, we can't do that. It's against regulations/policy/law/the boss's comments from two weeks ago/whatever." Do not allow that kind of hearsay when it is important. Do not rely on summaries or a staff member's or lawyer's opinion as to what the law says. Politely ask the staff to get you a copy and read it yourself. In many instances the leader's judgment applied to a situation will bring a different result. As the Navy says, "It is easier to beg forgiveness than to get permission." A related saying would be, "It is easier to get permission if you really understand the rules and regulations."

Organize yourself. This is a very personal item. Don't turn over personal organization to assistants, no matter how good they are. Much of the value of getting organized—putting things in the right folders, following up on memos sent, building a "day folder"—is that you are forced to think holistically about the events. The essential material thus gets into your head.

Make mentorship a priority. Good leaders, in addition to thinking consciously about the people with whom they work, are instinctive and proactive mentors. As you identify the sharp people on your team, write down their names. Keep a "good people" list. Make sure it is diverse in terms of background, race, gender, and other discriminators, but above all look for energy, enthusiasm, intelligence, and determination. Pull out that list from time to time and groom it: this means calling and e-mailing the people on it and keeping track of their progression, being available to advise them on the big decisions, knowing about their strengths and weaknesses, and looking for ways to allow them to develop their potential to the fullest. A mentor has to listen, learn, educate, and *lead*.

Things to Avoid

Just as good leaders know a few "tricks of the trade," they should learn to avoid the common pitfalls that will hold them back. All of the books we discuss here offer lessons of leadership failure as well as success. Below are a few common mistakes that must be avoided at all costs.

Refusing to delegate. Too often, leaders come to believe they are the "indispensable teammate." While they look upon their team with benign affection, they have succumbed to the idea that only they have the talent and energy to bring the really big wins to the table. This leads to a lack of delegation, which is essentially a lack of trust. There are few things more corrosive to overall team performance than a leader who views himself or herself as the one true source of competence. Avoiding this means sometimes putting up with minor failures, allowing subordinates to aim and miss, or enduring some overall team setbacks. Over the long haul, the best teams are the ones wherein the leader practices the right level of delegation, trains up his or her team in the process, and lets others gain credit for their good work.

Losing patience with people. Part of being a leader, of course, is holding people accountable when their performance is not acceptable. But losing your temper is always a failed approach. The essential job of a leader is to bring order out of chaos; when you are angry, shouting, losing your temper and patience, you are only injecting more chaos into what is presumably already a disordered situation. Leaders are the most effective when they are patient and kind. This does *not* mean giving your people a free pass when they do not perform. But performance corrections can and should be done in a professional, impersonal way in order to maintain organizational morale and ensure that the task at hand is the focus, not the spectacle of a leader blowing up.

Obsessing over little things that don't matter in the long run. Part and parcel of ensuring you do not lose patience is not obsessing over minor details while missing the big-picture trends. Not everything will go perfectly, and not every organization will run with military precision. And believe me, in the military *lots* of things go wrong every day. Good leaders know when to cut some slack about the minor failures while keeping the team focused on the big mission that is front and center. Sometimes it just feels so good to overdramatize minor frustrations—it can make a leader feel powerful and in charge. But your people know that the minor things aren't going to determine success or failure, and they want a leader who focuses on the big picture. Be that leader.

Working to exhaustion. This is perhaps the most common fault of leaders who are facing serious challenges and highly changeable situations. Since most good leaders are highly dedicated and want to succeed at all costs, there is a natural human tendency to stay up late (or all night), to forgo vacation time or weekend breaks, to skip meals or medical appointments, to spend more time at work, and to generally overwork. This leads to both large and small mistakes, short-tempered outbursts, a culture of "pity me," and a collapse in morale as subordinates begin to follow the leader's example (or bail out of the organization). Leaders perhaps more than anyone else in the organization need to be fresh, rested, balanced, and ready to do the job—overwork is counterproductive.

Armed with these "tricks of the trade," good leaders should find their way to the most important roles in their profession and particular enterprise; and more important, they will be the strongest of contributors. In the end, leaders can draw and sustain both intellectual capital and deep personal enjoyment from the books we discuss here. The books will serve as a bridge to others, a way to connect with peers, subordinates, and seniors, and—above all—a compass to true north.

There are two truths that run through all of the books on *The Leader's Bookshelf*, and they are both deceptively simple and vitally important. The first is that a leader's first and most important task is to bring order out of chaos. So many of the books on this list reflect the collision of human character with high danger and stress: the essential reason for the need for leadership. The best leader is calm, collected, compassionate, and inventive in finding the solutions that can reject the darkness of chaos and steer the team toward the light of order and accomplishment. *A leader must bring order out of chaos.*

The other maxim that appears again and again is summarized by a phrase Napoleon was fond of deploying: *a leader is a dealer in hope.* So often, what a team wants from a leader is a sense of optimism—not an unfounded naiveté but a grounded sense that "we can do this." Colin Powell has said that "optimism is a force multiplier," meaning that a hopeful approach to even the most difficult tasks will increase the chances of success. Hope is the heart of the matter for leaders, and all of the books on this list contain at least a component of that philosophy. So as you build your own leader's bookshelf, assembling the intellectual capital that will make you an effective leader, remember that your job is to bring order out of chaos and that, always, a leader is a dealer in hope. Good reading and better leading!

AFTERWORD

A Play and Two Poems

Adm. James Stavridis

Throughout *The Leader's Bookshelf* we've spoken about the ways that *books* can improve our ability to lead. But in addition to books, both poems and plays can provide valuable leadership lessons. In terms of impact, word-for-word, a beautifully crafted poem can deliver the most meaningful of reading experiences and provide startling insights for a leader. Plays, which of course are essentially scripts written to be performed in front of us, often give us powerful voices to listen to and therefore sharpen our leadership skills. As we close *The Leader's Bookshelf*, let us briefly examine two gorgeous poems and talk about one of the oldest extant plays—each of which offers important insights into the role of leaders.

The Persians
by Aeschylus

Turning first to the play *The Persians* by Aeschylus, we open it knowing we are in the hands of a master craftsman and an experienced leader. Aeschylus lived more than 2,500 years ago and was by turns a writer, a politician, and a warrior—a combination seldom seen these days. He lived during times of extraordinary geopolitical tumult somewhat akin to the early-to-mid twentieth century. During the decades of his life,

Greece and its fractious system of city-states (led by Athens and Sparta) were under constant threat of invasion by the vast Persian Empire.

This threat materialized most dramatically in 480 BC when the mighty Emperor Xerxes I sent a massive army and a battle fleet to strike Greece. Fortunately for the Western world, the Greeks managed to stop their seemingly endless internal quarreling long enough to patch together a shaky coalition that turned the Persians away, most notably inflicting upon them a stunning upset defeat in a sea battle just off Athens in the Bay of Salamis. This victory came about largely because of better tactics and technology (more effective ships maneuvering in constrained waters); higher motivation (the Greeks were largely free men defending their homes while fighting a conscripted and enslaved Persian force); and, above all, better leadership from brilliant fighting admirals like Themistocles who could inspire the Greeks. Historical accounts vary, but there is general agreement that the Greeks destroyed a force that measured somewhere between three to five times larger than their own fleet.

The Persians is a play about that defeat told from the point of view of the Persians. First performed in 472 BC, it uses the classic Greek chorus as the narrative force throughout, but with a twist—the chorus is composed of Persian Elders describing the campaign, the epic battle of Salamis, and ultimately the hubris of the self-styled God-King Xerxes, who led the Persians to defeat. Written in verse as were most Greek dramas of the era, it is effectively one long poem, similar in that sense to *The Iliad* and *The Odyssey*. Given that it was written to be performed in front of Greek audiences, the play is strangely and beautifully sympathetic to the Persians. Unlike much of Greek literature, it eschews mythology and legend from the distant past to tell a story about events that had occurred just a decade or so previously.

At the heart of *The Persians* is a stirring description of the Battle of Salamis, beginning with the call to battle of the Greek sailors:

> From every part of this voice of exhortation
> Advance ye sons of Greece, from thralldom save
> Your country, save your wives, your children save,

> The temples of your gods, the sacred tomb
> Where rest your honored ancestors; this day
> The common cause of all demands your valor

Xerxes watched over it all from a high promontory over the battle site:

> And storms of arrows crushed them; then the Greeks
> Rush to the attack at once, and furious spread
> The carnage, till each mangled Persian fell.
> Deep were the groans of Xerxes when he saw
> This havoc; for his seat, a lofty mound
> Commanding the wide sea, over looked his hosts.
> With rueful cries he rent his royal robes,
> And through his troops embattled on the shore
> Gave signal of retreat; then started wild,
> And fled disordered. To the former ills
> These are fresh miseries to awake thy sighs.

Overall, this short, highly readable play is a treatise on leadership in the ultimate crucible of crisis—a battle at desperate odds to save an entire society. While it is often described as a historical play, at its center this is a play about leadership. The key lessons to be taken from it are deceptively simple. First, *The Persians* teaches leaders the pitfalls of pride. Xerxes is certain that his power and glory are unmatched and that the Greeks will lose heart and fall before him. So often leaders fail when they begin to believe they are infallible—a failure the Greeks gave name to, calling it "hubris." Second, when faced with overwhelming odds against their side, leaders use powerful and inspiring rhetoric backed by simple facts to create a narrative of hope. This was the genius of Themistocles, the Greek admiral, which is captured in the play in vivid terms. Finally, the play goes straight to heart of accountability for leaders. After the disastrous expedition, Xerxes' mother, the Queen Mother Atossa, tells the story of his failure in bleak terms, capturing the fall of leaders perfectly in three simple lines:

Xerxes, ill-fated, led the war
Xerxes, ill-fated, leads no more
Xerxes sent forth the unwise command

This ancient epic remains fresh and full of leadership lessons—a fine example of the power of plays to inspire and inform us.

"The Second Coming"
by William Butler Yeats
and
"Sailing to Ithaca"
by Constantine P. Cavafy

Poetry as well can be full of leadership lessons, and two poems that have shaped my own leadership journey over the decades of my career are "The Second Coming" by the great twentieth-century Irish poet, William Butler Yeats; and "Sailing to Ithaca" by the iconic Greek poet Constantine P. Cavafy, who wrote around the same time—about a century ago. Both poems seem especially meaningful today as we confront global challenges and wrestle with profound questions about national leadership. One embodies *fear*, which at times feels as though it has become the defining characteristic of our lives these days; and the other offers *hope*, showing us that savoring life's journey as we try to achieve an elusive goal is at the heart of the human experience. Leaders need to understand both fear and hope, and how these emotions are projected by leaders is in many ways a central part of a good leader's skill set.

In "The Second Coming," Yeats correctly foresees the disastrous early twentieth century, describing a world in which the center cannot hold together. Effectively depicting a vision of the fall of civilizations, Yeats uses the vivid image of a falcon that is wheeling in the sky in ever-widening circles, getting farther and farther from the falconer. He concludes the poem by drawing a dystopian parallel to the birth of Jesus, saying, "And what rough beast, its hour come round at last / Slouches toward Bethlehem to be born."

The Second Coming

Turning and turning in the widening gyre
The falcon cannot hear the falconer;
Things fall apart; the centre cannot hold;
Mere anarchy is loosed upon the world,
The blood-dimmed tide is loosed, and everywhere
The ceremony of innocence is drowned;
The best lack all conviction, while the worst
Are full of passionate intensity.

Surely some revelation is at hand;
Surely the Second Coming is at hand.
The Second Coming! Hardly are those words out
When a vast image out of Spiritus Mundi
Troubles my sight: somewhere in sands of the desert
A shape with lion body and the head of a man,
A gaze blank and pitiless as the sun,
Is moving its slow thighs, while all about it
Reel shadows of the indignant desert birds.
The darkness drops again; but now I know
That twenty centuries of stony sleep
Were vexed to nightmare by a rocking cradle,
And what rough beast, its hour come round at last,
Slouches towards Bethlehem to be born?

The poem first shows leaders the efficacy of image in creating a shared sense of danger and challenge. Including both the falcon and the terrifyingly unknown shape of the "rough beast" reminds us that leaders will face dark and uncertain times. We are not the first generation, nor shall we be the last, to feel as though "the center cannot hold." Yeats gives us an example of how leaders can provide visual images with powerful word pictures that can inspire or awaken a sense of the need for shared action.

The poem also provides a needed sense of perspective, a crucial quality for a leader. Written in 1919, "The Second Coming" anticipates perhaps the most dangerous century in human history—two massive world wars, an enormous Great Depression, and the long twilight of the Cold War in which we nearly managed to destroy civilization in a potential nuclear war in the early 1960s. Poems like this allow leaders to reflect on history and put our current troubles in a better perspective.

In contrast to "The Second Coming" and its dark tones, it seems appropriate to close this book with the leadership lessons of "Sailing to Ithaca," one of the most beautiful and evocative poems ever written about hope. In this short poem, written in 1911, Cavafy imagines the final voyage of Odysseus to his home in Ithaca, a small island off the mainland of Greece. It would be a lovely but less important poem if it centered on the need to come home and the determination to reach a long-sought goal. But the real power of "Sailing to Ithaca" comes from the evocative observations that the beauty of life is not the destination, but rather the journey.

Sailing to Ithaca

As you set out for Ithaca
hope the voyage is a long one,
full of adventure, full of discovery.
Laistrygonians and Cyclops,
angry Poseidon—don't be afraid of them:
you'll never find things like that on your way
as long as you keep your thoughts raised high,
as long as a rare excitement
stirs your spirit and your body.
Laistrygonians and Cyclops,
wild Poseidon—you won't encounter them
unless you bring them along inside your soul,
unless your soul sets them up in front of you.

Hope the voyage is a long one.
May there be many a summer morning when,
with what pleasure, what joy,

you come into harbors seen for the first time;
may you stop at Phoenician trading stations
to buy fine things,
mother of pearl and coral, amber and ebony,
sensual perfume of every kind—
as many sensual perfumes as you can;
and may you visit many Egyptian cities
to gather stores of knowledge from their scholars.

Keep Ithaca always in your mind.
Arriving there is what you are destined for.
But do not hurry the journey at all.
Better if it lasts for years,
so you are old by the time you reach the island,
wealthy with all you have gained on the way,
not expecting Ithaca to make you rich.

Ithaca gave you the marvelous journey.
Without her you would not have set out.
She has nothing left to give you now.

And if you find her poor, Ithaca won't have fooled you.
Wise as you will have become, so full of experience,
you will have understood by then what these Ithacas mean.

When Cavafy says, "Keep Ithaca always in your mind / Arriving there is what you are destined for / But do not hurry the journey at all / Better if it lasts for years," he is reminding us that goals are important, but what really matters in the long throw of our lives are the journeys we are privileged to have—each day full of hope to metaphorically arrive again in a place we cherish.

In closing *The Leader's Bookshelf*, earlier we observed that more than two hundred years ago Napoleon said that "a leader is a dealer in hope." Even as Yeats reminds us that there are always dangers and challenges looming on the horizon, Cavafy shows us in a handful of beautifully crafted words that our journeys in the end are about hope, not fear. Leaders must understand the role of both fear and hope, but in the end the very best effective leaders use hope to inspire us in the long voyages on which we all must sail. Poems and plays each have a role in helping leaders find their way not only to challenges, but to hope.

NOTES

Chapter Two. Making Time for Reading

1. John Hudson, "Admiral James Stavridis: What I Read," *The Atlantic,* August 31, 2012, http://www.thewire.com/global/2012/08/natos-supreme -allied-commander-europe-james-stavridis-what-i-read/55626/.

Chapter Three. The Leader's Bookshelf "Top 50"

1. Mike Gallagher, "In Defense of 'Once an Eagle,'" *Time*, August 29, 2011, http://nation.time.com/2011/08/29/in-defense-of-once-an-eagle/.

2. "Orson Welles Talks about Cornelia Lunt," YouTube video, from an interview on *The Dick Cavett Show* airing July 27, 1970, posted by "cavett-biter," May 6, 2008, https://www.youtube.com/watch?v=r1fauAc48tA& feature=related.

3. "James Buchanan," *Harper's New Monthly Magazine*, December 1883– May 1884, 260.

4. William O. Stoddard, *Abraham Lincoln: The True Story of a Great Life* (New York: Fords, Howard, and Hulbert, 1884), 265.

5. Noah Brooks, *Mr. Lincoln's Washington: Selections from the Writings of Noah Brooks, Civil War Correspondent*, edited by P. J. Staudenraus (South Brunswick, N.J.: T. Yoseloff, 1967), 136.

6. Doris Kearns Goodwin, *Team of Rivals* (New York: Simon and Schuster, 2005), 282.

7. Peter Mackay, "The Timeless Beauty of War," review of *The Art of War*, posted on Amazon.com, May 11, 2002, https://www.amazon.com/review /R2CMG2JKBK1JGR.

8. Patrick Shrier, review of *The Face of Battle* by John Keegan, posted on *Military History* web site, July 25, 2011, http://www.military-history .us/2011/07/book-review-the-face-of-battle-by-john-keegan/.

9. Army Field Manual 3-0, February 2008, A-1, http://downloads.army.mil /fm3–0/FM3–0.pdf.

10. William H. Ewing, "Nimitz, Reflections on Pearl Harbor," Nimitz Foundation, 1982.

11. "Stanley McCrystal's 6 Favorite Books," The Week.com, January 27, 2013, http://theweek.com/articles/468405/stanley-mcchrystals-6-favorite -books.

12. In *Future Soldiers and the Quality Imperative: The Army 2010 Conference*, ed. Robert L. Phillips and Maxwell R. Thurman.

13. Russell W. Glenn, "Men against Fire: How Many Soldiers Actually Fired Their Weapons at the Enemy during the Vietnam War," *Vietnam* magazine, April 2002.

14. "Robert D. Kaplan: Writing Career Reflections," RobertDKaplan.com, accessed August 23, 2016, http://www.robertdkaplan.com/robert_d _kaplan_reflections.htm.

15. "Jeff Shaara: Leadership at Gettysburg," *Anniston (Alabama) Star*, July 28, 1996, 36.

16. Oliver Jensen, "Working with Bruce Catton," *American Heritage*, February–March 1979, http://www.americanheritage.com/content/working-bruce -catton.

17. Warren Kozak's web site, accessed August 23, 2016, http://www.warren kozak.com/.

18. "Women's History Month: Vice Chief of Naval Operations Admiral Michelle Howard," *All Hands* magazine, March 1, 2016, http://www .navy.mil/ah_online/deptStory.asp?dep=13&id=93371.

19. Fox10News, Mobile, Alabama, February 16, 2016, http://www.fox10tv .com/story/31756133/first-african-american-woman-to-command-navy -ship-in-mobile."

20. August 27, 1988, interview: https://www.scribd.com/document/237325175 /Isaac-Asimov-Interview.

21. Isaac Asimov, interview with Slawek Wojtowicz, https://freedocs.net /interview-with-isaac-asimov/439494/.

22. CSPAN Interview, "After Words," July 9, 2010, https://www.c-span.org /video/?293989–1/words-karl-marlantes.

23. Robert E. Lee, letter to his wife, December 25, 1862, http://www.civilwar .org/education/history/primarysources/robert-e-lees-letter-to-his-1.html.

24. Col. Harry G. Summers Jr., http://www.historynet.com/battle-for-hamburger-hill-during-the-vietnam-war.htm; article reprinted from *Vietnam* magazine, June 1999.

25. Mark Bowden review of *Matterhorn* for Amazon.com, https://www.amazon.com/dp/B003V8BRTQ/ref=dp-kindle-redirect?_encoding =UTF8&btkr=1#nav-subnav.

26. Evan James, "A Vietnam Epic Uncovers Old Wounds: An Interview with Karl Marlantes," *Mother Jones*, April 2010, http://www.motherjones.com /media/2010/04/interview-karl-marlantes-matterhorn-vietnam?page=2.

27. Michael Keane, *George S. Patton: Blood, Guts and Prayer* (Washington, D.C.: Regnery, 2014), 5.

28. Adm. Mike Mullen, quoted in "Navy Professional Reading Program Debuts," http://navy.mil/submit/display.asp?.story_id=25810.

29. C. Peter Chen, review of *Goodbye, Darkness: A Memoir of the Pacific War*, Book Reviews, *World War II Database*, April 11, 2006, http://wwtdb.com.

30. Michael Freeland, "I'm the Only Journalist Alive to Have Interviewed Harper Lee—and It's All Thanks to Gregory Peck," *The Guardian*, July 13, 2015, https://www.theguardian.com/commentisfree/2015/jul/13 /interviewed-harper-lee-to-kill-a-mockingbird-sequel-go-set-a-watchman.

31. "To Kill A Mockingbird by Harper Lee—review," *The Guardian*, July 17, 2015, https://www.theguardian.com/childrens-books-site/2015/jul/17 /to-kill-a-mockingbird-harper-lee-review.

32. *Authors of the Mid-20th Century* (New York: Britannica Publishing, 2013), 57.

33. John Keegan, "A Generation of Victors," *New York Times*, August 16, 1987, http://www.nytimes.com/1987/08/16/books/a-generation-of-victors .html?pagewanted=all.

Chapter Seven. Building a Personal Library

1. Beatrice Ayer Patton, "A Soldier's Reading," *ARMOR*, November–December 1952; reprinted in *ARMOR*, July–September 2013. See http://www.benning.army.mil/earmor/eARMOR/content/issues/2013/JUL_SEP /ARMOR_JulSep13_Web.pdf. All of Mrs. Patton's quotes are from this source.

2. Roger H. Nye, *The Patton Mind: The Professional Development of an Extraordinary Leader* (Garden City Park, N.Y.: Avery, c. 1993).

3. Ardant du Picq, *Battle Studies: Ancient and Modern Battle*, trans. Col. John N. Greely and Maj. Robert C. Cotton (New York: Macmillan, 1921).

4. Frederick Ayer Jr., *Before the Colors Fade: Portrait of a Soldier, George S. Patton Jr.* (Boston: Houghton Mifflin, 1964).

5. Patton, "A Soldier's Reading."

ABOUT THE AUTHORS

A 1976 distinguished graduate of the U.S. Naval Academy, **Adm. James Stavridis** spent more than thirty-five years on active service in the U.S. Navy. He commanded destroyers and a carrier strike group in combat and served for seven years as a four-star admiral, culminating with four years as the sixteenth Supreme Allied Commander at NATO. He holds a PhD in international relations and is Dean of the Fletcher School of Law and Diplomacy at Tufts University. Admiral Stavridis has written six books and hundreds of articles on global security issues and leadership.

A former lieutenant commander in the Navy Reserve with periods of active duty, **R. Manning Ancell** has worked in media for decades. The author of more than two hundred articles in magazines, newspapers, and journals, he has authored or coauthored six books, including *Four-Star Leadership for Leaders* and *Who Will Lead? Senior Leadership in the United States Army*. He lives in Norfolk, Virginia, with his wife.

The Naval Institute Press is the book-publishing arm of the U.S. Naval Institute, a private, nonprofit, membership society for sea service professionals and others who share an interest in naval and maritime affairs. Established in 1873 at the U.S. Naval Academy in Annapolis, Maryland, where its offices remain today, the Naval Institute has members worldwide.

Members of the Naval Institute support the education programs of the society and receive the influential monthly magazine *Proceedings* or the colorful bimonthly magazine *Naval History* and discounts on fine nautical prints and on ship and aircraft photos. They also have access to the transcripts of the Institute's Oral History Program and get discounted admission to any of the Institute-sponsored seminars offered around the country.

The Naval Institute's book-publishing program, begun in 1898 with basic guides to naval practices, has broadened its scope to include books of more general interest. Now the Naval Institute Press publishes about seventy titles each year, ranging from how-to books on boating and navigation to battle histories, biographies, ship and aircraft guides, and novels. Institute members receive significant discounts on the Press' more than eight hundred books in print.

Full-time students are eligible for special half-price membership rates. Life memberships are also available.

For a free catalog describing Naval Institute Press books currently available, and for further information about joining the U.S. Naval Institute, please write to:

Member Services

U.S. NAVAL INSTITUTE

291 Wood Road

Annapolis, MD 21402-5034

Telephone: (800) 233-8764

Fax: (410) 571-1703

Web address: www.usni.org